"AMERICA'S BEST-SELLING TRUCK"

FORD
F-100/F-150
PICKUP

1953 - 1996

Robert Ackerson

"AMERICA'S BEST-SELLING TRUCK"

FORD F-100/F-150 PICKUP

1953 - 1996

Robert Ackerson

VELOCE PUBLISHING

THE PUBLISHER OF FINE AUTOMOTIVE BOOKS

Also from Veloce Publishing

First published in 2005 by Veloce Publishing Limited, 33 Trinity Street, Dorchester DT1 1TT, England. Fax 01305 268864/e-mail info@veloce.co.uk/web www.veloce.co.uk or www.velocebooks.com
ISBN 1-904788-76-9/UPC 36847-00376-0

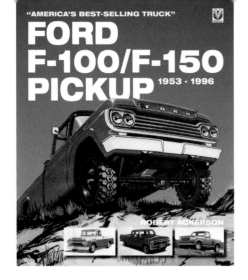

"AMERICA'S BEST-SELLING TRUCK"

FORD
F-100/F-150
PICKUP 1953 - 1996

ROBERT ACKERSON

Contents

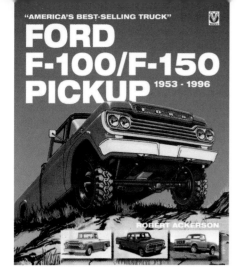

Thanks

Chronicling the development of these remarkable vehicles was greatly facilitated by the voluminous supply of rare Ford factory literature provided by Paul Politis. Mike Mullane also contributed Ford literature from his dealership. The help provided by Rebecca Gage was also appreciated. Karen Shaughnessy and Dan Bedore of Ford Public Relations provided valuable material concerning the 1997 F-150.

Thanks to Bonnie and Jim Banner for their company on trips to Rhinebeck, NY. Also acknowledged is the help extended by my daughter, Cindy Seymour, and her husband, Jack. A special note of appreciation goes to Dave Dorf who, like Gerald Frisbe, shared his extensive knowledge of F-100 restoration procedures. Dave also dug deeply into his photographic collection to assemble a fine portfolio of his truck's restoration. Special thanks go to Dave Marquart for his many contributions.

As always, personal appreciation is extended to my wife, Grace, for her patience and forbearance, and to my daughter, Susan, who faithfully logged crucial phone calls.

I would be very amiss if, in closing, I didn't include a sincere 'Thank You' to my publisher, Rod Grainger, who helped me see the light about the Ford F-100 and F-150.

Robert C Ackerson

FORD F-100/F-150 PICKUP 1953 - 1996

ROBERT ACKERSON

Introduction

Ford pickups underwent dramatic changes in design and appearance in the almost half a century that separated the 1948 models from those introduced in 1996. The 1948 F-1 was the first new pickup from Ford since 1938. It broke with the past in appearance, but was still intended for a market that had changed little from previous decades. Pickups were purchased by farmers to haul product, livestock, and supplies, and by contractors to transport building materials from the lumber yard to the construction site; just two examples of individuals using light duty trucks in the daily operation of their businesses.

The pickup's versatility and utilitarian character also appealed to a significant number of new vehicle buyers, who found it ideal for recreational purposes and weekend trips to the nursery or hardware store. It didn't happen overnight, but from this highly visible group grew the notion, by the mid-fifties, that ownership of a pickup was fashionable.

New conveniences such as air conditioning, automatic transmission, smoother suspension, brighter, more appealing exterior colors, two-tone color schemes, and attractive new interior appointments and features, along with expanded availability of options, drastically changed the pickup's public image. The pickup was increasingly chosen as the second vehicle in a two car family. Before long, the functionality and design of Ford pickups also attracted many buyers who purchased them as their main means of transportation.

In 1940 several Ford pickup models had front end styling resembling that of Ford's passenger cars. This approach was repeated in 1951 when a restyled F-1 was introduced with a grille similar in form to that used by the 1951 Ford cars. But overall, Ford styled its pickups to look like Ford trucks, not imitations of sedans, station wagons, or convertibles. This was one key to the success of the F-100 and F-150; regardless of their vintage, they possessed distinctiveness and character that instantly identified them as Ford pickups.

Ford was remarkably successful in detecting early indications of emerging consumer preferences. Modern Ford pickup history is filled with the result - Flareside or Styleside - let the customer choose: SuperCabs; 4x4s; luxurious Lariats; special edition models, and high performance Lightnings.

By 1996 the next generation of F-150s awaited the customer. An era of F-150 history characterized by unprecedented change was coming to an end; a time when the substance of the Ford pickup remained rock solid, a vehicle that, when called upon, delivered a solid day's work, off road or on, day after day, year after year.

Ford, whilst refining the design of its trucks to meet customer needs and expectations, had never lost sight of the single most important reason why the F-series pickup was so popular - each one was built 'Ford Tough'.

**Robert C Ackerson
Schenevus, New York**

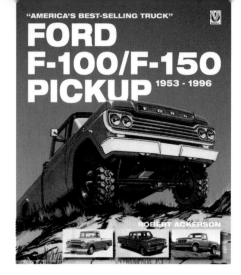

1

1953-1956

Reporting an investment of 30 million dollars in research, design, tooling, and plant facilities for a new line of trucks for 1953, Ford used the occasion of its 50th anniversary to adopt a new model nomenclature which identified its light duty pickup as the F-100.

With the pickup truck still primarily regarded as a utilitarian vehicle, primary emphasis was placed on the practical virtues of the F-100's all-new 'Driverized Cab' with its new five feet wide seat and

that pickups were increasingly being purchased as viable alternatives to the station wagon. Thus Ford noted that the F-100's 'capped roof' construction with a full drip rail added a "distinctive touch of beauty." Similarly, new push button door handles were depicted as "more easily operated" whilst also enhancing the F-100's appearance.

The design of the F-100, with its curvaceous hood and front fenders, and low mounted grille and headlights,

The Ford F-100 6.5ft bed Pickup. Ford claimed it was "... the sweetest handling truck ever built." (Courtesy Ford Motor Company)

increased leg, shoulder, and foot room. The F-100's interior had been developed in Ford's research laboratories using a full-scale cab model and the 'Measuring Man', a lifelike replica of the average driver.

This close attention to detail also demonstrated Ford's awareness

successfully combined functionality with good styling taste. An emblem positioned in the grille center provided engine identification. F-100s with V-8 engines carried a 'V-8' logo; those powered by a 6-cylinder engine had an inverted three-pointed star emblem. The F-100's curved windshield provided in excess of 400

F-1 v F-100 dimensions

Model	F-1	F-100
Overall length	188.78in	189.12in
Wheelbase	114in	110in
Overall height	75.64in	75.3in
Overall width	75.94in	71.3in
Front tread	58.08in	60.58in
Rear tread	60.0in	60.0in
Cargo capacity	45cu ft	45cu ft
Exterior box length	6.5ft	6.5ft
Load length	78.06in	77.9in
Load width	49in	49in
Load height	20.35in	20.3in

square inches more area than did the F-1's flat windshield. A much larger rear window, which Ford claimed was the largest in the industry, along with a lower (by two inches) window sill contributed to the F-100's visual appeal, and the driving comfort of its operator. The surface area of the rear view mirror was also increased. The F-100's optional heater produced 100 per cent greater air volume for full area defrosting of the windshield.

Detail refinements abounded in the F-100 cab. More durable rubber seals completely encircled the cab doors, along with tighter fitting, rotor-type door locks, providing improved weather protection. The accelerator linkage now passed through the firewall instead of the floor pan, as on previous pickups, preventing entry of water, dirt, and dust into the cab. Although repositioned for 1953, the linkage for both the clutch and brake pedals still exited through the floor. Serving as an 'insulating wall' against road heat was a new drop-ribbed, all-rubber floor mat. A new design enabled the entire seat to move four inches forward and back, whilst maintaining independent adjustment of the seat back angle. In addition, greater storage area was available behind the seat. The use of concealed 'goose-neck' type hinges allowed the cab doors to open through a wider arc than previously.

All instrumentation was positioned in a single dash cluster with controls located within easy reach of the driver. Ford reported that the 'Anniversary Medallion'

mounted in the center of the truck's three-spoke steering wheel "... marks the fiftieth year of progress for Ford ... builder of more than 17 million trucks for the American Road."

A new non-sag spring seat construction, and twin double-acting seat snubbers contributed to what Ford called the F-100's 'Hammock Comfort.'

Both cab versions - the standard and Deluxe - of the F-100 had new reinforced tailgates with quick operating, toggle-type latches. Replacing the traditional Ford script identification on the tailgate's outer surface was the Ford name in block letters. Also introduced on the F-100 was a diagonal-type spare tire carrier. The tire could be easily lowered from its position beneath the pickup box by removing the wing nut at the base of the tailgate and letting the tire slide down the carrier.

Although the overall length of the F-100 was virtually identical to that of the 1952 F-1 model, the exterior dimensions of the F-100 differed from those of its predecessor in several key areas, as shown in the table above.

The F-100's design blended new technical and engineering developments with well-proven components from earlier Ford pickups. This mixture was most apparent in the engine lineup. Both Ford's overhead valve 'Cost Clipper Six,' which had debuted in 1952, and the flathead 'Truck V-8' engine were carried over into 1953, with only minor changes such as larger capacity radiators, and redesigned motor mounts providing for easier servicing of the clutch, transmission, and water pump. The horsepower and torque ratings of both engines were unchanged from 1952.

The contemporary design of the overhead valve 6-cylinder merits a close review of its development. Few Americans had taken notice when Ford of England introduced the new Consul and Zephyr models in late 1950. Ford subsequently imported these cars into the US and, for the most part, they proved well suited for use in America. This should have come as no surprise to their owners since the engines for both cars were designed in Dearborn. But the engineers who worked on this project were not merely producing a new generation of engines for Ford's English operations; they were also developing the first ever Ford overhead valve engines. As a consequence, Ford, in 1952, introduced a new overhead valve 6-cylinder engine for use in American cars and trucks.

Work on this engine began in 1948, a time when the lifespan of Ford's side-valve 6-cylinder (introduced in 1941) was drawing to a close. Not surprising, since its flathead V-8 was scheduled for two more years of production, was Ford's assertion that the L-head engine was not obsolete. But Ford's position - as stated by Earl S. MacPherson, vice president of engineering - was equivocal. In a paper presented to the SAE in December 1951 he noted: "Ford does not consider the L-head engine obsolete, and will consider it so for several years ... But in looking to the future, and considering the fuels that probably will be available eight or ten years from now, it is likely that the overhead valve engine will give far better performance than the L-head type."

Aside from this aspect, the 6-cylinder's short stroke suggested a long service life. For example, whereas in

Ford L-head v Ford OHV engine specifications

Engine	Ford L-head	Ford OHV
Bore	3.3in	3.5625in
Stroke	4.4in	3.6in
Displacement	225.9cu in	215.3cu in
Comp. ratio	6.8:1	7.0:1
Horsepower	95@3600rpm	101@3500rpm
Torque	178lb/ft@1200rpm	185lb/ft@1300-1700rpm
Dry weight	538lb	502lb

one hour the piston in the L-head engine traveled 15 miles, the piston in the ohv engine traveled only 12.2 miles, while concurrently reducing connecting rod and main bearing loads.

With about 20 per cent more intake area compared to the valves of the L-head six, the relatively large valves of the ohv engine (made possible by its larger bore), provided much greater breathing capacity. The table above of the new Ford engine specifications with those of its predecessor, illustrates the degree of change its introduction represented.

Like the F-1, the F-100 used longitudinal, semi-elliptical leaf springs for front and rear suspension. The F-100's were longer, and had a reduced deflection rate. The specifications for the springs of the F-100 and the F-1 were as shown in the table (above right).

Standard for the F-100 were direct double-acting hydraulic front and rear shock absorbers.

The table (right) shows that the F-1 and F-100 were virtually identical in many major areas.

Both Fordomatic automatic transmission and overdrive were optional for the F-100, and provided the F-100 customer with a choice of five transmissions:

3-speed Synchro-Silent, column shift (standard).

3-speed heavy duty, Synchro-Silent, column shift (optional).

4-speed Synchro-Silent, floor shift (optional).

3-speed Synchro-Silent, column shift with overdrive.

Fordomatic torque converter automatic.

Tests involving two F-100 pickups, one with standard transmission and the other with Fordomatic, loaded 10 per cent over their maximum gross, offered impressive evidence of the performance of a Fordomatic-equipped F-100. Both were stopped on a 30 per cent grade on Ford's Dearborn Test Track. "The standard F-100" explained Ford, "just barely went up the grade. The Fordomatic F-100 not only moved up the grade smoothly ... it accelerated!"

The Ford overdrive transmission, produced by Warner Gear, provided a fourth forward gear that reduced engine

F-1 v F-100 spring specification comparison

	F-1	F-100
Front spring		
Length and width	36in x 1.75in	42in x 1.75in
Number of leaves	8	8
Capacity (at ground)	NA	1085lb
Rear spring		
Length and width	45in x 2.0in	48in x 2.0in
Number of leaves	10	6
Capacity (at ground)	NA	1035lb

F-1 v F-100 general comparison

Model	F-1	F-100
Brakes		
Type	Hydraulic	Hydraulic
	Two-shoe	Two shoe
	Single anchor	Single anchor
Front dimensions	11.0in x 2.0in	11.0in x 2.0in
Rear dimensions	11.0in x 1.75in	11.0in x 1.75in
Lining area	178sq in	178sq in
Tires:	6.00 x 16, 4-ply	6.00 x 16, 4-ply
Optional:	6.00 x 16, 6-ply	6.00 x 16, 6-ply
	6.50 x 16, 6-ply	6.50 x 16, 6-ply
Wheels:	16 x 4.5K, drop	16 x 4.5K, drop
	center steel discs	center steel discs
Rear axle	Semi-floating	Semi-floating
	Hypoid	Hypoid
Ratio	3.92:1	3.92:1 (4.27:1 and others optional)
Clutch	10.0in	10.0in
Clutch area	85.5sq in	85.5sq in
Fuel tank	20 gall	17 gall

Transmission	Ratios				
	1st gear	2nd gear	3rd gear	4th gear	Reverse
3-speed H-D	3.71	1.87	1.00	-	4.59
3-speed OD	2.78	1.62	1.00	0.78 (OD)	3.375
4-speed	6.40	3.09	1.69	1.00	4.59
Auto	2.44	1.48	1.00	2.10*	2.00

F-100 optional transmission specifications

*Converter ratio

speed by approximately one third. For example, an F-100 equipped with standard transmission, rear axle, and tires had, at a speed of 50mph, an engine speed of 2410rpm. The same vehicle's equivalent engine speed with overdrive was 1760rpm. Operation of the overdrive unit was not complicated. When the lock-out handle (positioned beneath the instrument panel) was pulled out, overdrive was operative. To shift the truck into overdrive, the driver momentarily released the accelerator pedal after the truck had reached a speed of approximately 27mph. The truck would remain in overdrive until road speed dropped to about 21mph. The driver could, for added acceleration, also shift out of overdrive by firmly pressing the accelerator to the floor, causing the transmission to 'kick-down' to a lower gear ratio. To return to overdrive the driver momentarily released accelerator pressure. Standard and optional equipment of the F-100 comprised the items shown in the table on page 12.

It was also possible, through Ford dealers, to equip an F-100 pickup with a power take-off (4-speed transmission only), a reinforced canvas pickup box cover or 4-wheel drive.

Production of the F-100 for the 1953 model year totaled 116,437, which compared favorably with the output of 81,537 F-1 pickups in 1952.

In 1954, production of the F-100 pickup, priced at $1318, reached 101,202 units. Interior and exterior changes were minor in nature. The grille now had a forward canted main section with a wide center bar, beneath which were three small rectangular air openings and a wider air intake. Deluxe Cab models had three chevrons on each side of the engine identification logo. The V-8 emblem was unchanged for 1954. The 6-cylinder

emblem was now a four-pointed star.

The Deluxe Cab's upholstery and door trim panel designs were revised, and a new, 'full-breathing' woven vinyl upholstery material used.

Exterior colors for 1954 were Raven Black, Sea Haze Green, Meadow Green, Sheridan Blue, Dovetone Gray (subsequently replaced by Goldenrod Yellow), Glacier Blue, and Vermilion.

Joining the F-100's unchanged Cost Clipper 6-cylinder for 1953 was a truck version of Ford's new overhead valve Y-block V-8. Work on this engine started in 1948. In an SAE paper presented on January 13, 1954, Ford's chief engine engineer, Robert Stevenson, noted that: "In establishing the initial design concepts for this new engine, we found it was easy to decide on the number and arrangement of cylinders, since the V-8 had already earned worldwide acceptability in our vehicles since 1932."

Stevenson cited five major design aims for the new engine:
1. Displacement, overall size, and weight were to approximate those of the L-head V-8.
2. Maximum structural rigidity was to be attained to maintain a high standard of smoothness, and make future compression ratio increases possible.
3. A short stroke was to be used for mechanical and thermal efficiency.
4. Use of overhead valves arrangement would permit maximum volumetric efficiency, and full advantage of future compression ratio increases.
5. Consistent with traditional Ford manufacturing, the new engine would possess maximum mechanical simplicity.

Other objectives included lower valve temperatures, rotating valves, full flow oil filtration, a single water pump, a chain-driven camshaft, combustion

chambers with maximum quench area and, as expected, increased horsepower and torque.

Ohv V-8 development required nearly 600,000 man hours and the building of over 400 experimental engines. These engines were tested on dynamometers for over 160,000 hours, and were installed in vehicles accumulating more than 2.5 million miles. During this process engines were rebuilt as many as eight times to facilitate testing of individual components. "As a result of this extensive and thorough testing," Mr Stevenson noted, "we are introducing the new Ford V-8 engine with every confidence that it not only meets our design objectives, but that it will establish for itself a reputation as enviable as its famous predecessor."

Highlights of the new design included a one-piece, high grade iron alloy cylinder block casting carrying the crankcase skirts well below the crankshaft centerline. Five bulkheads provided structural rigidity and support for the crankshaft and camshaft bearings. Overall, 14 cylinder block cores were required, compared to the 29 cylinder block cores of the 1953 V-8.

The new V-8's crankshaft had five main bearings instead of three as previously, and was precision molded of alloy iron. Whereas the old crankshaft weighed 65 pounds, the new version weighed 49 pounds. Due to their much deeper cross-section, the new cylinder heads were far more rigid than those used previously and, as a result, the number of hold-down bolts reduced from 24 to 10.

The overhead-valve V-8 had a 3.5 inch bore and a 3.1 inch stroke, as compared with the 3.19 inch bore and 3.75 inch stroke of the L-head V-8. Piston travel was reduced by 17 per cent. Eclipsing the L-head's ratings of 106 horsepower at 3500rpm, and 194lb/ft of torque at 1900-

F-100 equipment (1953)

Standard
Chromed front bumper
Hub caps
Oil bath air cleaner (one quart capacity)
Dual windshield wipers (overlapping)
Left-side sun visor
Push button starter
Inside rearview mirror
Jack and tool kit
Ash receptacle
Dispatch box
Electric horn
Sealed beam headlights with floor dimmer control
Parking lights
17 gallon fuel tank

Optional
Axle ratios: 4.10:1 and 4.27:1/overdrive, 3.92:1/automatic.
Rear bumper
Deluxe Cab
Heavy duty cooling system
Fresh air heater and defroster
Re-circulating type heater and defroster
Oil filter
Heavy duty radiator
Right side tail light
Tinted glass
3-speed heavy duty transmission
Overdrive on standard transmission
3-speed automatic transmission
4-speed transmission
Positive action dual windshield wipers
Dual electric windshield wipers
Five 6.00 x 16, 6-ply tires with wheels
Five 6.50 x 16, 6-ply tires with wheels
Five 15 in 6-ply tires with wheels
Five 15 in 8-ply tires with wheels
100, 120 or 130 amp-hr battery

11in clutch with standard transmission (provided 123.7sq in area)
Fuel and vacuum pump for positive action wiper control
32amp low cut-in generator
40 or 60amp generator
Governor
Hand throttle
Chrome yellow or white exterior paint
Heavy duty front and rear shock absorbers
Progressive rear springs
Heavy duty front springs
Heavy duty rear springs
Light duty rear springs
Front tow hooks

These F-100 accessories were available through Ford dealers
Directional turn signals (flasher-type)
Fire extinguisher (1.5 quart capacity)
Locking gas cap
Engine compartment light
Road lamps
Spotlight with bracket
Reflector flares (3) with flags
Radiator grille guard (both light and heavy duty)
Radio (five tube) with rectifier and single knob control
Exterior, 6in adjustable rear view mirrors (left and right sides)
Seat covers
Windshield washers
Tow hooks
Outside mirror braces
Governors
Handbrake signal
Heat and defroster (both recirculating and MagicAire systems)
Stop lamp

2100rpm, was the new V-8's output of 130 horsepower at 4200rpm, and 214lb/ft of torque at 1800-2200rpm.

Clues to the pickup truck market's fundamental restructuring were provided by Tom McCahill's test of a 1954 F-100, published in *Mechanix Illustrated* of October 1954. After giving his 6-cylinder pickup plenty of opportunity to prove its mettle as a rough and ready vehicle, McCahill noted that pickup trucks were rapidly replacing the station wagon since they "... have all the dig and high speed performance of the average sedan ..." while being "... quick to load and just right for carrying feed, lumber, and a million other things that have to be hauled." Readily conceding that the Ford pickup had a lot of tail bounce when unloaded, and that it was very easy to spin the rear wheels on dry concrete, he also noted that "... if you think the standard Ford Six pick-up [sic] will be a pushover in a drag race, let's look at the facts." The supporting performance data was impressive; the Ford needed just 4.3 seconds to accelerate from zero to 30mph. The zero to 50 run was completed in 9.9 seconds, and zero to 60mph averaged 17.7 seconds. "As you can see," McCahill wrote, "this is really good passenger car performance."

Further evidence of the F-100's changing character was found in a road test of a 1955 F-100 pickup published in the October 1955 issue of *Motor Life*. "It drives like a truck .." *Motor Life* noted, "... now means it's comfortable, handles well, is economical to run and operate, and has fair performance. What more could anyone ask?" This perspective dominated the *Motor Life* test which, whilst recognizing the F-100's "ruggedness and efficiency" based its evaluation of the F-100 primarily on passenger car features.

In terms of performance, the V-8 engined F-100, equipped with Fordomatic, achieved the following:

0-30mph:	3.9 seconds
0-45mph:	9.8 seconds
0-60mph:	18.5 seconds

After adding an extra 5 pounds of pressure to the F-100's tires, *Motor Life* reported the F-100's handling as "easy and fairly sure."

Motor Life's assessment of the F-100's styling as "... not the most advanced in the field, but ... up-to-date, clean and neat" was probably influenced by the arrival in late March 1955 of Chevrolet's all-new 'second series' of 1955 model year trucks. It took a well informed Ford truck

The 1956 F-100's modern full-wrap windshield was combined with a traditional windshield visor. (Courtesy Ford Motor Company)

The surface area of the 1956 F-100 extra cost, full-wrap rear window exceeded 823.5sq in. (Courtesy Ford Motor Company)

enthusiast to identify the styling changes of the 1955 F-100. Most apparent was a new grille format with two crossbars, the uppermost of which dipped to form a center V-shape. The engine designations (V-8 for the Y-block V-8, or a four-pointed star for the I-block 6-cylinder) were placed in this indentation. New side hood medallions positioned the Ford name and F-100 designation within a chrome circle. Unlike previous models, which were delivered with wheels painted to match the body color, the 1955 F-100, priced at $1460, left the factory with white-painted wheels.

Both the Standard and Custom Cab interiors continued to use the woven plastic seat upholstery introduced in 1954. The Custom Cab now had five inch thick foam rubber padding over the entire width of the seat, as well as a three inch thick foam rubber seat back pad. The exterior of Custom Cab F-100 pickups had door mounted Custom Cab name plates, and chrome framed air vent windows. The grille's leading edge was chromed, and six rectangular recesses were positioned in the upper grille bar. These features, said Ford, "... add design balance and give a definite feeling of advanced styling."

The F-100's color selection consisted of Raven Black, Aquatone Blue, Banner Blue, Waterfall Blue, Meadow Green, Goldenrod Yellow, Sea Sprite Green, Snowshoe White, and Torch Red. Custom Cab pickups were available with optional two-tone paint schemes consisting of the roof and upper back panel painted Snowshoe White, with the remainder of the body in any of the other available colors.

Both the V-8 and the Cost Clipper Six with higher 7.5:1 instead of 7.2:1 compression ratios were slightly more

powerful for 1955. The 6-cylinder engine developed 118 horsepower at 3800rpm and 195lb/ft of torque at 1200-2400rpm. Its net power ratings were 109 horsepower at 3600rpm and 189lb/ft of torque at 1000-2300rpm. The V-8's new ratings were 132 horsepower at 4200rpm and 215lb/ft of torque at 1800-2200rpm (net ratings were 113 horsepower at 3600rpm and 209lb/ft at 1500-2000rpm). Both engines now used an inverted fuel pump and 18mm sparkplugs. The 6-cylinder had revised piston rings and an improved head gasket. The V-8 received a larger capacity water pump. Also adopted for 1955 was a larger capacity water pump, and a higher maximum - 5500lb - GVW. Total production for 1955 was 124,842 units.

Ford offered a fairly drastically restyled F-100 pickup for 1956. The most apparent aspect of what Ford called the F-100's 'Leadership Look' styling was the new, 'full-wrap' windshield. Often generically referred to as a wraparound windshield, this arrangement was a sine qua non of contemporary American car and truck styling. With nearly 1000sq in of glass

area, Ford's version was promised to give drivers "... a new feeling of confidence at the wheel that markedly relieves the strain of driving." An apparent by-product of the use of the new windshield was the change in the windshield wiper format. Previously the wipers' individually swept areas overlapped; for 1956 the wipers operated through separate arcs of travel. Adding to the F-100's wide expanse of glass was an optional 'full-wrap' rear window with an area of over 823sq in Emphasizing the F-100's new vertical post windshield was a prominent windshield visor that Ford considered "... a distinctive trademark ..." The side hood-mounted series identification now consisted of a chrome F-100 designation within a red-finished circle, with bright surround attached to a chrome spear which carried red-finished FORD lettering.

The same general grille format as that used in 1955 was carried over into 1956 with minor revisions. A touch of 1955 Ford car styling was evident in the visors positioned above the headlights. Whereas V-8 engined F-100 pickups had a chrome alphanumeric 'V-8' plaque mounted in

F-100 wheel sizes (1955-1956)		
Model year	1955	1956
Standard wheel	16 x 4.5K	15 x 5K
Optional	-	16 x 4.5K
		16 x 5K

1955 V-8 v 1956 V-8		
	1955 V-8	1956 V-8
Bore	3.50in	3.62in
Stroke	3.10in	3.30in
Displacement	239cu in	272cu in

the grille's center, those with a 6-cylinder engine no longer carried a grille-mounted engine identification.

Exterior colors offered for 1956 were Vermilion, Diamond Blue, Nocturne Blue, Meadowmist Green, Platinum Gray, Goldenrod Yellow, Meadow Green, and Raven Black. Two-tone combinations - Colonial White on the roof and upper back panel, plus any of the previously listed colors - were available on trucks fitted with the Custom Cab option.

The F-100's interior bore evidence of Ford's commitment to extend its Lifeguard design philosophy to include both cars and trucks for 1956. All F-100s were equipped with Ford's Lifeguard steering wheel, with its deep-dished center section. Ford reported that this wheel "... brings new security to truck driving. Exclusive deep-center design gives added protection against contact with the steering column in case of accident. With this and new preventive features, Ford answers a very real need of today's driver - and again points the way for the entire truck industry."

Among other safety features that Ford incorporated into the F-100 for 1956 were new Lifeguard door latches, with a double grip designed to provide extra protection against doors springing open in an accident, and optional seat belts. The dash panel was revamped to provide for a new 'high dial' instrument cluster.

The standard F-100 interior was finished in a gray plaid pattern with red vinyl facings. The Custom Cab was fitted with black and white chain-stripe upholstery with vinyl bolster and facing. The bolster and facings were color-keyed, red or copper-tone, to harmonize with the truck's exterior finish. Additional Custom Cab features included specific door trim and hardware, perforated thermacoustic header backed by one inch thick glass wool insulation, sound deadener on floor and rear cab panels, grip-type armrest on left door, large dome light with manual switch, two adjustable sun visors, and an illuminated cigar lighter. The Custom Cab's exterior features consisted of a 'Custom Cab' identification plate positioned just below the door window, bright-finish reveal molding for the windshield, and a bright metal grille. This latter feature had not been available on a Ford truck since 1938.

Joining the 110 inch wheelbase F-100 pickup was a new model, the 8 foot Express, mounted on a 118 inch wheelbase. This truck, which was subsequently identified as the 8 foot pickup, had box dimensions of 96.0in (length) x 54.0in (width) and 22.2in (height) which resulted in a volumetric capacity of 65.4 cubic feet. The 6.5ft F-100 was priced at $1577, and the 8ft version at $1611.

Several technical revisions characterized the 1956 F-100. A new 10.5in clutch, providing a surface area of 96.2sq in, was standard on all models powered by the V-8 engine. Introduced as a new option was power steering.

Both the F-100's 6-cylinder engine (identified as the Cost Cutter Six for 1956) and its Power King V-8 had increased power for 1956. Use of a 7.8:1 compression ratio and a freer-breathing manifold provided the Cost Cutter Six with 133 horsepower at 4000rpm and 202lb/ft of torque at 1600-2200rpm. Also introduced on the Cost Cutter Six were new triple seal oil rings. The Power King was credited with 167 horsepower at 4400rpm and 260lb/ft of torque at 2100-2600rpm.

In addition to its higher 7.8:1 compression ratio, the V-8 also received a substantial increase in displacement.

Ford offered new tubeless tires on all its 1956 truck models. The standard tires for 1956 were 6.70 x 15 units with a 4-ply rating. Three optional tires were available for the F-100: 6.70 x 15 (6-ply); 7.10 x 15 (6-ply), and 6.50 x 16 (6-ply). Associated with the F-100's new tire format was the use of new wheel sizes for 1956.

Replacing the heavy duty 3-speed in the optional transmission lineup for the F-100 pickup was the Warner T89B, which was rated as a medium duty unit. Its gear ratios were 3.17:1 (first gear), 1.75:1 (second gear), 1.00:1 (third gear), and 3.76:1 (reverse). Available axle ratios for 1956 were slightly revised with a 3.73:1 ratio replacing 4.27:1 as the V-8's standard axle ratio. The standard 6-cylinder axle ratio remained at 3.92:1. Overdrive ratio for F-100s with the 6-cylinder engine was 4.09:1. Those with V-8 engines and overdrive had ratios of 3.92:1.

Manufacture of 137,581 F-100 6.5ft pickups, in addition to 25,122 models with the 8ft bed closed out the final year of production of the first generation F-100 pickups. For 1957 Ford truck dealers not only would have new F-100 pickups to sell, but also a new Truck Market Manager whose name was Lee Iacocca.

FORD F-100/F-150 PICKUP 1953 - 1996

ROBERT ACKERSON

2
1957-1960

As Ford's new Truck Marketing Manager, Lee Iacocca's first message to Ford's sales staff began with the obvious: "1957 can be a big truck sales year for you for two important reasons. First, the 1957 line of Ford trucks is a completely new line with new styling and new models, offering greater sales potential than ever before ... The completely new Styleside pickups, plus the Ranchero, provide every Ford salesman with a strong product edge over competition. You have the line of trucks to really make the most of your truck sales opportunity."

Iacocca's second point that "... the truck market is growing, and growing fast," was underscored by his report that "... the number of trucks on the road has almost doubled from 5.1 million in 1946 to 9.2 million trucks in 1955. The average age of all trucks in operation is 6.7 years old. Fourteen per cent of all trucks on the road today are prewar models. 1,122,000 trucks now in use are 14 years old or older. Trucks in use by 1965 is estimated at 12 million units."

Looking towards that time, Ford claimed that "... the 1957 Ford trucks have stepped over and beyond the rest of the industry in five major areas:

Functional styling - which means a superior appearance as a result of matching beauty to power with a practical purpose.

Driver comfort and convenience - which means the utmost in ease of operation - minimizes driver fatigue for a more efficient trucking operation.

Exclusive safety factors - pioneered by Ford for greater protection of lives and property - a plus benefit for any trucking operation.

Load handling ability - no equal in the industry in providing maximum payload capacities matched by rugged and powerful operating components.

Power - a broad line of engines, transmissions, and rear axles matched to provide the right power for the job."

Although Ford abandoned the rounded outer surfaces of the 1953-1956 models in favor of a squared-off appearance, with distinct body surfaces for the new F-100, the truck successfully retained a visual kinship with the older F-Series. A major contributor to this 'Ford Look' was a 'wide sweep' grille with a prominent center bar with six rectangular cutouts, and headlights with squared-off 'hoods' positioned at the grille's outer extremities. The circular parking/directional lights, positioned within separate nacelles, were still located directly beneath the headlights.

The ribbed surface of the F-100's hood joined the air intake of a new 'Hi-Dri' ventilation system at the windshield base. The intake was fitted with an integral rain trap, and was operated by dual controls that could provide fresh air to the driver's area, passenger area, or both.

Mounted on the hood side was model trim consisting of bright-finish FORD letters and F-100 identification positioned within a field of bright red enamel. Only the faintest vestige, in the form of raised ribs over the wheel cutouts, remained of what had once been the F-100's distinctive front fenders. Now the impression was of a vehicle designed with previously separate elements coming together in a unified fashion.

Underscoring this development was the designation of a new Styleside pickup box with flush rear fenders as per the standard F-100 pickup model. The older pickup box design, with its wood floor (with steel skid strips) and outside running boards positioned between the cab and body, was still offered as the

F-100 interior dimensions (1956-1957)		
	1956	*1957*
Seat width	56.75in	56.75in
Hip room	60.75in	63.12in
Door height (from floor)	45.19in	43.78in
Door width	35.62in	37.02in

F-100 model dimensions (1957)

Flareside models

Wheelbase	110in	118in
Box length	78in	96in
Box width:	49.0in	54.0in
Box height:[1]	20.3in	22.1in
Box Height:[2]	17.6in	19.4in
Cubic capacity	45.0cu ft	65.4cu ft

Styleside models

Wheelbase	110in	118in
Box length	76.44in	94.44in
Box width:	73.20in	73.20in
Width between wheelhousings	49.0in	49.0in
Box height:[1]	19.09in	19.09in
Cubic capacity	56.05cu ft	70.55cu ft

[1]Measured to top of sides
[2]Measured to top of tailgate

Flareside model. Both pickups carried identical prices. The 110in wheelbase models listed for $1789, and the 118in wheelbase versions retailed at $1828. The latest F-100 was 2 inches wider and 3.5 inches lower than the 1956 version. Also increased in size for 1957 was the F-100's windshield which, at 61.5 inches, was over 2 inches wider than in 1956. Total windshield area now measured 1020sq in. The area of the 1957 model's standard rear window was reduced from 448sq in in 1956 to 407sq in. Similarly, the optional rear window in 1956 measured just over 823sq in; its 1957 counterpart had an area of 767sq in.

Another small change, new hubcaps of greater depth, and with a squared-off appearance, were accentuated by black-finished fluted surfaces.

Exterior colors offered for 1957 consisted of Vermilion, Midnight Blue, Starmist Blue, Woodsmoke Gray, Raven Black, Colonial White, Meadow Green, and Inca Gold. The Styleside pickup was available in any of these colors (except Colonial White) in combination with Colonial White to create a two-tone color scheme. All models were also offered in prime, if a customer desired a non-standard color scheme.

While defining the new Styleside F-100 as the 'Pacesetter of the Light Duty' line, Ford emphasized that, with its larger capacity and steel floor with integral skid strips, the Styleside was "truly functional."

Whereas the Flareside still retained taillights that were attached by brackets to the pickup box, the new Styleside's were incorporated into the rear fender format. Both pickup versions carried new style FORD lettering on their tailgates consisting of elongated letters with white surrounds and body-colored inner areas.

Although Ford reported that the F-100's new inboard step stayed free of slush and snow in bad weather, a year earlier it had touted the virtues of the 1956 model's old style running board format by noting that "Instead of moving the running board up inside the door, Ford keeps it low ... an easy intermediate step from ground to curb." In any case, the 1957 F-100's inboard steps were positioned 6.8 inches below floor level, thus still providing for a low step height to the ground. The use of suspended pedals for the brake and clutch eliminated the old clearance holes in the floor that had, for many years, allowed dust, water and, depending on the season, heat or cold, into the cab.

Ford achieved greater cab strength in 1957 by using a heavier, 18-gauge floor pan and fabricating the entire cab from heavy gauge steel, welded together into a single unit. Examples of this construction included welding the ventilation system to the cowl, providing double-wall strength in the major part of the cowl, and support to the cowl side panels and front door pillars. All-in-all, Ford claimed the F-100 had "... the strongest, sturdiest Light Duty Cab ever to bear the Ford name."

The instrument panel positioned all the dials within a dash flange, and included red warning lights for the oil pressure and generator battery voltage. Gauges were provided for engine coolant temperature and fuel level.

Ford, continuing to promote driver safety, included in the 1957 Light Duty

trucks sales brochure an illustration of an F-100 equipped with the standard Lifeguard steering wheel, and optional, dealer installed front safety belts. Customers were told that "... the exclusive Lifeguard steering wheel is designed to absorb the impact force of the driver when an accident occurs. The three-spoke, deep-dish safety steering wheel is designed so that the upper surface of the rim is approximately 3⅛ inches above the horn button. It will absorb impact forces uniformly and, after deformation, will maintain the plane of the rim well above the steering column no matter how the wheel is turned at the moment of impact. The wheel will be permanently deformed under such conditions and will not spring back to its original shape or position."

In the event of an accident, the F-100's redesigned rotor-type door locks tended to tighten on impact. "This is a definite safety factor," said Ford, "in helping prevent the driver or passenger from being thrown from the cab." Offered as extra cost options were padded sun visors and a padded instrument panel.

Key aspects of the standard cab equipment included a dispatch box, right door lock, dual windshield wipers, hub caps, left taillight, light switch, mechanical jack and tools, interior safety mirror, single electric horn, sound deadener on doors, underframe spare tire carrier, and a left side sun visor.

Interior features of the Custom Cab option consisted of two adjustable

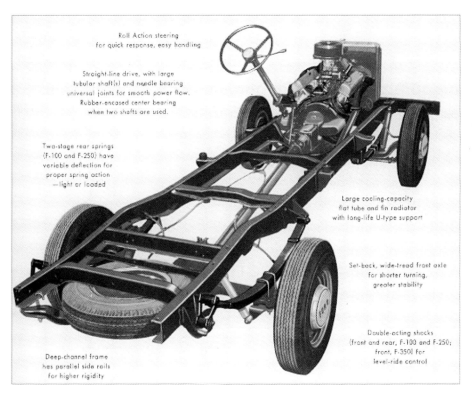

Roll Action steering for quick response, easy handling

Straight-line drive, with large tubular shaft(s) and needle bearing universal joints for smooth power flow. Rubber-encased center bearing when two shafts are used.

Two-stage rear springs (F-100 and F-250) have variable deflection for proper spring action —light or loaded

Large cooling-capacity flat tube and fin radiator with long-life U-type support

Set-back, wide-tread front axle for shorter turning, greater stability

Double-acting shocks (front and rear, F-100 and F-250; front, F-350) for level-ride control

Deep-channel frame has parallel side rails for higher rigidity

The chassis of the 1957 F-100 with 110in wheelbase. Two-stage springs were used at the rear. (Courtesy Ford Motor Company)

This view of a 1957 F-100 shows the Custom Cab interior, its chain stripe woven plastic upholstery, and optional, dealer installed seat belts. (Courtesy Ford Motor Company)

sun visors, a perforated thermacoustic headliner backed by 0.5 inches of glass wool insulation, a dome light with manual switch, armrests on both doors, three-tone chain stripe woven plastic seat upholstery color-keyed to cab exterior color (the standard cab had tan and brown woven plastic seat upholstery), a five inch foam rubber seat pad and two inch seat pad (both versions had new, non-sag formed wire springs), sound deadener on the floor and rear cab panels, insulation on the cab cowl wall, and hardboard door cowl-side trim panels. Custom exterior features included door locks on both doors, a bright metal grille bar and headlight assembly (the standard cab's grille was painted white, rather than ivory as had been the case previously), bright metal parking light rims, bright metal windshield reveal molding, door-mounted 'Custom Cab' emblems, and dual door locks. All F-100 pickups with the optional 'full-wrap' rear window also had a bright metal reveal molding for the rear window.

Numerous changes were made to the F-100's chassis and suspension for 1957. The front axle kingpin was longer, and a heavier spindle with a larger base

diameter was used. As the table on page 18 shows, the specification of both front and rear F-100 springs was revised.

As in 1956, a total of five transmissions were available for the F-100 pickup. The manual units had a new hydraulic clutch that reduced clutch chatter and required less foot pressure to operate.

The F-100 '223 Six' and '272 V-8' engines were more powerful for 1957. The 6-cylinder developed 139 horsepower at 4200rpm; net horsepower was 126 at 4000rpm. Maximum torque increased to 207lb/ft at 1800-2700rpm and maximum net torque was 198lb/ft at 1600-2500rpm. Ford attributed this additional power to the use of a higher 8.3:1 compression ratio and a new high lift cam. The V-8's ratings were 171 horsepower at 4400rpm (145 net horsepower at 4100rpm) and 260lb/ft of torque at 2100-2600rpm (net torque was 249lb/ft at 1900-2400rpm). Both engines were fitted with self-locking tappet adjustment screws, two-point, insulated front engine mounts and, in place of the old oil bath air filter, a cellulose filter.

Major options for the F-100 included a transistor radio, MagicAire heater and defroster, windshield washers, directional

signals, 70-amp/hr battery, chrome front and rear bumpers, oil filter (223 six), full-wrap rear window, armrest, cigar lighter and domelight (for standard cab), and side-mounted spare tire carrier.

Identifying the 1958 F-100 were its new grille with a center egg-crate design, hubcaps without the black-finished surfaces used for 1957, dual headlights, and front fender-mounted identification. The power ratings of the 272 V-8 were now 181 horsepower at 4400rpm and 262lb/ft of torque at 2200-2700rpm. Net ratings for 1958 were 153 horsepower at 4100rpm and 249lb/ft of torque at 1900-2400rpm. Early in 1958 the 272 cubic inch V-8 was replaced by a 292 cubic inch version with a 3.75in bore and 3.3in stroke. Its horsepower ratings were 186 at 4000rpm (gross) and 158 at 4000rpm (net). Torque ratings were 269lb/ft at 2200-2700rpm (gross) and 254lb/ft at 1900-2400rpm (net). This engine would be carried unchanged into 1959.

Three new colors - Azure Blue, Seaspray Green, and Gunmetal Gray - were introduced for 1958. Goldenrod Yellow, last available in 1956, was reintroduced. Carried over from 1957 were Vermilion, Midnight Blue, Raven Black, Colonial White, Meadow Green, and prime. All of these colors, except for prime and Colonial White, were available with Colonial White to create a two-tone color scheme.

F-100 suspension specifications (1956 v 1957)

Front suspension

	1956	1957
Length x width	42in x 1.75in	45in x 2.0in
Number of leaves	8	6
Capacity:(at pad)	950lb	950lb
Capacity (at ground)	1095lb	1090lb

Rear suspension

	1956	1957
Length x width	52.0in x 2.0in	52.0in x 2.25in
Number of leaves	6	7
Capacity (at pad)	1025lb	1025lb
Capacity (at ground)	1235lb	1245lb

F-100 transmission ratios (1957)

	Ratios[1]				
Trans	1st	2nd	3rd	4th	Rev
3-speed	2.78/2.574	1.62/1.634	1.00	–	3.375/3.125
3-speed/OD	2.78/2.574	1.62/1.634	1.00	0.70[2]	3.375/3.125
Fordomatic	2.40	1.46	1.00	2.10[3]	2.00
MD 3-speed	3.17	1.75	1.00	–	3.76
4-speed	6.40	3.09	1.69	1.00	7.82

[1]The first ratio cited is for trucks with the 6-cylinder engine; the second ratio is for trucks with V-8 engines.
[2]Overdrive ratio.
[3]Converter ratio.

F-100 standard and optional axle ratios (1957)

Transmission	Standard ratio	Optional ratio
6-cylinder models		
All manual transmission	3.70	3.89[1]
Fordomatic	3.89	4.11[2]
Overdrive	4.11	4.29[2]
V-8 models		
All manual transmission	3.70	3.89[2]
Fordomatic	3.70	3.89[2]
Overdrive	4.11	3.89[2]

[1]4.29 and 4.11 were available as pre-approved options only.
[2]Available as pre-approved option only.

As in previous years the latest Ford F-100 and its competitors were evaluated by both the press and the public as possible alternatives to station wagons and passenger cars. Typical of this approach was a road test of a 1959 Styleside pickup published by *Motor Life* in its September 1959 issue. Although unhappy about the poor fit of the rubber floor mat and lack of a secure storage area for the tire changing tools, *Motor Life* was generally impressed with the F-100. It found the steering, with only four turns lock-to-lock "... light and easy to manage." On the open road the F-100 was judged to be "... quite stable with no noticeable tendency to wander."

Although it was easy to spin the rear wheels of the V-8-powered F-100, *Motor Life* also discovered that acceleration was impressive with the zero to 60mph run requiring only 12.3 seconds. Also noteworthy was the F-100's overdrive-equipped fuel economy. Overall it delivered 15.9mpg, with one run in traffic yielding 17.8mpg. In conclusion, *Motor Life* reported that "... the test crew was very favorably impressed with the Ford F-100. With its light steering, it was a pleasant truck to drive, performance and economy were both above par, the cab was comfortable, and hauling capacity was among the largest in its class."

Due primarily to a new grille, the object of *Motor Life*'s approval was easy to distinguish from the 1958 F-100. An arrangement of four horizontal bars was mounted below a large air scoop with a mesh anodized aluminum insert, upon which, in bold block letters, was the word 'FORD.' The parking lights were rectangular in shape and positioned in the grille area just below the headlights. A new contoured front bumper with a center recess for the license plate was also used, as was a new side hood-mounted 'gear and lightning' model identification.

Four new exterior colors were introduced for 1959 - Indian Turquoise, April Green, Academy Blue, and Wedgewood Blue. Carried over from 1958 were Goldenrod Yellow, Vermilion, Meadow Green, Colonial White, and Raven. As in 1958, two-tone color combinations were possible. The F-100 was also available from the factory in a prime finish.

The F-100's standard cab was

The 1957 F-100 standard 6-cylinder and optional V-8 engines. Both had compression ratios of 8.3:1.
(Courtesy Ford Motor Company)

freshened for 1959 by the use of an easier to clean, more durable and breathable woven nylon-saran upholstery. New fresh air outlet grilles and a domelight were also provided. Added to the content of the Custom Cab option was new nylon-saran 'candy' striped upholstery, color-keyed to the exterior, a white steering wheel with a chromed horn ring, and a two-tone instrument panel. The interior cab step on all pickups was now constructed of 25 per cent thicker steel for increased strength.

The new 4-wheel drive F-100 pickup on the 118in wheelbase chassis was offered in Styleside and Flareside forms.

Key aspects of the 4-wheel drive F-100, including its hypoid front axle and two-speed transfer case, are listed in the table on page 20.

Instructions for operating the two-speed (1.87:1,1.0:1) Spicer transfer case were attached to the driver's sun visor, and engraved on the shift control knob. Gear positions for the 4-wheel drive F-100 consisted of the following:
4L: 4-wheel drive - low gear
N: Neutral
2H: Rear wheel drive
4H: 4-wheel drive, direct drive

With a base price of $2512.46, the 6-cylinder F-100 (the 292 V-8 was also offered) 4-wheel drive pickup was available with only one optional transmission, a 4-speed manual gearbox. Prices for the other F-100 pickups were as follows:
6.5ft Flareside: $1932
6.5ft Styleside: $1948
8.0ft Flareside: $1971
8.0ft Styleside: $1987

In June,1959 Ford introduced two features for the F-100 pickups. The first was a Powr-Lok locking differential for 2-wheel drive models. This new $50.10 regular production option automatically supplied driving force to the wheel with the greatest traction, and was offered with either the 6-cylinder or V-8 engine. Available axle ratios were 3.73:1 and 3.92:1.

Also entering production at approximately the same time was a revised F-100 frame that, Ford reported, represented "... considerable research and testing to provide a more rugged frame with increased durability to withstand the severe stresses produced by rough roads." Major features included the use of 50 per cent heavier gauge steel for rear crossmembers numbers five and six. The gauge previously had been 0.118 inches

and was now 0.180 inches. Also added were upper and lower flange gussets at the junction of number five crossmember and the side rail. This latter change gave the frame 18 per cent greater torsional rigidity. To ensure maximum strength the new crossmember and gussets were secured by twenty additional rivets. Another four rivets (for a total of eight) were added to the junction of number six crossmember and the side rail.

When Ford entered the factory-built 4-wheel drive pickup field, Willys controlled 64.7 per cent of the market; International followed with a market share of 15.1 per cent. The remaining market segment was divided between Dodge (10.8 per cent), Chevrolet (4.0 per cent), and GMC (3.1 per cent). In the years to follow, this division would change dramatically. Overall, Ford accounted for 31.09 per cent of all new truck registrations in 1959. Production of F-100 Flareside pickups totaled 26,616, whilst output of Styleside models reached a level of 112,082 units.

In 1960 the F-100 was significantly redesigned with a new grille consisting of a large, full-width crossbar enclosing the dual headlights, and a lower portion containing an insert of rectangular

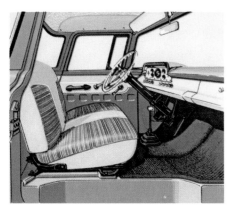

The Custom Cab interior for 1959 featured a new two-tone treatment for the instrument panel and door panels. The seats were covered in a candy-striped nylon-saran fabric. (Courtesy Ford Motor Company)

4-wheel drive F-100 specifications (1959)

Maximum GVW	5600lb
Front axle capacity	3000lb
Front axle ratio	3.92:1
Rear axle capacity	3300lb
Rear axle ratio	3.89:1
Steering ratio	18:11
Turning radius	48.32ft[2]
Frame side dimensions*	6.0in x 2.25in x 0.19in
Section modulus[1]	3.34
Front springs[1]	
Size	45in x 2.0in
Number of leaves	6
Standard capacity	950lb (at pad)
Optional capacity	1050lb (at pad)
Rear springs	
Size	52in x 2.25in
Number of leaves	7
Standard capacity	1025lb (at pad)
Optional capacity	1350lb, 1650lb (at pad)

[1]Identical to the specifications of the component used for the 2-wheel drive, 118in wheelbase F-100 pickup.
[2]Turning diameter as measured to center line of outer wheel. By comparison, the turning diameter for the 2-wheel drive F-100 was 37.26ft.

dividers. The parking lights, positioned below the headlights, were integrated into this element. The leading edge of the hood carried two narrow recessed air intakes separated by a reformatted Ford gear and lightning crest. The hood side-mounted series identification was revamped to include a stylized rocket with bright red FORD lettering, and chrome F-100 identification positioned in a bright red field.

A new 'Diamond Lustre' enamel exterior paint, resistant to scratching and

Styling highlights of the 1959 F-100 included floating grille, rectangular parking lights, and new model identification plate. (Courtesy Ford Motor Company)

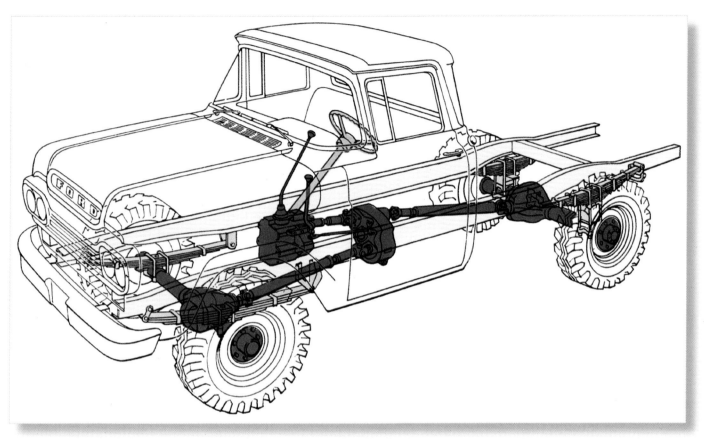

This cutaway view of a 1959 F-100 4x4 illustrates front and rear differentials, transfer case, and transmission.
(Courtesy Ford Motor Company)

chipping, was offered in Monte Carlo Red, Goldenrod Yellow, Academy Blue, Skymist Blue, Caribbean Turquoise, Adriatic Green, Holly Green, Corinthian White, or Raven Black. Any standard color could be combined with Corinthian White for a two-tone color theme.

Refinements found in the F-100 interior included improved weatherstripping, coat hooks, and a sturdier inboard support for the sun visor. The door locks were also easier to operate. New plaid nylon-plastic seat upholstery, with vinyl bolsters sporting a 'rib and stitch' effect, along with a light gray, spatter-patterned headliner, was used in the standard F-100 cab. Replacing the cotton seat pads of the previous standard cab was a new 1.25 inch thick foam seat pad. Although no changes were made in the instrument panel design for 1960, a white cover plate

*The 1958 F-100 Styleside pickup box provided cab-wide body sides and an expansive bed space.
(Courtesy Ford Motor Company)*

for the control cluster area was used for the standard cab. The optional heater was capable of keeping the cab ten degrees warmer, and provided better defrosting than the 1959 unit.

Several refinements were made to the content of the Custom Cab option for 1960, the most obvious of which was new striped nylon-saran seat upholstery with a ribbed vinyl center panel. The dials

1960 FORD TRUCKS
LIGHT DUTY MODELS

F-100
F-250
F-350

The 1960 F-100 was easily identified by its recessed air intake, full-width center crossbar, and new grille gridwork. The model illustrated has the Custom Cab and Tu-Tone paint options.
(Courtesy Ford Motor Company)

mounted in the two-tone instrument panel were highlighted by chrome rings.

Both the 223 6-cylinder and 292 V-8 engines were upgraded with new rocker arm covers and neoprene gaskets to minimize oil leaks, improved and more durable cooling systems, and new crankshaft knurling in the rear oil seal area for better oil retention and economy. The 6-cylinder engine had a higher - 8.1:1 - compression ratio, a generator with permanently lubricated sealed commutator end bearing, and a new 'depth-type' oil filter that promised to deliver 20 per cent more filter efficiency and longer element life. Introduced as a running change during the 1959 model run, and carried over for 1960 was a new

The Custom Cab option for 1960 included two-tone styling on the instrument panel and door panels, and a striped woven nylon-saran upholstery with gray vinyl bolsters and seat facings.
(Courtesy Ford Motor Company)

F-100 power ratings (1960)		
Engine	*223 6-cylinder*	*292 V-8*
Gross horsepower	139 at 4200rpm	172 at 4000rpm
Net horsepower	126 at 4000rpm	146 at 3800rpm
Gross torque (lb/ft)	203 at 2000-2600rpm	270 at 2000-2600rpm
Net torque (lb/ft)	192 at 1600-2500rpm	254 at 1900-2400rpm

FORD TRUCKS

rotor-type oil pump providing 54 per cent more oil pressure at idle speed, as well as a more constant oil pressure at all speeds.

A combustion chamber design with increased squish area in the combustion area, new sparkplug location, and new intake valves on the 292 V-8 were considered to deliver "... more complete, more economical combustion using regular grade gasoline." The piston rings were also of a new design, incorporating

A 1960 F-100 Styleside 4x4 with after-market towing equipment and special order tires. (Courtesy Ford Motor Company)

1960 F-100 prices

Model	Price	
110in wheelbase	6-cylinder	V-8
Pickup, 6.5ft box	$2032.00	$2167.00
118in wheelbase		
Pickup, 8.0ft box	$2070.00	$2205.00

Option	Price
4-wheel drive[1]	$567.00
Fresh air heater and turn signals	$94.00
Locking rear axle	$51.00
Rear bumper	$26.00
Chrome bumpers	$48.00
Custom Cab	$77.00
Heavy duty seat covering	$8.00
Side mount tire carrier	$15.00
Heavy duty radiator	$17.00
Heavy duty rear springs	$13.00
Power steering	$125.00
Wrap-around rear window	$29.00
Tinted glass	$22.00
Tu-Tone paint	$27.00
Electric wipers (6-cylinder)	$8.00
3-speed, medium duty transmission	$81.00
4-speed transmission	$87.00
Overdrive	$109.00
Fordomatic	$200.00
6.70 x 15, 4-ply WSW tires	$31.00
6.70 x 15, 6-ply, BSW tires	$45.00
7.10 x 15, 6-ply BSW tires	$49.00
6.50 x 16, 6-ply PT BSW[2]	$80.00
6.50 x 16, 6-ply TT BSW[2]	$122.00
7 x 17.5, 6-ply BSW[2]	$148.00

[1]118in wheelbase only.
[2]Includes heavy duty rear springs.

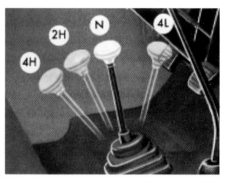

The 4x4 2-speed transfer case provided direct drive and a low ratio of 1.86:1. (Courtesy Ford Motor Company)

An illustration of the 1960 F-100's 4x4 transfer case shift lever, and its four positions. (Courtesy Ford Motor Company)

a three-segment oil control ring with 150 per cent more chrome plating on the ring-side rails. The anticipated result was greater ring stability and reduced oil consumption. An ignition distributor assembly previously used on the heavy duty version of the 292 V-8 engine was now standard for the F-100's 292 V-8. Its breaker plate design improved overall engine performance. Also used on the 292 V-8 was an improved oil pump with a stronger steel cover in place of the older, cast iron unit. Also found on the latest oil pump was a new relief valve that virtually eliminated sticking caused by sludge and varnish accumulation.

Other technical changes for 1960 included a new neoprene seal for the driveline center bearing, and more durable brake linings. The drum surfaces were more highly polished to provide greater equalization of braking action and thus reduce erratic braking performance. All models also had a stronger battery support system.

Structural changes made to the body of F-100 4-wheel drive models involved new cab reinforcement and a more rigid door opening area. The standard front springs rating was 1050lb at pad. In 1959 this rating had been optional. Similarly, the rear spring's standard rating of 1350lb

at pad had been optional in 1959. The steering ratio was changed from the 1959 model's 18.2:1 to 20.4:1 for 1960.

Production of F-100 pickups for 1960 comprised 27,383 Flareside models, 113,875 Styleside models, 964 4-wheel drive Flareside models and 4334 4-wheel drive Styleside models.

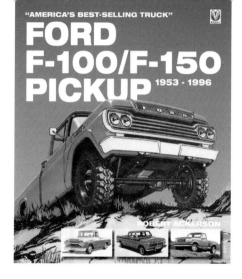

"AMERICA'S BEST-SELLING TRUCK"

FORD F-100/F-150 PICKUP 1953 - 1996

ROBERT ACKERSON

3

1961-1966

On October 13, 1960 Ford introduced what it regarded as "... the greatest commercial vehicle expansion in Ford Motor Company's 58 year history." Ford Truck Marketing Manager, Wilbur Chase, noted that "... the dramatic change in Ford truck appearance results directly from incorporation of more functional design of components, rather than the addition of 'ginger bread' styling." In addition, Chase explained that "... the 1961 Ford truck line exemplifies Ford's efforts to supply truck operators with durable, reliable tools, while incorporating the latest proven engineering advancements that will maintain Ford's historic leadership in truck economy."

Highlighting the F-100 pickups was a new Styleside model with an integral cab and body. The result, said Ford "... was a smooth, clean appearance ... greater rigidity and longer life." The new Styleside truck's cargo capacity was 9 cubic feet more than the previous model's, and the tailgate was 13 inches wider with a new, non-rattling latch which could be operated with one hand. The result was a load space of over 65 cubic feet on the 6.5 foot box, and nearly 80 cubic feet on

the 8 foot body. The inside width of both boxes was 76.56 inches, 3.65 inches wider than in 1960. The boxes were also longer for 1961: the 6.5 foot box extended to 78.19 inches and the 8.0 foot box to 98.19 inches.

Ford asserted that the new type of construction "... provides greater sheet metal life by eliminating the gap between the cab and the box - a major source of rust and corrosion." Greater load area strength was credited to the use of box girder construction at the rear corners.

The new F-100 cab was two inches wider and, due primarily to the frame's 'step down' in the cab area, four inches lower than its 1960 counterpart. Ground clearance was marginally increased, while step-in height was reduced by 1.5 inches.

Exterior colors consisted of Monte Carlo Red, Goldenrod Yellow, Raven Black, Mint Green, Holly Green, Caribbean Turquoise, Academy Blue, Starlight Blue, and Corinthian White. The Styleside model was available in any of these colors in a two-tone combination with Corinthian White.

One of the most obvious exterior

F-100 Styleside dimensions (1960 v 1961)		
Model	1960	1961[1]
Wheelbase	110in/118in	114in/122in
Windshield area	1020sq in	1247sq in
Std. rear window area	407sq in	600sq in
Seat width	56.75in	56.75in
Hip room	63.12in	63.42in
Door height[2]	43.38in	42.0in
Door width	37.00in	37.48in

[1]The 4-wheel drive models for 1961 had a 120 inch wheelbase, which was two inches longer than that of the 1960 model.
[2]As measured from the floor.

FORD LEADS THE WAY FOR 1961

WITH THE MOST ADVANCED LIGHT AND MEDIUM DUTY TRUCKS IN THE INDUSTRY

Here Are The New Features On Your 100 Through 600 Series
DESIGNED TO OUTSELL COMPETITION

features of the new F-100 was a single 7 inch headlight design. Abandonment of the dual headlight system was explained by Wilbur Chase: "Ford trucks have single headlights to reduce headlamp replacement by 50 per cent." At the same time Ford noted that the new headlight still provided full-range illumination. The headlight was positioned within a new, one-piece grille design with bright metal FORD block lettering, a wide chrome surround, and rectangular parking/directional lights mounted inboard of the headlight. Directly above the grille was a prominent crease line containing four recessed air intakes.

The hood, with two broad indentations and a new Ford logo, was wider and lower than in 1960. Opening and closing the hood was easier due to a new hood latch and spring-loaded hinges. Installed at the windshield base was a larger 'hi-cowl' air intake providing increased fresh air flow to the cab. A new windshield design eliminated the old dog-leg front post while concurrently providing over 22 per cent greater glass area. The F-100's hubcaps

Highlights of the 1961 Custom Cab interior included a chrome-trimmed instrument cluster, a two-tone color scheme, and twill stripe woven seat upholstery. (Courtesy Ford Motor Company)

New styling for 1961 featured a lower silhouette, a lower and wider hood, single headlights, and elimination of the cab dog-leg. (Courtesy Ford Motor Company)

still had FORD identification in bold red block letters, but were somewhat flatter than in 1960, and carried a ring of black rectangular ornamentation on the outer edge. Two-speed electric windshield wipers, standard for all models, operated in tandem to sweep a larger surface area.

A redesigned instrument panel provided theft-resistant ignition and large

223 6-cyl v 292 V-8 engine specifications

Engine	223 6-cylinder	292 V-8
Compression ratio	8.4:1	8.0:1
Gross horsepower	135 at 4000rpm	160 at 4000rpm
Net horsepower	114 at 3600rpm	135 at 3800rpm
Gross torque (lb/ft)	200 at 1800-2400rpm	270 at 1800-2000rpm
Net torque	186 at 1600-2000rpm	245 at 1800-2000rpm

F-100 general specifications

Maximum gross vehicle weight	5000lb
Standard front axle capacity	2600lb
Standard rear axle capacity	3300lb
Standard front spring capacity[1]	1145lb
Standard rear spring capacity[1]	1180lb
Turning diameter	38.18ft (114in wheelbase) 40.27ft (122in wheelbase)
Total brake lining area	169.2sq in
Clutch size	10.0in (6-cylinder) 11.0in (V-8)
Clutch area (sq in)	96.2 (6-cylinder) 124.0 (V-8)
Standard tires	6.70 x 15, 4-ply

[1]At ground.

F-100 prices (1961)

Flareside, 11in wheelbase, 6.5ft bed, 6-cylinder	$1920.83
Flareside, 114in wheelbase, 6.5ft bed, V-8	$2039.23
Flareside, 122in wheelbase, 8.0ft bed, 6-cylinder	$1956.03
Flareside, 122in wheelbase, 8.0ft bed, V-8	$2074.43
Styleside, 114in wheelbase, 6.5ft bed, 6-cylinder	$1935.73
Styleside, 114in wheelbase, 6.5ft bed, V-8	$2054.13
Styleside, 122in wheelbase, 8.0ft bed, 6-cylinder	$1971.93
Styleside, 122in wheelbase, 8.0ft bed, V-8	$2090.33

circulator defroster deflectors for quicker eye level defrosting. Both the optional fresh air and recirculating type heaters possessed up to 60 per cent greater heating capacity than those used in 1960. The standard upholstery was a brown basket weave vinyl with 1.25 inches of foam seat padding. Principle interior and exterior components of the Custom Cab were:

Exterior:
Bright metal grille and headlight assembly.
Bright metal windshield molding.
Door locks on both doors.
Custom Cab emblem on doors.

Interior:
5 inch foam rubber padding in seat cushion.
Approximately 2 inches of foam rubber padding in seat back.

Key elements of the 1961 F-100 chassis included shot-peened front springs, a heavier gauge metal radiator header, and recirculating ball steering. (Courtesy Ford Motor Company)

White steering wheel with chrome horn ring.
Chrome-trimmed instrument panel.
Two-tone interior with twill stripe wovenplastic seat upholstery.
Insulation installed on cab cowl wall.
The 223 6-cylinder and 292 V-8 engines had new crankcase oil seals, new fans, improved crankcase ventilation, 180 degree thermostats, and oil bath air cleaners for 1961.
A heavier gauge metal radiator header with lock seam construction made for a more durable and leak-resistant cooling system. Other technical refinements included the use of a moisture-proof wiring harness and cab-mounted fuse

Ford introduced the 1962 F-100 on September 21, 1961. (Courtesy Ford Motor Company)

boxes. A new high output heater/defroster was optional.

All F-100 pickups were based on a new frame with greater resistance to twisting and bending. Front springs were shot-peened for increased durability and longer life. The 4-wheel drive models had springs that were 3 inches longer and 0.5 inches wider than those used in 1960. The frame's maximum side rail dimension was increased from 6 to 6.96 inches. All models had more durable front and rear shock absorbers that gave a smoother ride. Replacing the old worm and lever steering system was a recirculating ball system with a 20:1 ratio. Changes in the design of the standard 3-speed transmission made it sturdier while allowing for smoother and more positive shifting. Also utilized for 1961 was a new mechanical clutch linkage, in place of the hydraulic system, that reduced both pedal effort and the need for maintenance.

Ford released its 1962 model trucks on September 21, 1961 and, understandably, changes for 1962 were limited. A revamped front end appearance was achieved by moving the FORD lettering from its 1961 position within the grille to a location just below the air intakes. The grille now carried a narrow horizontal bar and a thin vertical divider. Except for some units with red lettering found on early production models, the FORD lettering on the F-100 hubcaps was now argent.

Replacing Fordomatic as F-100 optional automatic transmission was a heavy duty Cruise-O-Matic unit. In lieu of any other major development for 1962, Ford's News Bureau reported that the company's primary focus for 1962 would be to concentrate "... its 1962 light truck engineering effort on reducing truck operating costs." Specifically, Ford

A 1962 F-100 Flareside with an 8 foot pickup box. (Courtesy Ford Motor Company)

Integral *v* Separate cab and box Styleside box measurements (1962)

	Integral Styleside		Separate Styleside		Flareside	
Box length (ft)	6.5	8.0	6.5	8.0	6.5	8.0
Inside length (in)	78.2	98.2	76.4	94.4	78.0	80.0
Inside width (in)	76.6	76.6	73.0	73.0	49.0	54.0
Inside width[1] (in)	49.0	49.0	49.0	49.0	-	48.4
Tailgate opening (in)	64.5	64.5	51.6	51.6	49.0	54.0
Height[2] (in)	19.6	19.6	19.1	19.1	20.3	22.1
Cubic capacity (cu ft)	65.1	79.7	56.1	70.6	45.0	65.4

[1]Measured between wheelhousings.
[2]Measured from floor to top of sides.

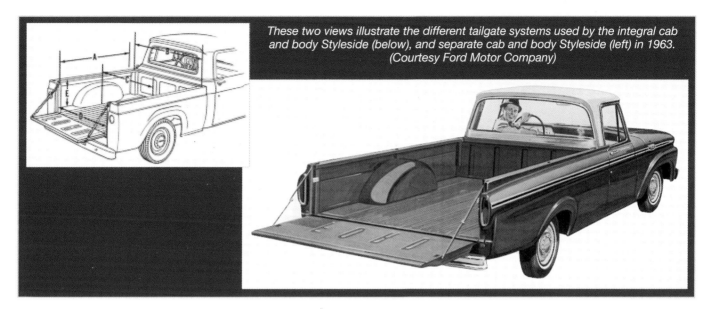

These two views illustrate the different tailgate systems used by the integral cab and body Styleside (below), and separate cab and body Styleside (left) in 1963. (Courtesy Ford Motor Company)

Division's Truck Marketing Manager, John F. Mclean, said that "... in a deliberate effort to help businessmen combat inflationary-type operating costs, Ford has focused its prime attention on engineering improvements rather than body changes."

Due to a fair amount of buyer resistance to the integral cab Styleside model of 1961, early in 1962 Ford reintroduced a Styleside body with separate cab and box. After being initially limited to use as the standard Styleside model for the 4-wheel drive models, this format was also offered for the 2-wheel drive F-100 models.

Color selection for 1962 was revised: Rangoon Red, Goldenrod Yellow, Raven Black, Sandshell Beige, Holly Green, Caribbean Turquoise, Academy Blue, Baffin Blue, and Corinthian White. Once again, Styleside models could be finished in a two-tone combination of Corinthian White and any of the standard colors.

1963 was a year of major refinements in the design of the F-100, as well as the final year of production for the integral cab and bed Styleside model. Adding substance to the assertion that the F-100 was "... built like the big ones ..." was Ford's new 24,000 mile or 24 month warranty which replaced the 12,000 mile or 12 month warranty of 1962.

As part of Ford's program to improve driver comfort, clutch and brake pedal height was lowered for 1963. This seemingly minor change was readily apparent to drivers who appreciated the resulting reduction of leg lift required when transferring the right foot from the accelerator to the brake pedal, and the left foot from the floor to the clutch pedal. Probably even more appreciated by the typical buyer of a 1963 F-100 pickup was the 1963 model's standard equipment fully synchronized, Ford-built 3-speed transmission. This transmission used self-energizing ring and blocker type synchronizers which enhanced overall shifting characteristics. In addition to these improvements, its design also lowered gear stress and shaft deflection. The respective gear ratios of the 1963 Ford-built transmission, and those of the 1962 version, were as shown in the table below.

Use of new amber colored parking lights was consistent with a recommendation from the Automobile Manufacturers' Association, and provided a contrast with the white headlight for better turn signal visibility. Less apparent was the F-100's more durable and reliable new turn signal flasher. Its longer life was achieved by the use of a temperature sensitive metal disc which changed from convex to concave during cycling. This

Gear ratios (1962/1963)

| | 1962 | | 1963 | |
	6-cyl	V-8	6-cyl	V-8
First gear	2.78	2.57	2.79	2.59
Second gear	1.61	1.63	1.70	1.58
Third gear	1.0	1.0	1.0	1.0
Reverse	3.38	3.12	2.87	2.66

Carry-over transmissions and ratios

| Manufacturer Identification | Warner[1] | | Warner[2] | | Ford |
	T-86G	T-86H	T-89C	T-98A	Cruise-O-Matic
1st	2.80	2.57	3.17	6.40	2.46
2nd	1.69	1.55	1.75	3.09	1.46
3rd	1.00	1.00	1.00	1.69	1.00
4th	-	-	-	1.00	2.20
Rev	3.80	3.49	3.76	7.82	2.40
Overdrive	0.70	0.70	-	-	-

[1]The T-86G was the overdrive unit supplied with the 6-cylinder engine; T-86H was the overdrive used with the 292 V-8.
[2]T-89C was the medium-duty 3-speed transmission, T-98 was the designation for the 4-speed manual.

"BUILT LIKE THE BIG ONES"

Two views of the 1963 F-100 Styleside. Top: the re-introduced model with separate cab and body; bottom: the integral cab and body version. (Courtesy Ford Motor Company)

F-100 prices and production totals (1963)

Production

Integral Styleside models	40,535
Flareside models	35,963
Separate Styleside	76,728
4-wheel drive Flareside	967
4-wheel drive Styleside	2809

Prices

114in wheelbase[1], 6-cylinder:

Flareside	$2001.74
Integral Styleside	$2137.14
Separate Styleside	$2184.64

112in wheelbase[1], 6-cylinder:

Flareside	$2038.24
Integral Styleside	$2055.24
Separate Styleside	$2066.24

120in 4-wheel drive[1]

Flareside	$2652.50
Separate Styleside	$2680.50

[1]Price listed is for 6-cylinder models; for V-8 models add $118.40.

Options	*Price*
42amp alternator	$21.55
60amp alternator	$134.50
Left side armrest (for standard cab)	$4.70
Right side armrest	$4.70
Locking type rear axle	$63.80
55amp battery (except 4wd)	$5.20
70amp battery (except 4wd)	$9.70
70amp battery (4wd)	$7.60
Chrome front bumper	$14.20
Rear painted contour bumper (Styleside)	$21.90
Front and rear chrome contour bumper (Styleside)	$47.90
Rear painted channel bumper (Flareside)	$20.60
Custom Cab	$89.20
Side-mounted spare wheel carrier	$14.10
Spare wheel carrier under frame (delete credit)	$3.10
Cigarette lighter	$4.20
11in heavy duty clutch (6-cylinder)[1]	$5.00
11in heavy duty clutch (V-8)[2]	NC
Tinted windshield glass	$14.20
Laminated sheet glass (doors only)	$4.30
Governor	$17.40
Brush-type grille guard	$38.00
Fresh air heater	$68.40
Recirculating heater	$49.10
Dual electric horns	$8.50
Bright metal hubcaps	$7.40
Free running front manual hubs (4-wheel drive)	$72.10
ICC emergency lamp flasher unit[3]	$11.60
ICC clearance lights (2 front center)	$5.30
ICC clearance lights (3 front center)	$8.00
Spare tire lock and chain	$6.40
Chrome left or right side outside mirror	$4.90
Inside safety mirror	$2.90
Right side 5.0in x 5.0in non-telescopic mirror	$4.90
Left side 5.0in x 5.0in non-telescopic mirror	$4.90

continued over

design replaced the older coiled wire construction version.

Similarly invisible was a new speedometer cable incorporating in its construction a wire casing, along with an outer rubber cover which improved cable lubrication and prevented damage from dirt and water. The cable assembly was pre-packed with grease; additional lubrication was not required.

Fitted to the F-100's front wheels was a new, thin, wheel bearing adjustment nut which gave much better precise control of adjustment than did the older castellated front wheel spindle nut. The new nut made possible a fifty per cent reduction in wheel bearing and play tolerance which, in turn, increased wheel bearing life.

A new option for the standard cab was a door-located stowage compartment. With a bezel and zippered vinyl cover measuring 20in x 12in x 2.5in, it provided a protected area for such items as a flashlight, flares, clipboard, etc. This compartment was standard in the left hand door of the Custom Cab, and optional in either door for all pickups. Another new option was a 40amp alternator.

Beginning in 1960, the design of the F-100 had incorporated a number of corrosion preventive features. For 1963, this effort was substantially upgraded to include the following:

1 Use of galvanized steps and risers.

2 Application of zinc-rich primer to:

    a) Fender 'eyebrows.'

    b) Rear of under-fender reinforcement.

    c) Inside of doors.

    d) Joining surface of running board reinforcement.

    e) Inside surface of front body crossmember.

    f) Underside of cowl vent intake.

3. Application of rust-resistant primer to:

    a) Cowl vent chamber.

F-100 prices and production totals (1963) (continued)

Options	Price
Right side 5.0in x 8.0in telescopic mirror	$7.40
Right side Western type 5.0in x 10.0in mirror	$12.70
Left side Western type 5.0in x 10.0in mirror	$12.70
Bright metal body side moldings (Styleside)	$21.60
Two-tone paint	$16.20
Chrome Yellow or White paint	NC
Extra cooling radiator	$21.40
Manual radio	$50.20
Front amber reflectors	$3.60
Rear reflectors	$3.60
Safety package A (padded dash and visor)	$19.60
Heavy duty vinyl seat trim	$7.80
Full foam seat cushion	$25.70
Heavy duty, 1100lb front springs[4]	$3.20
Rear, two-stage, heavy duty 1350lb springs[5]	$6.50
Heavy duty, 1650lb rear springs[6]	$12.30
Rear, two-stage, 1950lb heavy duty springs[7]	$7.10
Stowage compartment, left or right side	$10.30
Stowage compartment, left and right side	$20.60
3-speed medium,duty transmission[8]	$75.40
3-speed medium duty transmission[9]	$80.70
4-speed transmission[10]	$80.90
4-speed transmission[11]	$86.10
Overdrive 3-speed transmission[12]	$108.40
Heavy duty Cruise-O-Matic[13]	$243.40
Front fender mounted and integral rear turn signals	$17.40
Right side sun visor (for standard cab)	$4.50
Windshield washer	$11.60
Wrap-around rear window[14]	$43.00
Dual electric windshield wipers	$4.90
Tubeless tires	
6.70 x 15, 4-ply rated WSW, 5.5 K wheels	$31.50
6.70 x 15, 6-ply rated PT, 5.5 K wheels	$44.70
7.10 x 15, 4-ply rated PT, 5.5 K wheels	$15.70
7.10 x 15, 6-ply rated PT, 5.5 K wheels[15]	$48.30
6.50 x 16, 6-ply rated PT, 5.0 K wheels[15]	$71.60
6.50 x 16, 6-ply rated TT, 5.0 K wheels[15]	$99.40
7 x 17.5, 6-ply rated TT, 5.25 wheels[15]	$134.60
Tube type tires[16]	
6.50 x 16, 6-ply rated, PT 4.5 K wheels	$71.20
6.50 x 16, 6-ply rated, TT 4.5 K wheels	$99.40
7.00 x 15, 6-ply rated, TT 5.50F wheels	$149.40

[1] Not available for 6-cylinder with overdrive, standard on 4wd.
[2] Not available for V-8 with overdrive, standard on 4wd.
[3] Requires turn signals.
[4] Except 4wd. Standard with 122in wheelb
[5] Except 4wd.
[6] Except 4wd.
[7] Available for 4wd only.
[8] For 114in wheelbase models, includes 11in heavy duty clutch.
[9] For 122in wheelbase models, includes 11in heavy duty clutch.
[10] For 114in wheelbase models, includes 11in heavy duty clutch.
[11] For 120in and 122in wheelbase models, includes 11in heavy duty clutch.
[12] Not available for 4wd.
[13] Not available for 4wd.
[14] Available for Integral Styleside only.
[15] Optional rear springs required, except 4wd.
[16] Spare tires and wheels for virtually all sizes offered for the F-10 pickup were offered as delete options at credits ranging from $13.20-$23.20 for tires, and $3.80 to $8.40 for wheels.

b) Inside of body pillars.
4. Undercoating applied to critical stone spray areas of the lower dash panel and toe board.

Both the 223 6-cylinder and 292 V-8 engines had a new improved 'silenced' oil bath air cleaner for 1963. The improved silencing was achieved by revising the air cleaner cover to include a tuning shroud around the outside of the 1962 model air cleaner. The shroud added a narrow channel to the air stream, which effectively absorbed the objectionable peak frequencies of the induction system.

Also shared by these engines was a standard positive crankcase emission system, installed on all Ford vehicles built or sold in California since 1961, and optional for other applications. By utilizing manifold vacuum to draw fumes from the crankcase to the intake manifold, it removed approximately 40 per cent of engine hydrocarbons normally emitted into the atmosphere. No changes were made in the horsepower, torque or compression ratios of the F-100 engines for 1963.

Enhancing the external appearance of the F-100 was its new grille with a field of rectangular elements, and a new, full-length bodyside molding. The grille elements were painted white on standard cab models, and finished in anodized aluminum for F-100 models with the Custom Cab option. Both versions of the Styleside model were available with a new optional anodized aluminum body side molding with a red band. Custom Cab models without this option had 'Custom Cab' door handle escutcheon plates. If the side trim was ordered for a Custom Cab F-100, the 1962 style Custom Cab script was used. A new side body chrome diecast ornament with a plastic '100' insert was also used.

Standard F-100 colors were

114 inch v 128 inch wheelbase overall dimensions

	Styleside		Flareside	
Wheelbase (in)	114	122	114	122
Body length (ft)	6.5	8.0	6.5	8.0
Max. inside length (in)	78.7	98.7	77.9	96.0
Max. inside width (in)	70.0	70.0	49.0	54.0
Width between wheelhousings (in)	49.0	49.0	zero	48.4
Tailgate opening (in)	65.0	65.0	49.0	54.0
Height[1] (in)	19.3	19.3	20.3	22.1
Capacity (cu ft)	60.3	76.4	45.0	65.4

[1]Measured from floor to the top of sides.

Relationship between wheelbase/overall length of F-100

Model	Wheelbase	Overall length
Styleside, 6.5ft	114in	187.6in
Flareside, 6.5ft	114in	187.9in
Styleside, 8.0ft	128in	207.6in
Flareside, 8.0ft	128in	205.5in
4wd Styleside, 8.0ft	120in	203.7in
4wd Flareside, 8.0ft	120in	205.5in

The Custom Cab interior for 1964 used vertical pleating for the door panel insert as well as a new seat upholstery pattern. (Courtesy Ford Motor Company)

Rangoon Red, Driftwood Gray, Raven Black, Sandshell Beige, Holly Green, Caribbean Turquoise, Academy Blue, Glacier Blue, and Corinthian White. A new two-tone effect had the roof and cab back panel painted Corinthian White, and the remainder of the truck finished in any of the other standard colors (the previous format used Corinthian White for the hood and upper body portion).

New standard cab features included a gray block weave pattern vinyl metallic upholstery, matching door locks and a two-tone door panel area. The Custom Cab seat was finished in a candy stripe, woven plastic trim material. A 'Tee' bolster effect was created by covering the center seat back region in a vertical patterned metallic vinyl. This area also carried an embossed crest.

Ford combined several key design themes into a coherent "Built Like The Big Trucks - With A Big Comfort Bonus" philosophy for 1964. Acknowledging that F-100 buyers were increasingly buying pickups for casual use rather than strictly business or agricultural purposes, Ford noted that the F-100 had a "... quiet operation, convenience, and car-like comfort." Literally in the same breath, Ford added that an F-100 "... is solid truck through and through. It's built like the big trucks from axle to axle to give ... big truck reliability ... big truck durability."

Absent from the F-100 lineup for 1964 was the integral body/cab Styleside model. Its replacement, an F-100 Styleside with a separate box, was esthetically more pleasing than the separate box/cab 1962-63 Styleside model. Ford reported that "... this new Ford pickup box design has double-walled side panels and tailgate for extra strength and to protect exterior sheetmetal from damage caused by shifting loads."

This view of the 1964 F-100 4x4 chassis suggests that little had changed under the skin since 1959.
(Courtesy Ford Motor Company)

In place of the 122 inch wheelbase models of 1963 were F-100 pickups with a 128 inch wheelbase. Both the Flareside and Styleside models were available in this form as well as the carryover 114 inch wheelbase format. The 4-wheel drive F-100 continued to be based on a 120 inch wheelbase chassis.

The latest Styleside F-100 had a new tailgate latch, located at the top center of the gate, which could be operated with one hand. Latching was automatic. The tailgate straps were constructed of heavy steel and were capable of supporting a load of 2000 pounds. They were also designed to allow the gate to easily drop to a horizontal position.

Among the external appearance changes for 1964 was a revamped grille format, now with a stamped insert consisting of eight horizontal members, each with a blacked-out inner section. The bright metal FORD lettering was slightly larger than in 1963 and the distance between the letters was increased. Aside from its new tailgate, which was stamped

with larger FORD identification, the F-100 Styleside featured larger vertical taillights with increased reflector area.

Exterior colors offered for 1964 were Rangoon Red, Raven Black, Bengal Tan, HoLly Green, Pagoda Green, Caribbean Turquoise, Academy Blue, Skylight Blue, Wimbledon White, Pure White, and Chrome Yellow. With the exception of Pure White and Chrome Yellow, all standard colors could be combined with Wimbledon White in the optional two-tone version. A deluxe two-tone style available on Styleside models equipped with the optional bodyside moldings had Wimbledon White on the cab hood above the beltline, around the door frames and the area of the pickup box above the bodyside molding.

The F-100's standard vinyl interior was available in Red, Blue, Green or Beige, keyed to the exterior paint. The seat cushion and seat back trim was embossed with vertical stitching, surrounded by crush grained vinyl bolsters and sides. An embossed Ford crest was located in

the center of the seat panel. Except for 4-wheel drive models, the steering wheel, steering column, brackets, and levers were color-keyed to the exterior. Black rubber floor mats were included. The

262 6-cylinder specifications

Bore x stroke	3.719 x 4.03in
Displacement	262cu in
Compression ratio	8.0:1
Gross horsepower	152 at 4000rpm
Net horsepower	132 at 3600rpm
Gross torque	237lb/ft at 1800rpm
Net torque	224lb/ft at 1300-1600rpm
Intake valve dia[1]	1.775in-1.785in
Intake valve lift	0.369in
Exhaust valve dia	1.505in-1.515in
Exhaust valve lift	0.369in
Radiator capacity	13.5qt

[1]The 223 engine had identical valve size and lift specifications.

F-100 prices (1964)

Model	Price
114in wheelbase, 223 engine	
Flareside	$1963.74
Styleside	$1979.49
128in wheelbase, 223 engine	
Flareside	$2000.24
Styleside	$2015.99
4-wheel drive, 120in wheelbase, 223 engine:	
Flareside	$2626.99
Styleside	$2642.74

Option	Price
42amp alternator	$21.55
52amp alternator	$30.20
60amp alternator	$134.50
Premium anti-freeze	$2.15
Left side armrest (std cab)	$4.70
Right side armrest	$4.70
Limited-slip rear axle	$63.80
70amp battery	$7.60
Chrome front bumper	$14.20
Rear contour bumper[1]	$21.90
Front and rear chrome bumpers[1]	$47.90
Channel painted rear bumper[2]	$20.60
Custom Cab	$95.70
Side mounted spare wheel carrier[3]	14.10
Cigarette lighter	$4.20
11in heavy duty clutch[4]	$5.50
262 6-cylinder engine	$64.40
292 V-8 engine	$118.40
Tinted windshield glass	$14.20
Laminated side door glass	$4.30
Engine governor	$17.40
Brush-type grille guard	$38.00
Fresh air heater	$68.40
Recirculating heater	$49.10
Heavy Duty Equipment Package[5]	$38.60
Dual electric horns	$8.50
Bright metal hubcaps	$7.40
Manual free-running front hubs[6]	$78.50
ICC emergency flashing unit	$11.60
ICC clearance light packages	
Two front corner lights	$5.30
Three front corner lights	$8.00
Spare tire lock and chain	$6.40
Chrome, left or right side exterior mirror	$4.90
Inside safety mirror	$2.90
Non-telescopic 5in x 5in right side exterior mirror[7]	$4.90
Non-telescopic 5in. x 5in left side exterior mirror[7]	$4.90
Telescopic 5in x 8in left side exterior mirror[7]	$7.40
Telescopic 5in x 5in right side exterior mirror[7]	$7.40
Western style 7in x 11in right side exterior mirror[7]	$12.70
Western style 7in x 11in left side exterior mirror[7]	$12.70
Bright metal body side molding[8]	$32.30
Two-tone paint	$16.20
Deluxe two-tone paint[9]	$53.80

continued over

headliner, sun visor, inside mirror arms, and brackets were finished in light gray. If the optional armrests and door stowage compartments were ordered they were color-keyed to the seat trim. The headliner for both the standard and Custom Cab now extended along the rear quarter panel to the beltline for a more complete appearance.

The Custom Cab was offered in the same color selection as the standard cab. Its seat cushions and seat backs were covered with a woven plastic fabric, color-keyed to the exterior. The sides, top, and bolsters were finished in complementary shades of vinyl fabric. A Ford crest was embossed in the center vinyl panel of the seat back. The steering column steering wheel, plastic seat back pivot arm covers, levers, and brackets were color-keyed to the exterior. Color-keyed vinyl floor mats with a heel pad were installed on all models except those with 4-wheel drive. Also included was a color-keyed (except for 4-wheel drive) morocco grained, left-hand armrest, and a color-keyed, vinyl-covered door stowage compartment on the driver's side. The polyethylene door trim panels were surrounded by bright metal moldings. A perforated headliner was also used. A heavy duty black vinyl seat trim was available with all color combinations.

Other salient Custom Cab features included 5 inches of plastic foam in the seat cushion, and 1.75 inches in the seat back, a right side sun visor with inboard support, cigarette lighter, and sound deadener material on the floor between the floor pan and mat.

All 2-wheel drive Custom Cabs had bright anodized aluminum scuff plates positioned around the door step wells, a bright metal horn ring and headlining retainer molding, and a 'Custom Cab'

F-100 prices (1964) (continued)

Option	Price
Chrome Yellow or White paint	NC
Extra cooling radiator	$21.40
Manual radio	$50.20
Front amber reflectors	$3.60
Rear reflectors	$3.60
Safety package - padded dash and visor	$19.60
Heavy duty vinyl seat trim	$7.80
Full foam seat cushion	$25.70
Heavy duty, 1100lb front springs[10]	$3.20
Two-stage 1250lb heavy duty rear springs[10]	$6.50
Heavy duty 1650lb rear springs[10]	$12.30
Two-stage1950lb heavy duty rear springs[11]	$7.10
Auxiliary 550lb rear springs	$26.90
Positive engagement starter[12]	$22.70
Stowage compartment, left or right side	$10.30
Stowage compartment, left and right side	$20.60
Tool stowage box[13]	$31.20
Tool stowage box[14]	$35.40
3-speed medium duty transmission[15]	$75.20
3-speed medium-duty transmission[16]	$80.70
4-speed transmission[17]	$80.90
4-speed transmission[18]	$86.10
Overdrive with 3-speed transmission[19]	$108.40
Heavy Duty Cruise-O-matic[19]	$243.40
Turn indicators	$17.40
Right side sun visor for standard cab	$4.50
Windshield washer	$11.60
Dual electric 2-speed windshield wipers	$4.90
Tubeless tires	
6.70 x 15, 4-ply rated, WSW 5.5 K wheels	$32.00
6.70 x 16, 6-ply rated, PT 5.5 K wheels	$46.60
7.10 x 15, 4-ply rated, PT 5.5 K wheels	$16.00
7.10 x 15, 6-ply rated, PT 5.5 K wheels[20]	$50.70
6.50 x 16, 6-ply rated, PT 5K wheels[20]	$69.40
6.50 x 16, 6-ply -rated, TT 5K wheels[20]	$111.40
7 x 17.5, 6-ply rated, TT 5.25 wheels[20]	$140.10
Tube type tires	
6.50 x 16, 6-ply rated, PT 5K wheels	$69.70
6.50 x 16, 6-ply rated, 5K wheels	$11.40
7.00 x 15, 6-ply rated, 5.5F wheels	$151.10

[1]For Styleside models.
[2]For Flareside models
[3]Left or right side in lieu of standard carrier position. Available for right side for Flareside only.
[4]Ford 6-cylinder engine models. Optional for V-8 at no charge. Not available for overdrive; standard with 4wd.
[5]Not available for 4wd.
[6]For 4wd.
[7]Shipped loose.
[8]For Styleside only, not available with 4wd.
[9]Includes bright metal side moldings, available for Styleside only.
[10]Except 4wd.
[11]Available for 4wd only.
[12]Available with heavy-duty Cruise-O-Matic and 223 engine.
[13]For 114in wheelbase Styleside models.
[14]For 128in wheelbase Styleside models.
[15]For 114in wheelbase models, includes 11in heavy duty clutch.
[16]For 128in wheelbase models, includes 11in heavy duty clutch.
[17]For 114in wheelbase models, includes 11in heavy duty clutch.
[18]For 120in and 128in wheelbase models , includes 11in heavy duty clutch.
[19]Not available for 4wd.
[20]Requires optional rear springs, except for 4wd.

script located below the instrument cluster face.

The same external features of the 1963 Custom Cab continued for 1964. Joining the 292 cubic inch V-8 as an alternative to the F-100's standard 223 cubic inch 6-cylinder engine (both the 223 and 292 engines had unchanged power ratings for 1964), was a 262 cubic inch, overhead valve 6-cylinder engine. This engine - which was not available with the 4-wheel drive F-100 - had first been introduced early in 1961 for Ford's medium duty C-550 and C-600 models. Its cylinder block was a one-piece casting of special high grade steel with heavy cast ribs for extra strength. The cylinder head was also cast of a special high grade iron, and provided a wedge-type combustion chamber. Four main bearings were used, as were cast aluminum pistons.

All 1964 F-100 pickups were equipped with brakes that adjusted automatically when applied while the truck was reversing. In addition, thicker secondary brake lining was used to provide a claimed 32 per cent longer service life.

A new option, available only for the Styleside pickups, was a lockable tool box located ahead of the right rear wheel. Measuring 6.625in x 18in x 17.5in with the 6.5ft pickup box, and 6.625in x 32in x 17.5in with the 8.0ft box, the compartment was fabricated from heavy gauge sheet metal and welded into a single unit. It was located below the pickup box floor and did not interfere with the cab or load space. Its full-length door, when opened, stopped at a horizontal position. Weatherstripping seals were provided to keep out moisture and dirt when the door was closed. A locking pullout-type latch was included. Also optional for the Styleside was a right-hand side spare tire carrier location. A left

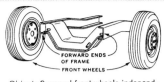
Object: Suspend front wheels independently, yet retain big-truck durability of solid I-beam axles.

Forged steel I-beam axle attaches wheel to frame, locks in wheel camber. Axle pivots in husky, chatter-proof bushing.

Big-truck radius rod secures axle to frame side rail. Stabilizes front end, locks in wheel caster.

Heavy-duty, non-sag coil spring gives entire suspension low-friction, easy-riding action.

Opposite wheel is similarly suspended. Each wheel has its own forged steel I-beam axle, radius rod and spring.

Each front wheel—on its own axle—operates independently to smooth the ride on the roughest roads.

The primary features and operation of the 1965 F-100 new Twin-I-Beam front suspension. (Courtesy Ford Motor Company)

side mount continued to be available.

Offered for all F-100 pickups was a new Heavy Duty Equipment Package consisting of a 70amp-hr battery with 66 plates, a heavy duty, 11.0in clutch with a surface area of 123.7sq in, an extra cooling radiator, front springs with a 1100lb (at pad) rating, and rear auxiliary springs rated at 450lb at pad. 6-ply tires were required with this option.

Heading a long list of major developments for 1965 was Ford's new Twin-I-Beam independent front suspension system for the F-100, which suspended the wheels independently whilst retaining the big truck capability of the older I-beam axle and leaf springs. Separate forged steel I-beam axles attached each wheel to the frame, thus locking in the wheel camber. The axles pivoted in large, chatter-proof bushings. Forged I-beam radius arms secured the axles to the frame side rail, providing stability and locking in the wheel caster.

Replacing the old elliptical leaf springs were new, non-sag coil springs. While the axles were held parallel to each other by the I-beam radius arms, they were permitted to move freely up and down until reaching their maximum high and low points, where they were constrained by mechanical stops. All driving thrusts from the frame to the axle - and braking forces from the axle to the frame - were transmitted via the radius rods and flexible insulating bushings. The shock absorbers were located just outside the coil springs in order to quickly respond to road surface irregularities. The shock absorbers used for 1965 were larger

than those for 1964, and had a new 'all-weather', multi-viscosity fluid providing more consistent ride quality over a wider temperature range. Also introduced was a new Haltenberger steering linkage. The F-100's service interval was extended to 6000 miles, and the wheelbase of both the short and long bed models was extended by 0.80 inches.

A more massive-looking grille with 18 rectangular openings was new for 1965. Standard cab models had white-painted divider bars with bright aluminum bars used for the Custom Cab. The upper grille panel opening was longer and wider for increased airflow through the engine compartment. The FORD lettering - located just above the grille in 1964 - was moved into the upper grille panel opening for 1965. Parking lights were mounted high in the grille, directly over the headlights. Ford reported that this new arrangement provided improved visibility

to oncoming traffic, thus increasing overall safety. A newly-designed, optional brush-type grille guard nicely complemented the F-100's grille and front end appearance. The guard's low profile fully protected the front end whilst allowing for unrestricted headlamp and parking lamp visibility. It was attached to the top edge of the bumper and held rigid by diagonal braces extending from the guard to the frame rail sides.

The hood ornament now had a V-8 insert for those F-100 pickups with V-8 engines. Those with the 6-cylinder engine retained the 'Geared Lightning' design used in 1964. The Custom Cab models were externally denoted by a bright metal 'Custom Cab' script located approximately in the center of the doors and on a horizontal line with the cab door handles. This identification replaced the 'Custom Cab' inscribed door escutcheon plate used in 1964.

Standard 6-cyl, optional 6-cyl and V-8 specifications (1965)

	Std. 6-cylinder	Optional 6-cylinder	Optional V-8
Bore	4.0in	4.0in	4.0in
Stroke	3.18in	3.98in	3.50in
Displacement	249cu in	300cu in	352cu in
Comp. ratio	9.2:1	8.0:1	8.9:1
Gross horsepower	150 at 4000rpm	170 at 3600rpm	208 at 4400rpm
Net horsepower	129 at 4000rpm	150 at 3600rpm	172 at 4000rpm
Gross torque (lb/ft)	234 at 2200rpm	293 at 2400rpm	315 at 1400-2400rpm
Net torque (lb/ft)	218 at 2000rpm	272 at 1400-2400rpm	
Carburetion:	1 barrel	1 barrel	295 at 2000rpm
			2 barrel

F-100 pickup prices (1965)	
Flareside, 6.5ft box	$1966
Styleside. 6.5ft box	$1981
Flareside, 8ft box	$2002
Styleside, 8ft box	$2018

Production (1965)

Model	Production
Flareside models:	34,184
Styleside models:	178,581

F-100 turning diameter (1965 v 1966)

Model	Diameter
(as measured by center line of outer wheel)	
4-wheel drive	
1965 (120in wb)	49.1ft
1966 (115in wb)	39.8ft
1966 (129in wb)	43.6ft
2-wheel drive 1965 & 1966	
115in wb	38.7ft
128in wb	42.3ft

For the purpose of comparison the turning diameter of the 2wd F-100 is included.

Four new exterior colors were introduced for 1965: Marlin Blue; Tropical Turquoise; Navajo Beige, and Phoenician Yellow. Continued from 1964 were Raven Black, Wimbledon White, Rangoon Red, Pure White, Holly Green, and Caribbean Turquoise.

The standard seat cushion pad and seat back panel was a new, beige-colored vinyl material accented by a wicker weave pattern. The seat cushion bolsters and seat back were a matching beige, highlighted by a crushed grain pattern. Cab interior metal surfaces were painted the same color as the lower cab exterior. The headlining, visor, inside mirror arm, and brackets were the same light shade of gray used in 1964.

Ford repositioned the windshield wipers and headlight controls for 1965. The new positions, reading from left to right on the dash, were: 'LIGHTS,' 'WIPER', and 'LIGHTER.' Relocating the headlight knob, now separated from the lighter, was done, explained Ford, "... to help prevent accidental shutting off of the headlights when the driver attempted to push in the cigar lighter." The F-100's upper instrument panel surface was stamped in production with a perforated area which served as an integral radio speaker grille. The new grille was a permanent part of the instrument panel, even if a radio was not fitted. This facilitated dealer installation of accessory radios, since only four screw holes had to be drilled to mount a speaker underneath

the instrument panel (previously, it was necessary to drill five, 2 inch holes in the instrument panel surface). A speaker grille was then mounted over the holes and the speaker mounted from underneath the instrument panel. The 1964 speaker grille was carried over for use on 1965 F-100 pickups ordered with the padded instrument panel option.

The Custom Cabs had new fabrics and fabric colors. The seat cushion and seat back trim panel material, available in Red, Blue, Green or Beige, was of woven plastic highlighted by a horizontal striped pattern. The trim panel bolsters were of crushed vinyl and color-keyed to the seat panel color. The Custom Cab package included a right side armrest. The door stowage compartment previously included as part of the Custom Cab package was deleted for 1965.

The F-100's optional seat belts, available for all pickups with full-width seats, were constructed of black nylon webbing with a black, plastic-coated buckle. The belt bases were anchored to the undercab crossmember, and met all SAE specifications for seat belt material and strength. Ford reported that "Estimations of the National Safety Council are that over 5000 lives could be saved each year if seat belts were installed and used on every vehicle."

Ford also offered a new fresh air heater possessing many advantages, including a very competitive price, compared with the older recirculating heater. Whereas the previous unit interfered with passenger

The 1966 F-100 new grille design is apparent in this view of a Styleside 4x4 model. (Courtesy Ford Motor Company)

Both the F-100 Styleside and Flareside 4x4 models had lower profiles for 1966. (Courtesy Ford Motor Company)

F-100 pickup prices (1966)

115in wheelbase:
  Flareside:................$2069
  Styleside:................$2085

129in wheelbase:
  Flareside:................$2105
  Styleside:................$2121

4x4 major specifications (1966)

Standard GVW rating	5600lb
Front axle capacity	3000lb
Rear axle capacity	3300lb
Axle ratio	3.70 (6-cylinder). 3.50 (V-8)
Clutch	Heavy duty,11.0in
Frictional area	123.7sq in
Frame section modulus	3.71 (115in wb), 4.14 (129in wb)
Front spring capacity (at pad)	1125lb (6-cylinder), 1250lb (V-8)
Rear spring capacity (at pad)	1250lb
Transfer case	Dana single speed
Transmission	4-speed, New Process 435

foot and leg room, the new heater was mounted up on the cab firewall well away from the cab floor. It was operated by a single, dash-mounted control knob: rotating the knob set the speed of the blower motor in any of three positions: 'off,' 'hi,' or 'lo.' Pulling the knob out controlled the amount of fresh air passing by the heater core. Defroster action was determined by a hand-operated crank on the plenum chamber, and could be set for varying degrees of air for defrosting.

Replacing the standard 30amp alternator of 1964 was an increased capacity unit rated at 38amp. Alternators rated at 45 and 55amps were optional. A new fuse panel containing the dome light, taillight, cigarette lighter, and other accessory fuses was mounted on the inside cab firewall, just to the left of the steering column. The 1964 fuse box (except for the cigarette lighter fuse which had been located on the back side of the lighter) had been an integral part of the headlamp switch. Optional was an improved Autolite

The 1966 F-100 4x4 was equipped with a new 'Mono Beam' front suspension. (Courtesy Ford Motor Company)

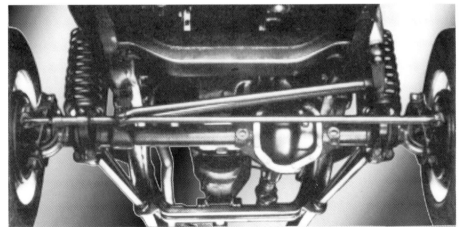

'sta-ful' 55amp-hr battery with increased durability and performance.

The F-100's standard 6-cylinder engine, along with its optional 6-cylinder and V-8 engines, had increased displacement for 1965.

Joining the F-100 option list was a new Camper Special Package consisting of an extra-cooling radiator, 70amp-hr battery, dual Western mirrors, extended

tailpipe, oil pressure gauge, and special side fender identification.

Perhaps the most important option for 1965, in terms of indicating the future path of development for the F-100, was the new Ranger option. Ford advised its sales personnel that the Ranger package "... is designed to appeal to the luxury and sports-minded light truck operator. This type prospect is looking for the same kind of vehicle that the Mustang, XL [Cougar] or Thunderbird buyer demands, but to accomplish a different purpose. He needs the hauling capacity or load space of a truck, and also wants the comfort, styling, prestige and, many times, the performance of an expensive automobile. The Ford 'Ranger' is ideally suited for this expanding market."

The Ranger Package, which was not available for the 4x4 model, included bucket seats, carpeting, gas tank cover panel, and a Ranger medallion insert ornament. It was offered with or without a center console. The retail price with the console was $155.20. If the console was not included the cost was $120.40.

The 4-wheel drive models were priced at $696 above the amounts in the accompanying table.

Leading the parade of changes for 1966 was a new 'Low-Silhouette' 4-wheel drive model with a single speed Dana transfer case. Although over two inches lower than its 1965 counterpart, the latest F-100 4 x 4 had an improved break-over angle that reduced, said Ford, "... the possibility of 'hanging up' in rough cross-country terrain."

The 4x4's improved maneuverability was due mainly to its new Mono-Beam, coil spring front suspension. Similar to the Twin I-Beam system, and very closely related to the design introduced on the 1966 Bronco, the Mono-Beam system used forged steel radius bars and a track bar to maintain axle alignment. The radius rods absorbed the driving and braking torque, and were insulated from both the frame and front axle by heavy insulating bushings, which also absorbed road shocks and appreciably reduced vehicle vibration. Ford asserted that this system virtually eliminated axle twist, reduced strain on universal joints, and increased joint life.

The new 4x4 was offered in either 115in or 128in wheelbase form in a choice of Styleside or Flareside pickup boxes.

The 1966 F-100's new grille positioned two long and narrow slots above 18 rectangular inserts, smaller in size than those used in 1965. Exterior colors for 1966 were Rangoon Red, Sahara Beige, Raven Black, Holly Green, Springtime Yellow, Caribbean Turquoise, Marlin Blue, Acadian Blue, Wimbledon White, Pure White, and Chrome Yellow. The two-tone option was offered in any combination of color except Pure White and Chrome Yellow with Wimbledon White. Carried over from 1965 was the Deluxe two-tone option for all Styleside models.

The 4-wheel drive models were

F-100 pickup option prices (1966)

Option	Price
45amp alternator	$22.00
55amp alternator	$30.50
60amp alternator	$90.00
Left or right side armrest (standard cab)	$5.00
Limited-slip rear axle	$64.00
55amp battery	$4.00
70amp battery	$8.00
Chrome, contour front bumper	$14.50
Contour rear painted bumper[1]	$22.00
Contour front and rear chrome bumpers[1]	$48.00
Rear channel painted bumper[2]	$21.00
Vacuum brake booster[3]	$45.50
Custom Cab	$96.00
Camper Special Package[4]	$58.00
Spare tire side mounted carrier, left or right side	$14.50
Spare tire side mounted carrier, left side	$14.50
Cigarette lighter (standard cab)	$4.50
Heavy-duty 11in clutch[5]	$5.50
Closed crankcase emission	$5.50
Deluxe Appearance Package	$52.00
Exhaust emission control[6]	$55.50
Ammeter and oil pressure gauges[7]	$8.00
Tinted glass, windshield only	$14.50
Tinted glass, all windows	$15.50
Laminated glass, doors only	$5.50
Governor, 6-cylinder engines	$11.00
Governor, V-8 engine	$17.50
Brush type grille guard	$38.00
Dual electric horns	$6.50
Bright metal hub caps[8]	$7.50
Manual free-running front hubs for 4x4	$78.50
ICC clearance lights	
2 corner, front	$11.00
3 center front	$16.50
Exterior mirrors	
Chrome, right side	$5.00
Non-telescoping 5in x 5in left side[9]	$NC
Non-telescoping 5in x 5in right side[9]	$5.00
Telescopic 5in x 8in left side[9]	$3.00
Telescopic 5in. x 8in right side[9]	$7.50
Western style 7in. x 11in left side[9]	$9.00
Western style 7in. x 11in right side[9]	$13.00
Bright metal body side moldings for Styleside	$32.50
Regular two-tone paint	$16.50
Deluxe two-tone paint[10]	$54.00
Power steering[11]	$108.00
Extra cooling radiator	$21.50
Manual radio and antenna	$50.50
Ranger package with bucket seats[12]	$97.00
Console for Ranger package[13]	$51.50
Front amber reflectors	$4.00
Heavy duty black vinyl seat trim	$17.00
Full foam cushion seat for standard pickup	$22.00
Front springs	
1125lb[14]	$3.50
1250lb[15]	$3.50

continued next page

F-100 pickup option prices (1966) (continued)

Option	Price
Rear springs	
1250lb, progressive (not available for 4x4)	$6.50
1650lb, single stage (not available for 4x4)	$12.50
1650lb, single stage for 4x4 only	NC
380lb, auxiliary[16]	$27.00
Stowage compartment, left or right side	$10.50
Stowage compartment, left and right side	$21.00
Right side sun visor for standard cabs	$4.50
Padded sun visors	$4.50
Extended length tailpipe for 129in wb	$7.00
Tool stowage box for 115in wb Styleside	$31.50
Tool stowage box for 129in wb Styleside	$35.50
Transistorized ignition perma-tuned ignition	$64.50
Transmissions	
4-speed with heavy duty clutch[17]	$81.00
4-speed with heavy duty clutch[18]	$86.50
3-speed with overdrive[19]	$108.50
3-speed Cruise-O-Matic[19]	$212.50
Bright wheel covers[19]	$21.50
2-speed electric windshield wipers	$5.00
Tubeless tires	
7.75 x 15, 4-ply rating, PT, WSW, 5.5 K wheels[20]	$32.00
7.75 x 15, 8-ply rating, PT, 5.5 K wheels	$47.00
8.15 x 15, 4-ply rating, PT, 5.5 K wheels	$16.00
8.15 x 15, 8-ply rating, PT, 5.5 K wheels	$51.00
8.15 x 15, 8-ply rating, PT, WSW, 5.5 K wheels	$84.00
6.50 x 16 6-ply rating, PT, 5K wheels	$69.50
6.50 x 16 6-ply rating, 5K wheels	$111.50
7 x 17.5, 6-ply rating, 5.25 wheels	$140.50
Tube-type tires[21]	
6.50 x 16, 6-ply rating, PT, 5K wheels	$70.00
6.50 x 16, 6-ply rating, 5K wheels	$111.50
7.00 x 15, 6-ply rating, 5.5F wheels	$151.50

priced at $718 above equivalent 2-wheel drive models. Purchase of the 300cu in, 6-cylinder engine added $93; the 352 V-8 was priced at $128 above the equivalent model with the 240 6-cylinder engine.

[1] For Styleside pickup.
[2] For Flareside pickup.
[3] Not available for 4x4.
[4] For 129in wheelbase only.
[5] For 150hp engine and standard transmission only.
[6] Included closed crankcase emission.
[7] Not available with 60amp alternator.
[8] Not available with 4-wheel drive.
[9] Shipped loose.
[10] Includes bright metal bodyside moldings. Available only for Styleside models.
[11] Not available for 4x4.
[12] Custom Cab required.
[13] Required bucket seats, not available with 4x4.
[14] For 6-cylinder models only, not available for 4x4.
[15] For V-8 models only, not available for 4x4.
[16] Not available with 16590 lb. main springs or 4x4.
[17] For 115in wheelbase, except 4x4.
[18] For 129in wheelbase, except 4x4.
[19] Not available with 4x4.
[20] Passenger-type tires, all other tires indicated are truck-type tires.
[21] All tube-type tire options required optional rear springs, except for 4x4.

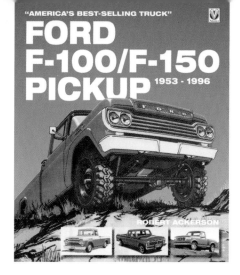

4

1967-1972

Although based on developments that occurred in 1965 and 1966, the F-100 pickups were extensively updated for 1967. The F-100's 'straight-line' styling was characterized by a broad, flat hood, a new windshield with sharp, nearly perpendicular corner posts, and a grille with vertical dividers for its horizontal members. Accentuating this styling theme was a broad side body crease that, on Styleside models, extended into the pickup bed side panel, and a secondary character line located along the lower rocker panel region. The headlights and parking lights were integrated into a single assembly positioned at the grille's outer extremities. Broad FORD lettering was located on the hood's leading edge.

Exterior colors offered for 1967 were Rangoon Red, Pebble Beige, Raven Black, Holly Green, Springtime Yellow, Frost Turquoise, Harbor Blue, Lunar Green, Wimbledon White, Pure White, and Chrome Yellow. The regular two-tone option included Wimbledon White paint on the entire cab roof, including the drip rails and back panel above the belt line molding, and extending around the cab corners to the door openings. The rest of the truck was painted with the selected standard color. The Deluxe two-tone for Styleside models included a Wimbledon White finish on the sheetmetal below the side moldings and lower tailgate section. The remaining surfaces were painted in the basic color selected. This package included bright body side molding, lower tailgate molding, and tailgate bezels. It was now possible to combine the Deluxe two-tone with the regular two-tone option on Styleside pickups.

The F-100's interior was completely redesigned with a 3 inch wider seat, a standard Deluxe fresh air heater - defroster and instrumentation formatted into a more car-like cluster.

Under the broad umbrella of Ford's 'Lifeguard Design' were many important safety features, including standard seat belts, safety door latches, safety hinges, outside mirror, windshield washer, two-speed electric windshield wipers, padded sun visors, thick laminate safety plate glass windshield, turn indicators, backup lights, ICC 4-way flashers, front seat shoulder anchor harnesses, and reduced glare instrument panel, wiper arms and blades. The standard padded dash panel

An appealing profile of the all-new F-100 for 1967 equipped with the Ranger package. (Courtesy Ford Motor Company)

An interior view of a 1967 F-100 4x4 equipped with the Ranger option. (Courtesy Ford Motor Company)

now included a warning light for the new dual hydraulic brake system. This system contained a tandem piston master cylinder operating two separate hydraulic brake sub-systems (front brakes and rear brakes). In the event that one sub-system was damaged, the other remained operative.

Appointments of the standard cab included a one-piece hardboard headlining, slide-action cowl-side air vents, cowl liner panels, and vinyl seat trim offered in red, blue, green or beige. The Custom Cab option provided a woven plastic seat trim in blue, red, green or beige, a deep-foam cushioned seat, color-keyed armrests and floor mat, bright-finish horn ring, custom instrument panel, bright metal headlining retainer, windshield and door panel moldings, and headlight assembly.

Reinforcing the public's image of the F-100 as a dual purpose vehicle (Ford liked to refer to the F-100 as a vehicle that "Works like a truck ... Rides like a car ...") was the Ranger option "... for those who prefer the ultimate in custom appearance, comfort and convenience." Major elements of the F-100 Ranger, which was offered for Styleside models only, included bright finish interior, and exterior trim items such as hub caps, front bumper, grille and headlight assembly, horn ring, instrument cluster, window frames, rocker panel, and wheel lip moldings. A Ranger script was applied to the side of the pickup box. In addition, the F-100 Ranger was fitted with wall-to-wall carpeting, courtesy lights door switches, deluxe seat belts with retractors, deep foam seat cushion, and a cloth-like vinyl seat trim.

But the new F-100 was not just a

pickup with a growing array of driver/passenger comforts, since its body assembly also included double-wall hood sections for added strength, rigidity, and stability.

No major changes were made to the F-100's engine, transmission or drivetrain for 1967. Models with the 8ft box now had a 131 inch wheelbase that, due to a longer cab-to-rear axle dimension, permitted more load to be transferred to the front axle for improved ride and handling. The long wheelbase version also used a stronger frame with a section modulus of 3.06; it had been 2.98 in 1966. The 6-cylinder models now had standard front springs rated at 1055lb instead of 1005lb as in 1966. Those with V-8 engines had 1175lb front springs in place of units rated at 1125lb in 1966. Base tire size was increased to 8.15 x 15in from 7.75 x 15in. The optional 17.5 inch tire was dropped in favor of a 15 x 5.50 inch unit.

Ford extended its warranty to include a 5 year or 50,000 mile warranty on the F-100 drivetrain. The warranty applied to the engine block, cylinder head(s), internal parts, water pump, intake manifold, transmission, transfer case and internal parts (4x4), driveshafts, universal joints, differentials, and driving axles and their bearings. Items such as ignition, electrical, cooling, fuel and braking systems, engine or transmission controls, and clutch assemblies were not included.

Supporting its assertion that the latest F-100 was "... an accumulation of everything an owner would want in a pickup" was Ford's 'Pickup Challenge Of The Year,' conducted at the Riverside International Raceway in California. Participating were three F-100 pickups and three "... of the competitor's '67 models." Although Ford never made the assertion directly, the belief that this competitor was Chevrolet was supported by Ford's comment that the "... competitive make [was] standard in every way, right off the production line - comparable to Ford in all equipment. But with its standard 250cu in engine - five more rated horsepower - the competition on paper has a slight power edge. Ford must live with it." For the record, the 1967 Chevrolet C-10 had a 250 cubic inch, 6-cylinder engine rated at 155 horsepower at 4200rpm.

The contest consisted of first testing and evaluating the pickups in four categories ride, handling, performance, and economy. After the first phase was concluded the pickups participated in an endurance run intended to replicate over two years of actual use involving 702 hours (29 days and nights) of continuous running, in which the trucks carried a 500 pound payload for alternate 6000 mile intervals. Mile-by-mile records were kept. At the conclusion, the same pickups were subjected to the same set of original tests. As Ford said "The proof will be in the comparisons." (see table).

Federally mandated front and rear body side reflectors helped identify the 1968 F-100. Joining the carry over 240 and 300 cubic inch 6-cylinder engines were two V-8 engines with displacements of 360 and 390 cubic inches.

All F-100 engines had new tuned passenger-type mufflers and quieter cooling fans. Installed on F-100s with optional heavy duty springs was a new suspension feature called Flex-O-Matic. It combined longer rear leaf springs with a compensating shackle device that, when a load was added, pivoted to automatically adjust the spring length for varying load conditions.

A new kingpin with a high density polyurethane-filled bearing cap used on F-100 4x4 pickups automatically

'Pickup Challenge of the Year'

Fuel economy

	Ford		Competitor	
	Initial	30,000 mile	Initial	30,000 mile
At steady 45mph (mpg)	19.1	22.2	19.2	20.2
At steady 60mph (mpg)	14.7	17.7	14.5	15.5
Average mpg	16.9	20.0	16.9	17.9

Ride index (initial)[1]

	Ford	Competitor
35mph, gravel road	8.2	8.7
35mph, smooth pavement	4.1	4.3
60mph, smooth pavement	5.6	5.5

Ride index (30,000 miles)

	Ford	Competitor
30mph, rough pavement	14.8	15.7
30mph, smooth pavement	3.4	4.1
55mph, smooth pavement	3.8	4.7

[1]In developing this data Ford used five different electrical attachments mounted on the trucks to feed impulses into an analog computer. Ford reported that it used different public roads for this part of the testing.

Handling

	Ford		Competitor	
	Initial	30,000 mile	Initial	30,000 mile
Static steering effort	3.3	3.4	3.9	3.3
Dynamic steering effort				
at 5mph	2.5	1.9	3.6	2.5
at 8mph	3.7	3.1	4.7	3.8
at 10mph	5.0	3.9	5.8	5.1
at 12mph	6.2	4.9	6.8	6.3

Performance

	Ford		Competitor	
Acceleration	Initial	30,000 mile	Initial	30,000 mile
0-60mph (seconds)	16.86	19.37	18.77	17.98
0-¼ mile (seconds)	20.52	20.99	20.34	20.31
¼ mile speed (mph)	64.64	62.67	63.19	63.92

Braking				
60-0mph (seconds)	6.23	5.47	5.57	5.72

Ford also conducted the same range of tests with its pickups after they had traveled a total of 67,000 miles. Among the highlights of the results were these

Acceleration
  0-60mph .... 19.92 seconds
  0-¼ mile .... 21.11 seconds

Braking
  60-0mph .... 5.63 seconds
  ¼ mile speed 61.90mph

Fuel economy
  At steady 45mph 20.2mpg
  At steady 60mph 15.7mpg

Production totals (1967)

Flareside pickups 18,307
Styleside pickups 204,710
4x4 Flareside pickups 481
4x4 Styleside pickups 3455

Prices of F-100 pickups[1] with standard 6-cylinder engine (1967)

Flareside, 6.5ft box $2198
Styleside, 6.5ft box $2237
Flareside, 8ft box $2237
Styleside, 8ft box $2273

[1]Add $651 for 4-wheel drive.

Prices of F-100 pickups[1] with standard 6-cylinder engine (1968)

Flareside, 6.5ft box......... $2318
Styleside, 6.5ft box $2357
Flareside, 8ft box............ $2357
Styleside, 8ft box $2393

[1]Add $647 for 4-wheel drive.
The Ranger option added another $238.

V-8 engine specifications (1968)

	360 V-8	390 V-8
Bore x stroke	4.05in x 3.50in	4.05in x 3.78in
Gross horsepower	215 at 4400rpm	255 at 4400rpm
Net horsepower	179 at 4000rpm	190 at 4000rpm
Gross torque (lb/ft)	327 at 2600rpm	376 at 2600rpm
Net torque (lb/ft)	302 at 2900rpm	324 at 2000rpm
Compression ratio	8.41	8.61
Carburetion	single 2-bbl	single 2-bbl

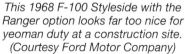

This 1968 F-100 Styleside with the Ranger option looks far too nice for yeoman duty at a construction site. (Courtesy Ford Motor Company)

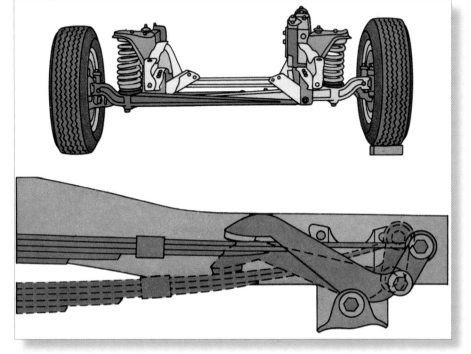

A sketch of the optional Flex-0-Matic rear suspension for the 1968 F-100 showing loaded and unloaded positions. (Courtesy Ford Motor Company)

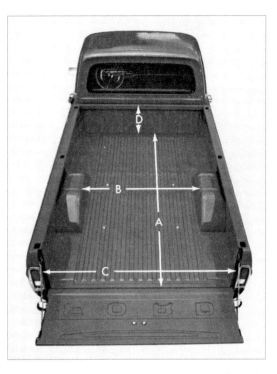

The 1968 Styleside pickup featured an all-steel floor and 65in wide tailgate opening. (Courtesy Ford Motor Company)

The F-100 could be equipped with the 390 cubic inch V-8 in 1968. (Courtesy Ford Motor Company)

Below: An F-100 Ranger with the Farm & Ranch Special option. (Courtesy Ford Motor Company)

Above: This 1969 F-100 with the Contractor Special package was also equipped with the extra cost rear step bumper. (Courtesy Ford Motor Company)

The Ranger dash was dressed up with woodgrain inserts for 1969. This F-100 was also equipped with air conditioning. (Courtesy Ford Motor Company)

These two views show the optional spare tire carrier offered for the 1969 F-100 Styleside (left), and Flareside (right). (Courtesy Ford Motor Company)

This 1970 F-100 Styleside Ranger was equipped with the optional Convenience Group, which included a cargo area light. (Courtesy Ford Motor Company)

302 cubic inch V-8 specifications

Bore x stroke ....4.00in x 3.0in
Gross horsepower ....205 at 4600rpm
Gross torque ....300lb/ft at 2400rpm

area was increased by 45 per cent. The new brake dimensions were as follows

| Front | 11.03in x 3.0in |
| Rear | 11.03in x 2.25in |

A revised grille with a wide center horizontal bar and four rows of thin horizontal bars identified the 1968 F-100. The interior color selection consisted of red, blue, black or beige. The heater controls were now integrated into the instrument panel. Ford claimed that the F-100's new air conditioning system, integral with the Deluxe fresh air heater, would keep the cab 35 degrees cooler than the older unit, even when the outside temperature was 110 degrees. Added to the Ranger package was a sound deadener, new grille identification, and a cargo area light which, in 1967, had been an exclusive Ranger option.

Standard exterior colors for 1968 were Rangoon Red, Pebble Beige, Raven Black, Meadowlark Yellow, Holly Green, Lunar Green, Sky View Blue, Harbor Blue, Wimbledon White, Chrome White, and Pure White. The same two-tone variations offered in 1967 were available.

Introduced for the 1969 F-100 were Contractor Special, Heavy Duty Special, and Farm & Ranch Special models. The Contractor Special was offered in two forms Package No.1 contained heavy duty front and rear springs, rear step bumper, convenience group (included cargo area light, courtesy light door switches, inside day/night mirror and engine compartment light), dual chrome Western swing-lock mirrors, contractor box on both sides with key-lock fold-down doors, and a 'Contractor Special' insignia on the cowl side. The Contractor Package No. 2 added an underhood Electric Power Pak to this equipment.

compensated for wear while providing improved anti-shimmy capability. The optional free-wheeling hubs had improved lubricant sealing and were redesigned for easier operation. Although Ford offered front disc brakes as options for the F-250 and F-350 series, these were not available for the F-100. Instead, the F-100's lining

Prices of F-100 pickups[1] with standard 6-cylinder engine (1969)

Flareside, 6.5ft box	$2354
Styleside, 6.5ft box	$2393
Flareside, 8ft box	$2393
Styleside, 8ft box	$2430

[1] Add $644 for 4-wheel drive.

Above: The new-for-1970 Sport Custom option had bright taillight bezels and tailgate applique. (Courtesy Ford Motor Company)

The base trim level for 1970 was the Custom, shown here as an F-100 Styleside pickup. (Courtesy Ford Motor Company)

A composite view of the Ranger XLT interior for 1970. (Courtesy Ford Motor Company)

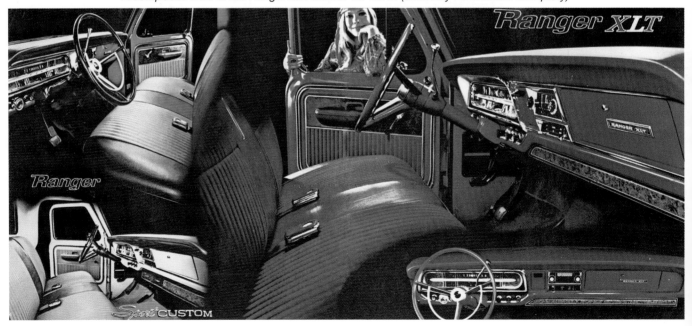

48

The 1970 F-100 4x4 in Styleside and Flareside versions. (Courtesy Ford Motor Company)

FORD TRUCKS

A 1970 F-100 Sport Custom Styleside with the Explorer Special Package that included chrome front bumper guards, mag-style wheel covers and Western-style mirrors. (Courtesy Ford Motor Company)

The Farm & Ranch Special option contained heavy duty battery, alternator and front and rear springs, as well as a rear step bumper, bright body side moldings, dual chrome Western swing-lock mirrors, front and 9in high side cargo boards, and a cowl side 'Farm & Ranch Special' insignia.

The Heavy Duty Special for 131in wheelbase models provided a heavy duty, 55amp-hr battery, heavy duty 70amp alternator, heavy duty rear springs, rear step bumper, oil pressure and ammeter gauges, bright dual swing-lock mirrors, and a cowl side 'Heavy Duty Special' insignia.

The 1969 F-100's grille used vertical bars that were bright finished rather than black. Initially, standard models had an ivory-painted grille but, beginning on February 10, 1969, all models had bright metal grille work. The Custom Cab option now included a bright finished front bumper and, for Styleside models, new taillight bezels.

The interior color selection for 1969 was black, blue, red or parchment. The Custom Cab had revised trim and seat insert patterns. Added to the Ranger package were dash and door trim woodgrain inserts, a red-striped grille divider, and blacked-out headlight bezels.

A mid-year 'White Sale' offering was the Explorer II model, based on the 8 foot Styleside F-100. It featured body side molding and wheel covers very similar to those used for the 1967 Thunderbird.

Initially, no changes were made in the F-100 engine line-up for 1969, but at mid-year a 302 cubic inch V-8 became optional for the 2-wheel drive models.

Exterior colors for 1969 were Raven Black, Wimbledon White, Norway Green, New Lime, Boxwood Green, Candyapple Red, Royal Maroon, Pebble Beige, Cordova Copper, Empire Yellow, Lunar Green, Reef Aqua, Sky View Blue, Harbor Blue, Chrome Yellow, and Pure White. Ford reported that a total of 42 different two-tones were obtained by using all the standard colors (except Chrome Yellow and Pure White). Wimbledon White could be used as the accent for all colors and Raven Black could be used as an accent for all colors except Harbor Blue. In the regular two-tone option the accent color was applied to the roof and upper back panel with a belt line molding from door to door around the back of the cab. In the Deluxe version, for Styleside pickups only, the accent color was applied to the area below the body side and lower tailgate moldings which were included in this package. The combination two-tone option remained available. As a result, the Styleside pickup could be painted in a total of 140 different ways.

Referring to the 1970 F-100's new grille with its two-piece egg crate design, Ford noted that "Now, behind one gleaming grille, Ford offers four better idea pickup models ..." This new F-100 hierarchy comprised Custom, Sports Custom, Ranger and Ranger XLT trim levels. Indicative of this strategy's success was the F-100's status as one of Ford's pickup models that collectively outsold all other Ford vehicles except the full-size Ford passenger cars. This formidable achievement began a three year string of full-size pickup sales victories over arch rival Chevrolet. At year's end, full-size pickup sales in the US totaled 1,163,535 units. Of that figure Ford's share was 466,773, giving it a lead of 58,697 trucks over Chevrolet's sale of 408,076 pickups.

All F-100 interiors for 1970 were color co-ordinated and equipped with a swept-away, padded instrument panel, energy-absorbing sun visors, and armrests with squeeze-type door latches. Additional standard items included windshield washers, two-speed windshield wipers, day/night mirror, a bright left side exterior mirror, backup lights, turn signals, and emergency flashers. In addition to a new grille design, all F-100 pickups had the blacked-out headlight bezels first used on the 1969 Ranger. Styleside models had side body reflectors and lights integrated into the body side character line. Common to all models were parking lights positioned outside of the headlight grille structure and extending into the side body where they functioned as side markers.

The 1970 Custom F-100 had an impressive array of standard interior and exterior features belying its status as Ford's least expensive full-size pickup. They included a bright grille, chrome front bumper, a deluxe 3-speed fresh air heater, hi-dri all-weather ventilation, door courtesy switches, ash tray, hardboard headlining, black floor mats with heel pads, aluminum scuff plates, deluxe instrument cluster bezel, color-keyed steel door trim panels and a vinyl seat trim with embossed patterned rib vinyl inserts offered in black, blue, red, parchment or green.

The Sport Custom level offered (in addition to, or in place of, Custom items) a deep-foam seat cushion and foam padding in seat back, pleated basket weave vinyl seat trim inserts, grained vinyl bolsters, color-keyed, pleated vinyl door panels with bright moldings, color-keyed floor mats, cigarette lighter and horn ring. Exterior trim for the Sport Custom included bright windshield, rocker panel and wheel lip moldings. Styleside versions also had bright taillight bezels and tailgate applique.

F-100 prices (1970)

115 inch wheelbase models
  Custom Flareside $2509.24
  Custom Styleside $2548.24

131 inch wheelbase models ....
  Custom Flareside $2548.24
  Custom Styleside $2584.75

4-wheel drive model
115 inch wheelbase
  Custom Flareside $3155.49
  Custom Styleside $3192.24

131 inch wheelbase models
  Custom Flareside $3192.24
  Custom Styleside $3231.24

Optional equipment

42amp Autolite alternator $21.60
55amp Autolite alternator $30.20
65amp Autolite alternator[1] $89.90
Ford Traction-Lok rear axles
  Ford 3300[2] $63.80
  Ford 3600[3] $63.80
  Ford 3600 for 390 V-8 .... $134.50
70amp-hr battery $8.90
Vacuum brake booster $45.30
Engines
  300cu in 6-cylinder $90.10
  302cu in V-8[4] $90.10
  360cu in V-8[4] $127.50
  390cu in V-8[5] $263.90
Engine equipment
  Oil bath air cleaner $6.50
  Evaporative fuel system[6] $50.30
Reduced sound level exhaust system[7] $6.50
Extra Cooling Package[8] $24.10
Velocity governor $18.30
Ammeter and oil pressure gauges $10.20
21.5 gallon fuel tank (less standard tank) $48.90
21.5 gallon fuel tank (with standard tank) $64.40
Electric Power Pak-120 volt, 2500 watt $468.50
Shock absorbers
  Heavy duty front $7.50
  Heavy duty rear $8.60
  Heavy duty front and rear $16.20
Front springs[9]
  1175lb (for 6-cyl. only) $4.60
  1250lb (for V-8 only) $4.60
Rear springs
  1250lb Progressive Flex-O-Matic, NA for 4x4 .... $9.70
  1650lb Progressive Flex-O-Matic, NA for 4x4 .... $21.30
  420lb auxiliary[10], NA for 4x4 .... $29.60
  365lb auxiliary[11] $29.60
Power steering $127.50
Transmission
  4-speed (115in wb) $86.10

continued over

The Ranger Styleside interior had (in addition to, or in place of, Custom items) woodtone instrument panel trim, bright headlining retainer molding, color-keyed pleated vinyl door panels with bright moldings and woodtone inserts, bright seat-pivot arm covers, and a Ranger plaque on the glovebox door. The Ranger exterior was highlighted by bright finished side, rear window and roof drip moldings, plus bright hub caps. A bright finish tailgate latch and a full tailgate panel were also included.

The top-of-the line Ranger XLT had, said Ford "... the highest-style appointments in the industry. *Four Wheeler* magazine, February 1970 noted that the XLT's interior upholstery and trim "... rival [that] of the Ford line of passenger cars." Its equipment included (in addition to, or in place of, Ranger items) pleated cloth and vinyl seat upholstery, color-keyed, wall-to-wall carpeting, special weather and sound insulation, convenience group (cargo and engine compartment lights, glovebox door lock, 12 inch day/night mirror), sound-absorbing perforated headlining, bright instrument panel molding on right side and heater modesty panel with woodtone insert. The XLT's exterior decor included bright side moldings with woodtone inserts, bright rocker panel and wheel lip moldings, and a woodtone tailgate panel.

Comprising the exterior color selection for 1970 were Raven Black, Wimbledon White, Norway Green, New Lime, Boxwood Green, Candyapple Red, Royal Maroon, Mojave Tan, Yucatan Gold, Pinto Yellow, Diamond Blue, Reef Aqua, Sky View Blue, Harbor Blue, Chrome Yellow, and Pure White. The same two-tone color schemes as offered in 1969 were retained for 1970, but this year a total of 48 different two-tones were available. In addition, the number of possible color

F-100 prices (1970) (continued)
Optional equipment

4-speed (131in wb)	$91.50
3-speed with overdrive	$118.40
3-speed SelectShift Cruise-O-Matic (6-cylinder)	$222.70
3-speed SelectShift Cruise-O-Matic (V-8)	$231.70
Air conditioner[12]	$406.80
Cigarette lighter	$4.20
Convenience Group[13]	$20.60
Tinted glass, all windows	$18.80
Shoulder harnesses	$29.60
Horn ring (for Custom Cab)	$7.10
Exterior mirrors	
Chrome, right side	$4.90
Chrome remote control, left side	$14.20
Chrome remote control, left side, fixed right side	$19.20
5in x 8in non-tel., left side	$3.20
5in x 8in non-tel., left and right side	$10.30
Western style mirrors	
7in x 11in fixed, left side	$8.70
7in x 11in fixed, left and right side	$24.00
6in x 10in bright swing lock, left side	$15.10
6in x 10in bright extended arm, left side	$15.10
6in x 10in bright extended arm, both sides	$36.90
Two-tone paint	
Regular, includes beltline molding	$19.00
Deluxe, Styleside only	
Custom and Sport Custom[14]	$59.20
Ranger and XLT Ranger	$21.50
Combination-Styleside only	
Custom and Sport Custom[14]	$72.10
Ranger and Ranger XLT	$34.40
Push button radio and antenna	$65.70
Black, texture painted roof	$58.00
Center passenger seat belt for bench seat	$6.70
Heavy duty black vinyl seat trimfor bench seat	$16.80
Sport Custom seat (Custom Cabs with bench seat)	$28.40
Bucket-type seats	
Sport Custom and Ranger	$114.20
Ranger XLT	$87.30
Special packages	
Sport Custom	$146.80
Ranger (Styleside)	$238.20
Ranger XLT (Styleside)	$347.50
Behind seat lockable stowage compartment[15]	$21.30
Lockable sliding rear window	$58.00
Rear contour chrome bumper (Styleside)	$37.80
Rear channel painted bumper (Flareside)	$23.70
Rear step type painted bumper (Styleside)	$48.60
Side mounted spare tire carriers	
Left or right side (Styleside)	$14.10
Left side only (Flareside)	$14.1
Dual electric horns	$6.50
Bright metal hub caps (Custom and Sport Custom)	$7.40
Cab roof ICC clearance and marker lights	$26.80
Bright moldings	
Narrow body side[16]	$37.70
Narrow rocker arm and wheel lip opening[17]	$43.20

continued next page

combinations for the F-100 Styleside rose to 144.

Technical changes for the F-100 were minor for 1970. G78-15 B (4-ply rating) bias-belted tires replaced the 8.25 x 15 B tires used in 1969. An automatic choke superseded the old manual system.

Ford offered White Sale Custom or Sport Custom Explorer Specials (in A, B, C or D package form) during the 1970 model year. Two exterior colors, Grabber Blue and Explorer Green, were exclusive to the Explorer Special. Other colors available for the Explorer Special were Raven Black, Wimbledon White, Harbor Blue, New Lime, Sky View Blue, Boxwood Green, and Yucatan Gold.

Explorer Specials with the Grabber Blue exterior had interiors finished in Blue Shetland plaid with blue vinyl non-metallic leather print. Matched to the Explorer Green exterior was a gold and red Shetland plaid with non-metallic leather print interior.

Primary features of the Explorer Special's Appearance A Package included bright body side molding, swing-lock bright Western mirrors, chrome front bumper guards with black rubber inserts, glovebox ornament, bright windshield molding, bright drip rails, bright box rails, door edge guards, and mag-type wheel covers.

The B Package added power steering, power brakes and SelectShift automatic transmission to the content of Package A. Package C added air conditioning to the content of Package A. Package D combined Package B with air conditioning.

As the 1971 model year began, Ford sales staff were told that "Ford light trucks for 1971 offer so much that they're destined to be No. 1 in trucks for the third straight year." At the end of the calendar

F-100 prices (1970) (continued)

Optional equipment

Special packages
- Left and right side contractors lockable boxes $257.50
- Contractors Special[18] $289.60
- Farm & Ranch Special[18] $109.60
- Heavy Duty Special[18] $122.30
- Heavy Duty Special[18] used with air conditioning $92.10
- Tool stowage box[18] $45.10
- Bright metal 15in wheel covers $23.20
- Mag-type wheel covers $51.50

Tubeless tires and wheels
- G78-15 4 ply rating WSW, 5.5 K wheels $30.70

Tubeless tires and wheels
- 8.25 x 15 8-ply rating PT-D, 5.5 K wheels $34.80
- 8.25 x 15 8-ply rating PT-D WSW, 5.5 K wheels $71.00

Tube-type nylon tires and wheels
- 6.50 x 16, 6-ply rating, 5K wheels $71.10
- 7.00 x 15, 6-ply rating, 5.5K wheels $98.80

Additional options for 4-wheel drive
- Dane free-running manual front hubs $78.50
- 1650lb single stage rear springs .... NC

[1]Includes ammeter and oil gauge.
[2]Not available with 4x4, 4-speed transmission or 390 V-8.
[3]Available with 4-speed transmission only, not available with 390 V-8.
[4]Includes heavy duty front springs.
[5]Includes 11.5in clutch and heavy duty front springs. Not available with 4x4.
[6]Required for California.
[7]Required for California and New York.
[8]Not available with air conditioning.
[9]Not available with Power Pak.
[10]Used with 1250lb main springs.
[11]Used with 1650lb main springs.
[12]Includes 55amp alternator and Extra Cooling Package.
[13]Includes Cargo area light, underhood light, glovebox lock, and 12in day/night mirror.
[14]Includes body side and tailgate moldings.
[15]Not available with standard fuel tank.
[16]For Custom and Sport Custom Styleside.
[17]For Ranger Styleside.
[18]For 8ft Styleside only.

year a total of 1,353,001 full-size pickups had been sold in the US; of that total Ford's share of 515,433 units gave it a lead of 20,506 over Chevrolet.

Noting that durability was the number one buying motive for pickups, Ford asserted that "... the 1971 F-Series Pickups are more durable than ever before. Durable in styling, in dependability, in performance and therefore, in popularity." Most changes for 1971 were in the form of new or revised standard equipment items. All F-100 pickups had a redesigned grille with a large rectangular pattern of argent-colored plastic. The grille's main frame and vertical center bar were constructed of bright polished-finish aluminum. A vertical stripe on the center bar and the area around the headlights had an anodized black finish. Sixteen exterior colors were available for 1971, including seven new colors Regis Red, Bahama Blue, Swiss Aqua, Mallard Green, Seafoam Green, Calypso Coral, and Prairie Yellow. Carried over from 1970 were Raven Black, Wimbledon White, Boxwood Green, Candyapple Red, Mojave Tan, Diamond Blue, Sky View Blue, Chrome Yellow, and Pure White. Three two-tone formats were once again available with 54 regular combinations offered.

A new steering wheel design highlighted the Ranger XLT option for 1971.
(Courtesy Ford Motor Company)

Changes made to the 1971 Ranger XLT interior included a repositioned woodtone door panel and revised upholstery pattern. (Courtesy Ford Motor Company)

The woodtone tailgate panel and body side molding of the 1971 Ranger XLT were virtually identical to those used in 1970. (Courtesy Ford Motor Company)

54

F-100 prices (1971 and 1972)

115 inch wheelbase models

	1971	1972
Custom Flareside	$2810.24	$2702.90
Custom Styleside	$2810.24	$2702.90

131 inch wheelbase models......................

Custom Flareside	$2846.74	$2738.90
Custom Styleside	$2846.74	$2738.90

4-wheel drive models
115in wheelbase

Custom Flareside	$3374.74	$3272.90
Custom Styleside	$3374.74	$3272.90

131in wheelbase

Custom Flareside	$3413.74	$3308.90
Custom Styleside	$3413.74	$3308.90

Optional equipment

42 amp Autolite alternator	$23.90	$22.81
55 amp Autolite alternator	$32.30	$30.81
65 amp Autolite alternator[1]	$95.30	NA
65 amp Autolite alternator[2]	63.20	NA
Ford Traction-Lok rear axles		
Ford 3300[3]	$66.90	$63.81
Ford 3600[4]	$66.90	$63.81
Optional axle ratios	$13.20	$12.51
70 amp hr battery	$17.40	$16.60
Vacuum brake booster (std in 1972 with 5500lb GVW)	$50.80	$48.46
Engines		
300cu in 6-cylinder	$90.10	NA
302cu in V-8[5]	$115.60	$100.27
360cu in V-8[5]	$161.10	$153.68
390cu in V-8[6]	$263.90	$251.73
Engine equipment		
Oil bath air cleaner	$6.50	$6.20
Emission Control System[7]	NC	$15.55
Reduced sound level		
Exhaust system[8]	$6.50	$6.59
Extra Cooling Package[9]	$29.60	$28.24
Super Cooling Package[9]	NA	$33.20
Ammeter and oil pressure gauges	$12.40	$11.83
21.5 gallon fuel tank (less standard tank)	$51.90	NA
21.5 gallon fuel tank (with standard tank)	$68.30	NA
20.5 gallon fuel tank (less standard tank)	NA	$49.51
20.5 gallon fuel tank (with standard tank)	NA	$65.16
Electric Power Pak-120 volt, 2500 watt	$468.50	NA
Shock absorbers		
Heavy duty front and rear	$16.30	$15.55

continued over

The Custom interior included a new 16.5in diameter, two-spoke steering wheel with a black vinyl horn-blow bar on the spoke area, new seat back cushions, new interior door panel finish, and new seat trim. Interior items that were color-keyed to the exterior included the door panels, armrests, padded instrument panel, seat belts and retractors. Gray sun visors and a black rubber floor mat were standard. An all-vinyl color-keyed seat trim was available in five different colors black, red, medium blue, parchment or medium green. The cabin headliner was a one-piece, sponged grain hardboard with gray-painted retainer molding. Bright metal interior highlights included outlines for the standard heater/defroster, door lock knobs, gearshift lever, and turn signal knobs.

Model emblems were mounted on the rear quarter panel on Styleside pickups and on the front fender behind the wheelhousing of the Flaresides. A new narrow aluminum applique with a contrasting black background was used on the tailgate of Styleside models. Smaller letters were used for Flareside tailgates.

New Sport Custom features included a revised script emblem, a color-keyed, two-spoke steering wheel, all-vinyl, color-keyed seat trim in the same colors offered for the Custom, and color-keyed vinyl door trim panels. The floor mats continued to be color-keyed to the exterior.

Ranger models had new bright metal hub caps with contrasting black striping. The Ranger emblem combined bright outlines with black-filled interiors. A smooth-colored vinyl horn bar cover with a burled-walnut woodgrain insert, plus Ford's corporate trademark mounted on a medallion attached to the horn bar cover, distinguished the Ranger's steering wheel from those of the Custom and Sport Custom models.

The Ranger's new color-keyed seat trim consisted of a one-piece pleated body cloth in the seat cushion and back, with a diamond design at the seat back top and vinyl bolsters and facings.

Ford described the 1971 Ranger XLT as "... the perfect answer for buyers seeking the ultimate in prestige." A new exterior Ranger XLT emblem had black Ranger letters with bright outlines. The XLT letters had red, white, and blue interiors. The tailgate continued to have a full panel simulated woodgrain applique.

The F-100's technical updates were limited to a new fuel evaporation control system that helped prevent vapors escaping from the fuel tank, and a redesigned fuel tank. A larger capacity windshield reservoir was adopted and, for trucks destined for California, a special exhaust emission control system was added. The 4-wheel drive models had a new ball joint steering front axle.

The A, B, C, and D variations of the Explorer Package for the Custom and Sport Custom Styleside models were offered in a choice of Lime Gold Metallic, Medium Blue Metallic or Saddletan Metallic exterior colors. Corresponding interior trim colors were Metallic Green, Metallic Blue, and Ginger. The upholstery combined a random striped cloth seat trim with vinyl bolsters. Major features of the Explorer Packages were carried over from 1970.

New options debuting in 1971 included Deluxe mag-style wheel covers (for 2-wheel drive only) with grey-gold metallic finish and bright centers and outer rim covers, a superior sound AM-FM stereo radio, larger, smoother-riding, heavy duty shock absorbers, and higher capacity G78 x 15B and D fiberglass-

F-100 prices (1971 and 1972) (continued)

	1971	1972
Front springs[10]		
1175lb (for 6-cylinder only)	$6.60	NA
1415lb[10]	NA	$6.30
1250lb (for V-8 only)	$6.60	NA
1500lb[10]	NA	$1.92
Rear springs		
1250lb Progressive Flex-O-Matic		
Rear springs		
NA for 4x4	$19.50	NA
1650lb Progressive Flex-O-Matic,		
NA for 4x4	$21.30	NA
420lb auxiliary[11], NA for 4x4	$31.30	$29.86
365lb auxiliary[12]	$31.30	NA
1475lb rear springs	NA	$6.30
1850lb rear springs (5000lb GVW)	NA	$4.87
1850lb rear springs (5500lb GVW)	NA	$2.49
Power steering	$134.50	$128.30
Transmission		
4-speed (115in wb)	$107.60	$102.63
4-speed (131in wb)	$113.00	$107.79
3-speed with overdrive	$125.50	NA
3-speed SelectShift		
Cruise-O-Matic	$247.50	$236.09
Air conditioner[13]	$461.90	$418.95
Chrome contour rear bumper		
for Styleside	$37.70	$35.95
Painted channel rear bumper		
for Flareside	$23.70	$22.61
Step-type painted rear bumper		
for Styleside	$51.80	$49.42
Left or right side mounted spare		
tire carrier for Styleside	$15.20	$14.50
Left side mounted spare tire carrier		
for Flareside	$17.40	$16.60
Cigarette lighter (Custom Cabs)	$4.70	$4.49
Convenience Group[14]	$22.00	$20.98
Tinted glass, all windows	$22.00	$20.98
Dual electric horns	$7.00	$6.69
Bright hub caps (for Custom		
and Sport Custom)	$10.80	$10.30
Clearance lights	$26.90	$25.65
Exterior mirrors		
Chrome, right side	$5.20	$4.96
Chrome remote control, left side	$15.10	$14.40
Chrome remote control, left side,		
fixed right side	$20.30	$19.37
5in x 8in non-tel., left and right side	$11.00	$10.50
Western style mirrors		
7in x 11in fixed, left and right side	$24.00	$22.90
6in x 10in bright swing lock,		
left and right side	$40.30	$38.44
6in x 10in bright extended arm,		
left and right side	$37.70	$35.95
Bright moldings		
Narrow bodyside (for Custom		

continued next page

F-100 prices (1971 and 1972) (continued)

	1971	1972
and Sport Custom)	$43.20	$41.22
Narrow rocker panel and wheel opening lip (for Ranger Styleside)[15]	$47.70	$45.51
Northland Special Package	NA	$122.29
Two-tone paint		
Regular, includes beltline molding	$26.90	$25.65
Deluxe, Styleside only		
Custom and Sport Custom[16]	$64.60	$61.63
Ranger and XLT Ranger	$26.90	$25.65
Combination-Styleside only		
Custom and Sport Custom[16]	$91.50	$87.28
Ranger and Ranger XLT	$53.80	$51.33
Protection Package	NA	$25.85
Push button AM radio and antenna	$72.60	$69.25
Push button AM/FM stereo radio and antenna	$229.50	$218.92
Black, texture painted roof	$61.50	$58.67
Center passenger seat belt for bench seat	$7.10	Std.
Heavy duty black vinyl seat trim for bench seat	$17.80	$16.99
Sport Custom seat (Custom Cabs with bench seat)	$30.20	$28.82
Sport Custom trim (Ranger cab with bench seat)	NC	NC
Bucket-type seats		
Sport Custom Cabs	$121.00	NA
Ranger	$113.30	NA
Ranger XLT	$94.10	NA
Shoulder harnesses (driver and passenger)	$31.50	$30.06
Special Packages		
Heavy Duty Special[17]	$122.30	NA
Heavy Duty Special[17] (with optional air conditioning)	$92.20	NA
Sport Custom	$155.50	$148.33
Ranger (Styleside)	$244.60	$233.33
Ranger XLT (Styleside)	$366.90	$349.98
Behind seat lockable stowage compartment[18]	$22.60	$47.93
Tool stowage box, right side[19]	$48.60	$46.37
Bright 15in wheel covers	$26.90	$25.65
Mag-style 15in wheel covers	$54.60	$52.09
Lockable sliding rear window	$53.80	$51.33
Tubeless tires and wheels		
G78-15 4-ply B rating WSW, 5.5 K wheels	$32.70	$31.76
8.25 x 15 8-ply D rating PT-D, 5.5 K wheels	$34.80	NA
G78-15D 8-ply rating, PT 5.5K wheels	NA	$34.48
G78-15D 8-ply rating, WSW, 5.5 K wheels for 5500lb. GVW	NA	$31.88
8.25 x 15 8-ply D rating PT-D WSW		

continued over

belted mud and snow tires.

Expanded standard equipment, minor styling changes and several new and revised options characterized the 1972 F-100. The grille's argent-colored insert retained its two-piece format with a polished aluminum divider creating a field of four rectangular elements. Added to all trim levels was a color-keyed center seat belt.

Six new exterior colors, three of them metallic, were included in a selection of sixteen colors for 1972. Fourteen colors could be combined in three different two-tone paint schemes (Regular, Deluxe and Combination) that Ford offered for the F-100.

Carried over from 1971 were Bahama Blue, Swiss Aqua, Mallard Green, Calypso Coral, Prairie Yellow, Tampico Yellow, Wimbledon White, Candyapple Red, Chrome Yellow, and Pure White. The new colors were Seapine Green Metallic, Winter Green, Royal Maroon, Wind Blue, Bay Roc Blue Metallic, and Sequoia Brown Metallic. The three two-tone combinations were once again available with 54 possible regular combinations.

Engine emission control equipment was added to all engines. The various Gross Vehicle Weight packages now included equipment required for specific ratings. The 4x2 F-100 had a higher GVW of 5500 pounds, up from 5000 pounds in 1971. The overdrive option was deleted for 1972. A new Northland Special option consisted of an engine block heater, 50/50 anti-freeze coolant, 70amp-hr battery, 55amp alternator and a limited-slip rear axle. Another new offering, the Protection Package, combined front bumper guards with door edge guards.

Initially, power-assisted brakes were listed as standard for the 4-wheel drive F-100, but, on October 1, 1971, Ford

F-100 prices (1971 and 1972) (continued)

	1971	1972
5.5 K wheels	$67.50	NA
G78-15 D 8-ply rating,WSW, PT, 5.5 K wheels	NA	$66.36
Tube-type nylon tires and wheels		
6.50 x 16, 6-ply rating, 5K wheels	$75.50	NA
6.50 x 16C 6-ply ratings, 5K wheels	NA	$74.57
6.50 x 16C 6-ply ratings, 5K wheels for 5500lb. GVW	NA	$40.09
7.00 x 15, 6-ply rating, 5.5K wheels	$103.10	NA
7.00 x 15C, 6-ply rating, 5.5K wheels	NA	$100.38
7.00 x 15C, 6-ply rating, 5.5K wheels for 5500lb GVW	NA	$66.50
Additional options for 4-wheel drive		
Dana free-running manual front hubs	$78.50	$74.87
1650lb single stage rear springs	NC	NA
1875lb single; stage springs (5200lb GVW)	NA	NC

[1]Not available with air conditioning.
[2]Available with Heavy Duty Special packages, not available with air conditioning.
[3]Not available with 4x4, 4-speed transmission or 390 V-8.
[4]Available with 4-speed transmission or 390 V-8.
[5]Includes heavy duty front springs.
[6]Includes 11.5in clutch and heavy duty front springs. Not available with 4x4.
[7]1971 required with 240 and 300 6-cylinder or 360 or 390 engines with Cruise-O-Matic for California. 1972: required in California with manual or Cruise-O-Matic.
[8]1971 required for California and New York. 1972 required for Chicago, Colorado, Minnesota, California, and New York.
[9]1971 Not available with air conditioning. 1972: Available with 360 and 390 engines only. Price listed is for use with air conditioner. When used without air conditioning the price was $61.43.
[10]1971: Not available with Power Pak. 1972: Not available with 131in wheelbase and air conditioning combination with 5500lb or 5000lb GVW or 390 V-8.
[11]Used with 1250lb main springs.
[12]Used with 1650lb main springs.
[13]Includes 55amp alternator and Extra Cooling Package.
[14]Standard with Ranger XLT. Includes cargo area and underhood lights, glovebox door lock and 12in day/night mirror.
[15]Also available for Ranger Flareside at $23.00
[16]For Custom and Sport Custom Styleside. Includes body side and tailgate moldings.
[17]With 8ft Styleside only.
[18]1971 not available with standard fuel tank. 1972 not available with standard fuel tank, Ford also reported it had limited availability.
[19]With 8ft Styleside only.

informed its dealers that these were now optional. F-100 4x4 models had a new standard Dana 3300lb rated front axle. This axle's capacity was 300lb more than the unit used in 1971. It also had longer wearing, impact-resistant, tapered roller bearings in the steering knuckles.

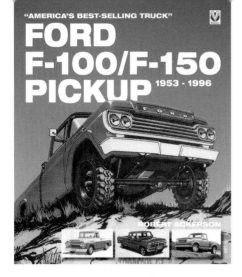

5

1973-1979

Introducing the F-100 pickups for 1973 on September 10, 1972, John Naughton, Ford vice president and Ford Division general manager, noted that "... the Ford pickup has become one of the best-selling vehicles in America because of its versatility and dependability. In the truck market, whether commercial or personal, form follows function - and for 1973 we have concentrated on providing the ever-growing number of pickup users with the features they have demanded, while retaining the rugged looks our customers want." In other words, the 1973 F-100 represented, in Naughton's view, "... a new generation of 'better ideas' that effectively answered an extremely difficult question - "... how could the number one pickup be improved?"

Appearance-wise, Ford explained that "Although the 1973 F-Series pickups have newly styled sheet metal, they retain the 'Ford Look' that has been so highly accepted by buyers over the past several years." All F-100 trim levels continued to have a standard bright grille and chrome front bumper, two items often cited as having helped acquire new customers for the F-100. The 1973 grille design, with its bright and black plastic insert, comprised four vertical dividers and three horizontal bars representing an updating of the 1972 divided motif. The FORD lettering was moved from the leading edge of the hood

to a space just above the grille, which also housed the high-mounted parking lights at its extremities. A new exterior contour, along with the use of full inner panels, made the hood more resistant to shaking and flexing. Viewed in profile the F-100 displayed a bold sculptured, full-length channel in which the front and rear side marker lights were placed. New recessed door handles were also used.

The F-100 cab glass area was increased by 2.21sq ft. The side glass was now curved and the backlight - 39 per cent larger than in 1972 - tilted slightly forward to reduce nighttime reflections in the rearview mirror. (See table below.)

The use of curved side glass and longer 117 and 133 inch wheelbases for the F-100 impacted on both interior and exterior dimensions, as shown in the table on page 60.

By moving the fuel tank (the 1973 tank had a capacity of 19.4 gallons; the 1972 unit's capacity was 18.2 gallons) out of the cab to a position under the rear of the pickup box, Ford provided the F-100 with a useful, behind-the-seat storage area. Incorporated into the instrument panel was a glovebox with a volume nearly twice that of the 1972 F-100. If the F-100 was equipped with optional power brakes, the brake pedal was located at a new, lower height. This feature - comparable to passenger car practice - was intended

F-100 Cab glass area (1973 v. 1972)

	1972	1973
Windshield	9sq ft	8.85sq ft
Side windows	5.7sq ft	6.13sq ft
Rear cab window	4.4sq ft	6.27sq ft
Total area	19.1sq ft	21.25sq ft

A 1973 F-100 Styleside with the Ranger XLT Package. Ford reported that its 1973 trucks represented a "New Generation of Better Ideas." (Courtesy Ford Motor Company)

An F-100 Ranger XLT with the new-for-1973 Deluxe box cover. (Courtesy Ford Motor Company)

to give the driver a more convenient accelerator-to-brake pedal transition.

Also noteworthy was a new, optional air conditioner with four adjustable air outlets fully integrated into the instrument panel. The system's four speed blower motor was mounted on the firewall under the hood; a new location which significantly reduced blower noise in the cab. As in 1972, a V-8 engine was required if air conditioning was ordered.

New options for 1973 included an easier to operate slide-out spare tire carrier, low-mount Western mirrors, bright chrome pickup box tie-down hooks for Styleside models, dual body side stripes (also limited to the Styleside models), intermittent windshield wipers, and revamped radios.

A simplified trim range for 1973 consisted of Custom, Ranger and Ranger XLT levels. In contrast to the base Custom F-100 (which was promoted as "... a fully trimmed pickup at an attractive price"), the Ranger was depicted as "... a more luxurious package designed to bracket and take the place of last year's Ranger and Sport Custom." Leaving no doubt in anyone's mind that the pickup market had changed dramatically in two decades, Ford asserted that the Ranger XLT was "... the ultimate in pickup elegance and luxury."

F-100 dimensions (1972 v 1973)

	1972	1973
Cab length	56.3in	58.3in
Leg room	38.3in	39.7in
Shoulder room	65.0in	66.0in
Hip room	65.7in	66.0in
Seat adjustment	4.5in	5.0in
Overall length		
1972 (115in wb)	187.8in	
1973 (117in wb)	189.3in	
1972 (131in wb)	202.3in	
1973 (133in wb)	205.3in	

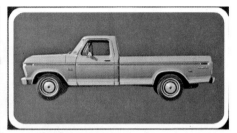

These four views of a 1973 F-100 Ranger XLT on the 133in wheelbase illustrate Ford's conservative approach to changing the appearance of its trucks. (Courtesy Ford Motor Company)

Key exterior elements of the Custom F-100 included a front bumper, left-side rearview mirror, tailgate handle depression (Styleside), and Custom script emblems. Among the Custom's major standard interior features was a dome light with door-operated switches, glovebox with push button latch, right and left side padded sun visors, bright plastic instrument cluster trim with instrument back-lighting in green, sponge grain hardboard headlining with white retainer moldings, vinyl seat trim, full-depth foam seat and seat back (in place of the 1.25 inch thickness used in 1972, Ford used 7 inch thick foam seat cushions on all 1973 F-100 models), three sets of deluxe seat belts with outboard extractors, bright shift and turn signal levers with black knobs, 10in day/night vinyl-framed mirror, and a black floor mat. The Custom interior was offered in blue, green, red or black.

The Ranger's exterior features, in addition to or in place of those of the Custom, included bright finishes for the rear window and windshield moldings, drip rail moldings, rocker panel and wheel lip moldings, Styleside tailgate applique, hub caps, taillight bezels (Styleside), and top and bottom tailgate moldings (Styleside). Key attributes of the Ranger interior included a color-keyed floor mat with heel pads, cigarette lighter, perforated headliner with bright molding, instrument panel molding with black accent, Ranger plaque on glovebox door, color-keyed pleated cloth seat trim with vinyl bolsters, added insulation, and sound-absorbing material under headliner and floor mat.

Key aspects of the Ranger XLT (in addition to or in place of Ranger features) were bright body side moldings with black vinyl inserts (this feature was also offered as an option for all other Styleside pickups), bright upper tailgate applique panel (Styleside), Ranger XLT grille and side script emblems, a black steering wheel with woodgrain insert, color-keyed carpeting, convenience group (under-hood light, cargo-box light, glovebox lock and light, 12in day-night mirror, door map pocket and ashtray light), door trim panels, color-keyed pleated-vinyl upper panel with woodgrain accented moldings and map pocket in lower panel, bright instrument panel with woodgrain accents, additional insulation and sound-deadener, high-style pleated cloth seat trim with vinyl bolsters, Ranger XLT glovebox door plaque, color-keyed vinyl sun visors, and bright seat pivot arm covers. The interiors of the Ranger and Ranger XLT models were available in Avocado, Blue, Ginger, Green, Red, and Black.

Sixteen exterior colors were offered for 1973: Raven Black, Wind Blue, Pure White, Chrome Yellow, Seapine Green, Wimbledon White, Winter Green, Sequoia Brown Metallic, Midnight Blue Metallic, Candyapple Red, Limestone Green, Mallard Green, Durango Tan, Royal Blue, and Tampico Yellow.

The Explorer Package for the F-100 Custom was offered in a choice of three exterior colors: Burnt Orange, Grabber Blue or Bright Lime. These colors were paired to interiors with the following combinations of random striped cloth/vinyl: Special Orange/Orange, Special Blue/Blue, and Special Avocado/Black.

Exterior appointments of the Explorer A Package (1973)

Bright front bumper guards.
Front bumper rub strips.
Bright box rails.[1]
Body side tape stripe.
Bright windshield moldings.
Bright drip moldings.
Explorer nameplates.
Bright low-mount Swing-Lok mirrors.
Mag-type wheel covers.

[1]F-100 long wheelbase only. Rope tie downs were used for the short wheelbase version.

Bright Box Rails*

Sporty Mag-Type Wheel Covers**

Bright Low-Mount Swing-Lok Mirrors

Handsome Bodyside Tape Stripe

These views highlight the features of the 1973 Explorer Package. (Courtesy Ford Motor Company)

For 1973 the optional air conditioning system was fully integrated into the instrument panel. (Courtesy Ford Motor Company)

The floor mats were color-keyed to the interior.

The B Package included all of Package A plus power steering and SelectShift Cruise-O-Matic. Package C contained all of Packages A and B plus air conditioning and tinted glass.

Although all 2-wheel drive F-100s, and the 117in wheelbase 4x4 model had new frames for 1973, no major technical breakthroughs were claimed for the 1973 F-100. Instead, Ford focused on several important refinements of the F-100's existing engineering. A 4 inch increase in the rear tread width of the 2-wheel drive F-100 made it, at 64 inches, essentially identical to that of the front wheels. This change also allowed the rear springs to be set further apart. The result, claimed Ford, was better tracking and load support, and greater handling stability.

The 1973 F-100 front springs were individually selected by computer to provide the softest ride consistent with

the capacity to handle the computed load. Also enhancing both the ride of the F-100 and its load capacity were the new H78 x 15 and L78 x15 tires available mid-1973 in place of the 8-ply tires offered in 1972. Their use was made possible by the added wheel space of the 1973 F-100. The 4-wheel drive F-100 was available with Cruise-O-Matic and power steering as options. A 2-speed (1.0:1, 1.96:1) New Process Model 205 transfer case was used with the automatic transmission.

Supporting Ford's claim that the 1973 F-100 "... should be more rust-resistant than any previous model" was the use of new galvanized front fender aprons. On Styleside pickups a new, special zinc-rich coating treatment called Zincrometal, and special rust-resistant primers provided increased corrosion protection to non-galvanized areas. The Styleside box was also produced with state-of-the-art stamping equipment which eliminated separate wheelwells and numerous joint seams vulnerable to rust. Other noteworthy features of the new F-100 Styleside pickup boxes included easier to clean coved corners, full double-panel design, including tailgate, wider 51 inch floor between wheel housings, rope tie holes in all corner stake pockets, and a new, pull-type tailgate handle. The short wheelbase Styleside also had a longer box for 1973 with a 6.75 foot nominal length.

Improving the F-100's road performance were standard front wheel single-piston floating caliper, Ford-designed disc brakes for the 2-wheel drive version. 4-wheel drive models had manual front drum brakes as standard, with power assist optional.

Engine changes for 1973 were confined mostly to improvements in emission control systems and, in some cases, altered compression ratios. A new

Exhaust Gas Recirculator System was added to engines with lower GVW ratings, and wider use was made of an IMCO (Improved Combustion Emission Control System).

A new, factory-installed option was a fiberglass pickup box cover for 8 foot Styleside models. The standard model, finished in textured white, was fitted with fixed clear glass side windows, tinted fixed rear window, and a lockable T-handle liftgate latch. The Deluxe model featured sliding side windows with screens, bright moldings for side and rear windows, roof vent, and dome light. The Deluxe model was also offered in a two-tone exterior paint combination. Additional new options for 1973 included low-profile swing-lock, 7in x 11in mirrors, bright chrome pickup box tie-down hooks (three hooks on each side of the Styleside box, plus two on the tailgate) and, for Styleside pickups, dual body side stripes and bright aluminum vinyl-insert body side moldings.

A 'Second-Level Super Cooling Package' was also introduced for all 4x2 F-100 pickups. If the truck was equipped with Cruise-O-Matic, the package included a heavy duty transmission oil cooler.

In spite of their many notable features, Ford's F-Series pickups were outsold by Chevrolet's all-new line of full-size pickups during the 1973 calendar year, by a margin of 37,187 units (the final tally was Ford: 693,989, Chevrolet: 731,176). But In a report to its dealers dated February 19, 1974, Ford noted that, according to R. L. Polk registration data based on state sources, buyers registered 995,156 Ford trucks as compared to 991,099 Chevrolet trucks.

In 1974, the impact of the Arab oil embargo weighed heavily upon the popularity of both Ford and Chevrolet full-sized pickups. At year's end, Ford sales

2-wheel drive F-100 brake specifications (1972 and 1973)

	1972	1973
Front brakes	Drum	Disc
Dimensions	11 x 3in	11.72in dia
Rear brakes	Drum	Drum
Dimensions	11.03 x 2.25in	11.03 x 2.25in

F-100 suspension and frame specifications (1972 & 1973)

	1972	1973
2-wheel drive		
Front suspension		
Front axle capacity	2750lb	2750lb
Standard spring rating	1290lb	1250lb
Rear suspension		
Number of leaves	5	4
Rear spring length	52in	56in
Rear spring width	2.25in	2.50in
Rear axle rating	3300lb	3300lb
Standard spring rating	1175lb	1225lb
4-wheel drive		
Front suspension		
Front axle capacity	3300lb	3300lb
Standard spring rating	1365lb/1490lb[1]	1365lb
Rear suspension		
Number of leaves	6	4
Rear spring length	52in	55.5in
Rear spring width	2.25in	3.00in
Rear axle rating	3300lb	3300lb
Standard. spring rating	1465lb	1475lb

[1]First figure is for 115in wheelbase model; the second is for the 131in wheelbase models.

Frame	Maximum side rail section (in)	Section Modulus
2-wheel drive		
1972/115in wb	6.04 x 2.42 x 0.156	2.98
1973/117in wb	6.65 x 2.38 x 0.146	3.09
1972/131in wb	6.09 x 2.40 x 0.164	3.06
1973/133in wb	6.66 x 2.39 x 0.154	3.26
4-wheel drive		
1972/115in wb	6.11 x 2.45 x 0.194	3.71
1973/117in wb	6.72 x 2.42 x 0.184	3.92
1972/131in wb	6.14 x 2.47 x 0.212	4.14
1973/133in wb	6.74 x 2.42 x 0.193	4.14

were down by nearly 133,000 trucks.

Whether the popularity of the 1974 F-100 was influenced by an appearance unchanged from 1973 is difficult to say. For the new truck buyer who was pleased with its styling, there were other significant developments. Making the 8 foot Styleside pickup more attractive to campers were revisions to its pickup box that provided added clearance for shorter slide-in campers. Beginning in early 1974, the 2-wheel drive F-100 was offered in all states except California with Ford's big 460 cubic inch V-8, with a 4.36in bore and 3.85in stroke and solid-state breakerless ignition. Returning as an optional engine was the 300 cubic inch 6-cylinder, last available in 1971. This engine was required in California as the F-100's base engine. Neither the 240 6-cylinder nor the 460 V-8 was available in California.

Eight new exterior colors were offered for 1974, including two 'Glow' paints - Ivy Glow and Ginger Glow (available February 1974). The other colors for 1974 were: Raven Black, Wind Blue, Chrome Yellow, Wimbledon White, Sequoia Brown Metallic, Midnight Blue Metallic, Candyapple Red, Limestone Green Metallic, Light Grabber Blue, Burnt Orange, Pastel Lime, Village Green, Samoa Lime, and Sandpiper Yellow. Interior colors, which were co-ordinated to the exterior and the specific trim level, consisted of Avocado, Blue, Ginger, Green, Black and Red. The optional tape strip was offered in Green, Black, Orange, White or Yellow, depending on the exterior color.

The simulated vinyl option was expanded for 1974 to include a white as well as black finish. It included a bright roof drip molding (standard on the Ranger), and bright back-of-cab beltline molding.

A midship fuel tank, located ahead of

Comparison of 1972 & 1973 engine power ratings

Engine: 240 6-cylinder	1972	1973
Compression ratio	8.5:1	8.1:1
Gross horsepower	118 at 3800rpm	115 at 4000rpm[1]
Net horsepower	105[2] at 3600rpm	105 at 3800rpm
Gross torque (lb/ft)	184 at 2400rpm	180 at 2400rpm
Net torque (lb/ft)	173[3] at 2400rpm	175 at 2400rpm

[1]Ratings are for models with manual transmission.

The ratings for trucks with automatic transmission were:

Gross horsepower	114 at 4000rpm
Net horsepower	100 at 3800rpm
Gross torque (lb/ft):	183 at 2400rpm
Net torque (lb/ft)	173 at 4000rpm

[2]Rating shown is for 115in wheelbase. Rating for use with 131in wheelbase was 104 at 3800rpm.
[3]Rating shown is for 115in wheelbase. Rating for use with 131in wheelbase was 172 at 2200rpm.

Engine: 302 V-8	1972	1973
Compression ratio	8.2:1	8.0:1
Gross horsepower	1541 at 3600rpm	1602 at 4200rpm
Net horsepower	134 at 3600rpm	139 at 3800rpm
Gross torque (lb/ft)	246 at 2400rpm	250 at 2600rpm
Net torque (lb/ft)	231 at 2400rpm	236 at 2000rpm

[1]Ratings are for 115in wheelbase model with manual transmission.
The ratings for trucks with automatic transmission and 131in wheelbase as well as those destined for California differed as indicated by the following:

California
115in wheelbase, automatic transmission

Gross horsepower	153 at 4000rpm
Net horsepower	133 at 3800rpm
Gross torque (lb/ft)	243 at 2800rpm
Net torque (lb/ft)	223 at 2200rpm

131in wheelbase, automatic transmission

Gross horsepower	153 at 4000rpm
Net horsepower	132 at 3800rpm
Gross torque (lb/ft)	243 at 2800rpm
Net torque (lb/ft)	222 at 2200rpm

131in wheelbase (except California with automatic)

Gross horsepower	154 at 4000rpm
Net horsepower	133 at 3800rpm

continued next page

the rear axle, was available for Styleside models either in lieu of the standard fuel tank or with it as an auxiliary tank.
Introduced on February 4, 1974 was a full-time, 4-wheel drive system for F-100 pickups equipped with the 360 engine and Cruise-O-Matic transmission. This system provided 4-wheel drive at highway speeds as well as off the road. Ford explained that the system was called 'Full-Time' because power was directed to all four wheels through a differential in the transfer case. While providing equal and constant power to the front and rear wheels, the older conventional system did not compensate for differences in front and rear axle ratios. Consequently, normal highway driving on hard dry surfaces in 4-wheel drive was not recommended since it could result in axle wind-up and increased tire wear.

The new, full-time system automatically compensated for differences in front and rear axle speeds. Included in the full-time transfer case was a mechanical lockout feature by-passing the third differential, thus eliminating the differential effect and essentially converting the full-time system to a conventional 4-wheel drive system with equal and constant power to the front and rear axles. This operation was controlled by moving the transfer case lever to either the high or low lock position. A special plate was installed on the dash which included a blue warning light to indicate to the driver when the transfer case was in the 'lock' position.

The transfer case also incorporated a two-speed gearbox with a high ratio of 1:1 for regular driving and a low 2:1 ratio for difficult conditions. The F-100 could be driven in either high or low range in either the differential 'full time' or the 'locked' position. Shifting between high full-time, four-wheel drive with differential action and high lock could be accomplished with the truck moving, as could a shift between low full-time, 4-wheel drive and low lock. Ford priced the full-time system for the F-100 at $78.00, which was the same as the cost of the free-wheeling front hubs.

In June, an equally important product development occurred when Ford's response to Dodge's Club Cab, the SuperCab, was introduced. Ford

Comparison of 1972 & 1973 engine power ratings (continued)

Gross torque (lb/ft)	246 at 2400rpm
Net torque (lb/ft)	230 at 2200rpm

Ratings for trucks with automatic transmission were as follows

Gross horsepower	159 at 4200rpm
Net horsepower	137 at 3800rpm
Gross torque (lb/ft)	241 at 2800rpm
Net torque (lb/ft)	219 at 2600rpm

[1]Ratings are for 115in wheelbase model. The ratings for trucks with 131in wheelbase differed as shown by the following:

	1972	*1973*
Engine: 360 V-8		
Compression ratio	8.0:1	8.0:1
Gross horsepower	193[1] at 4400rpm	189[2] at 4600rpm
Net horsepower	157 at 4000rpm	157 at 4000rpm
Gross torque (lb/ft)	290 at 2600rpm	287 at 2600rpm
Net torque (lb/ft)	269 at 2400rpm	265 at 2200rpm
Gross horsepower	193 at 4400rpm	
Net horsepower	156 at 4000rpm	
Gross torque (lb/ft)	290 at 2600rpm	
Net torque (lb/ft)	268 at 2400rpm	

[2]Ratings for 4x2 trucks with automatic transmission and 4x4 trucks were as follows:

4x2 automatic	
Gross horsepower	187 at 4200rpm
Net horsepower	151 at 3800rpm
Gross torque (lb/ft)	284 at 2600rpm
Net torque (lb/ft)	257 at 2000rpm

4x4	*Manual*	*Automatic*
Gross horsepower	189 at 4600rpm	187 at 4200rpm
Net horsepower	153 at 4000rpm	148 at 3800rpm
Gross torque (lb/ft)	287 at 2600rpm	284 at 2600rpm
Net torque (lb/ft)	262 at 2200rpm	256 at 2200rpm

	1972	*1973*
Engine: 390 V-8		
Compression ratio	8.2:1	8.2:1
Gross horsepower	200 at 4400rpm	189[1] at 4600rpm
Net Horsepower	165 at 4000rpm	157 at 4000rpm
Gross torque (lb/ft)	317 at 2600rpm	287 at 2600rpm
Net torque (lb/ft)	294[2] at 2400rpm	265 at 2200rpm

[1]The 390 engine was offered only with automatic transmission in 1973. It was not offered for the 4x4 model in 1972 and 1973.
[2]Rating for 131in wheelbase models was 296 at 2200rpm.

estimated that SuperCab sales for the remainder of the model year would represent nearly 25 per cent of all Ford pickup sales.

By extending the wheelbase of the F-100 by 22 inches, Ford provided the SuperCab with exterior dimensions which compared to those of the conventional pickups, as shown in the accompanying table.

The SuperCab provided a minimum of 44 cubic feet of behind-seat storage area; if the seat was moved to its farthest forward position, this increased to 49 cubic feet. The standard floor covering for the Custom SuperCab cargo compartment was a two-piece black, carpet grained mat running the full length of the cab. In Ranger models, the mat was color-keyed. For the Ranger XLT a full-length, color-keyed carpet was fitted.

Two seating options were offered. The first included two center-facing jump seats. Each seat had a foam cushion back and seat, and was supported by a swing-down leg. When not in use, these seats folded up against the cab wall. The jump seats were available in Blue, Green, Black, and Red for Custom models, and Blue, Green, Black, and Ginger for Ranger and Ranger XLT models. Optional seat belts were offered in black only.

The SuperCabs could also be equipped with a full-width, forward-facing bench seat. This had a vinyl-covered foam seat and seat back cushion and, via a handle positioned at the base of the seat, could be folded down to form a flat, steel-ribbed cargo region. The same interior colors offered for the Custom, Ranger, and XLT Ranger models with the jump seats were available for this option. Standard with either seat option were soft vinyl, color-keyed shoulder bolsters, molded rear compartment trim panels, and fixed quarter windows measuring 15in x 15in. Except for 4-wheel drive and the in-cab auxiliary fuel tank, most F-100 options were also available for the SuperCab. The F-100 SuperCab was available with the 360 engine only, and either a 3-speed manual or Cruise-O-Matic transmission.

Interior trim colors for the SuperCab were identical to those of comparable standard cab models, except that Red and Avocado were not offered for Ranger and Ranger XLT models.

F-100 prices (effective March 12, 1973)

	Price
117 inch wheelbase models	
Custom Styleside	$2778.90
133 inch wheelbase models	
Custom Flareside	$2814.90
Custom Styleside	$2814.90
4-wheel drive models	
117in wheelbase	
Custom Styleside	$3339.90
131in wheelbase	
Custom Flareside	$3375.90
Custom Styleside	$3375.90
Optional equipment	
Ranger trim level (Styleside)	$196.60
Ranger trim level (Flareside)	$161.80
Ranger XLT trim level (Styleside)	$349.98
Ranger XLT trim level (Flareside)	$331.58
302 V-8	$110.27
360 V-8[1]	$153.68
390 V-8	$251.43
4-speed manual trans. (117in wheelbase)	$102.63
4-speed manual trans. (133in wheelbase)	$107.79
3-speed Cruise-O-Matic[2]	$236.09
3300lb Traction-Lok rear axle	$63.81
3600lb Traction-Lok rear axle	$63.81
Optional axle ratios	$12.51
Air conditioner[3]	$418.95
42amp Motorcraft alternator[4]	$22.81
55amp Motorcraft alternator	$30.81
70amp-hr battery	$16.60
Power brakes, 10in vacuum brake booster (std. with 5450lb and 500lb GVW)	$48.46
Contour chrome rear bumper (Styleside only)	$35.95
Channel painted rear bumper (Flareside only)	$22.61
Stepside rear bumper (Styleside only)	$49.42
Side mounted spare tire carrier left or right side, for 8ft Styleside only	$14.50
Left side mounted spare tire carrier for Flareside - 5in x 8in or larger mirrors recommended	$16.60
Rear slide-out spare tire carrier	$23.70
Cigarette lighter (Custom Cab only)	$4.49
Convenience Group[5]	$35.60
Oil bath air cleaner[5]	$6.20
Extra Cooling Package	$28.24
Super Cooling Package[6]	$33.20
California emissions testings	$15.55
Required California exhaust emission control system for 360 and 390 engines	$15.55
Reduced sound exhaust system	$6.59
Ammeter and oil pressure gauges	$11.83
Evaporative emission control fuel system required for California	$51.40

continued next page

All SuperCab models had 'SuperCab' script on the rear quarter windows. Added to the Ranger and XLT Ranger models was a rear quarter window molding.

Ford's Explorer Packages, available in early March 1974, were again offered as Packages A, B, and C. Three special exterior colors - Brook Blue Metallic, Viking Red, and Parrot Orange - were offered. The interior was offered in Blue, Ginger or Red Stirling cloth, or a Tan 'Super Soft' vinyl. Aside from the use of new, below eye level, low-mount, swing-lok exterior mirrors, the Explorer Packages content was unchanged from that of 1973.

The 1975 F-100 exterior was virtually identical to that of the 1974 model. New 'high solid' enamel paint was introduced.

Custom level pickups were available with a Custom Decor Group consisting of knitted vinyl seat trim, color-keyed insulated floor mats, bright windshield, and rear window moldings, bright drip rails and bright hubcaps.

The Ranger used the super soft vinyl introduced in 1974 for the Explorer Packages. Other new Ranger features included simulated woodgrain steering wheel insert, color-keyed perforated headliner, 12 ounce, loop-style carpet and visors, bright wheellip, and Styleside body side moldings. The XLT Ranger also had the super soft vinyl as a no-cost option. New XLT features included 22 ounce cut-pile carpeting, and standard bright wheel covers.

1975 exterior colors were Raven Black, Viking Red, Candyapple Red, Wind Blue, Midnight Blue Metallic, Bahama Blue, Hatteras Green Metallic, Baytree Green, Glen Green, Sequoia Brown Metallic, Parrot Orange, Chrome Yellow, Vineyard Gold, Wimbledon White, Medium Green Glow, and Ginger Glow. Interior colors, coded to the exterior finish, consisted of

F-100 prices (effective March 12, 1973) (continued)

Optional equipment ....Price
22.5 gal. fuel tank (with standard tank) $77.30
Tinted glass, all windows $20.98
High output heater...$16.60
Dual electric horns..$6.69
Bright hub caps (Custom Cab only) $10.30
Roof clearance lights (five) $25.65
Outside mirrors
    Chrome right side...$4.96
    Left side remote control $19.37
    Non. tel., 5in x 8in left and right side $10.50
Western-type mirrors
    7in x 11in fixed left and right side....................................$22.90
    6in x 10in bright long arm, left and right side $35.95
    7in x 11in low mount swing lock, left and right side........$38.44
Moldings, bright metal
    Narrow body side (Styleside only, not available
    with Ranger XLT) $41.22
    Body side with vinyl insert[7]..$59.30
Rocker panel delete
    Ranger and Ranger XLT Styleside..................................$20.87
    credit
    Ranger and Ranger XLT Flareside..................................$10.22
    credit
Northland Special Package[8]...$91.48
Two-tone paint
    Regular, includes beltline molding...................................$25.65
    Deluxe (Styleside only)
    Custom Cab (includes bright body side and tailgate
    moldings and bright taillight bezels..................................$61.63
    Ranger (includes bright body side moldings) $61.63
    Ranger XLT $25.65
    Combination Regular and Deluxe Custom Cab
    (includes bright body side and tailgate moldings and
    bright taillight bezels...$87.28
    Ranger (includes bright body side moldings) $87.28
Ranger XLT:..$51.33
Body side tape stripe (for Styleside only, not available with
Deluxe or Combination two-tone paint options): $25.40
Pickup box cover, regular (8ft Styleside only): $299.00
Pickup box cover, deluxe (8ft Styleside only):........................$390.00
Protection Group (includes door edge and front
bumper guards): $25.85
AM push button radio:..$69.25
AM/FM stereo push button radio: $218.92
Black painted texture roof (includes bright drip rail
molding on CustomCab and bright back of cab molding): $58.67
Seat trim
    Heavy duty black vinyl:..$16.99
Knitted vinyl
    Custom Cab $12.80
Ranger and Ranger XLT ....NC
Shock absorbers: heavy duty front and rear $15.55
Dual shoulder harnesses (includes black seat belts)...............$30.06
Heavy duty front springs[9] $6.30
Rear springs
1475lb progressive (for 4550 and 4650lb GVW only)..............$18.61

continued next page

Blue, Gray, Ginger, Green, Heavy Duty Black (for Custom models), Black, and Red.

All F-100 pickups were fitted with catalytic converters. Their respective front and rear axle capacities were 3300lbs and 1675lbs. Unleaded fuel was required for all pickups under 6000lb GVW. For improved fuel economy, the F-100 was available with an optional 3.00:1 rear axle ratio. All F-100 engines were equipped with the breakerless, solid-state ignition system.

A Fuel Economy Warning Light was added to the optional Instrument Package: this light began flashing when intake manifold pressure indicated excessive use of fuel.

New for 1975 was the F-150, a heavy duty, 2-wheel drive ½ ton with a GVW rating of 6050lb. It was not fitted with a catalytic converter and thus did not require unleaded fuel. Major suspension aspects of the F-150 included a 3300lb front axle, 1250lb front and 1875lb rear springs, and a Ford-built rear axle rated at 3750lb. Initially, its standard tires were L78-15D but these were later replaced by H78-15D tires. Power brakes were standard. Engine availability consisted of the 300-6, 390, and 460 V-8 engines.

Optional for all 2-wheel drive models was a cruise control system requiring the 460 V-8, Cruise-O-Matic, and power steering.

SuperCab models were offered with the new Custom Decor Group as well as in F-150 form. The SuperCabs, offered with a $350 rebate during the model year, were now available with the 300 cubic inch 6-cylinder as well as the 390 and 460 cubic inch V-8 engines.

Effective December 2, 1974, the base F-100 engine became the 300 cubic inch 6-cylinder. At the same time the 360 V-8 with a 4-barrel carburetor replaced

F-100 prices (effective March 12, 1973) (continued)

Optional equipment	Price
1650lb progressive (for 4550 and 4650lb GVW only)	$20.32
1650lb progressive (for 4800 and 5000lb GVW only)	$1.82
420lb auxiliary[10]	$29.86
Power steering[11]	$128.30
Chrome tie-down hooks	$27.00
Right side tool storage box (for 8ft Styleside only)	$46.37

Light duty trailer towing packages up to 2000lb (360 or 390 engines required)

Styleside models	$81.20

Heavy duty trailer towing packages for trailers over 2000lbs (360 or 390 engines required)

With air conditioning	$62.85
Without air conditioning	$121.90
Transmission oil cooler (includes Extra Cooling Package, for use with V-8 engine and Cruise-O-Matic)	$50.44
Bright 15in wheel covers	$25.65
Mag-style 15in wheel covers	$52.09
Sliding, locking rear window, clear glass only	$51.33
Interval windshield wipers	$25.40

Tubeless tires and wheels

G78-15 4-ply B rating WSW, 5.5 K wheels	$31.76
G78-15D 8-ply rating, PT, 5.5 K wheels	$34.48
G78-15D 8-ply rating, PT, WSW, 5.5 K wheels	$66.36
H78-15B, 4-ply rating, PT, 5.5 K wheels	$16.40
H78-15B, 4-ply rating, PT, WSW, 5.5 K wheels	$48.40
HR78-15B, 4-ply rating, PT, WSW, 5.5 K wheels	$138.40
L78-15B, 4-ply rating, PT, 5.5 K wheels	$71.50
L78-15B, 4-ply rating, PT, WSW, 5.5 K wheels	$103.50

Tube-type nylon tires and wheels

6.50 x 16C 6-ply ratings, 5 K wheels	$74.57
7.00 x 15C, 6-ply rating, 5.5 K wheels	$100.88

Additional option for 4-wheel drive

1875lb single stage springs (5200lb GVW)[12]	NC

[1] Includes 1340lb minimum front springs with 133in wheelbase.
[2] Includes 55 AH battery and transmission cooler. 4-wheel drive models include 42amp alternator and 1490lb minimum front springs and minimum 1340lb front springs; H78-15B or G78-15D tires required.
[3] Includes 55amp alternator, 70 AH battery and heavy-duty cooling
[4] Not available with air conditioner.
[5] Not available with 360 and 390 engines in California.
[6] For manual transmission - available with 360 and 390 engines only. Price listed was for use with air conditioner. When used without air conditioning the price was $61.43. For Cruise-O-Matic includes heavy duty transmission oil cooler. Price with air conditioning was $55.60; without air conditioning $83.83.
[7] Price listed was for trucks without Deluxe or Combination two-tone paint. When either of these was ordered, the price was $18.08.
[8] Includes engine block heater 50/50 (-35°F) antifreeze, and limited slip rear axle. Price listed was for trucks with air conditioning. Price for trucks without air conditioning was $122.49. The package then included a 70 AH battery and 55amp alternator.
[9] Computer selected, not available for 133in wheelbase with combination of air conditioning and 5500lb GVW.
[10] Not available with standard GVW or 5000lb GVW with 360 V-8, 4-speed transmission and pickup box cover.
[11] Not available for 4550lb or 5450lb GVW with combination of 360 V-8 and Cruise-O-Matic.
[12] These are the only rear spring options offered for the 4x4 F-100.

the 2-barrel version in all pickups with a GVW exceeding 6000lb. These revisions, plus developments made to improve fuel economy and reduce emissions, resulted in a significantly revamped engine line-up for 1975 (see table page 73).

The auxiliary fuel tank was now equipped with an electric valve switching system in place of the older manual valve unit. Both the fuel gauge reading and the fuel tank selection was controlled by a single instrument panel switch.

Ford's mid-year Explorer pickups were offered for both the F-100 and F-150 in either regular or SuperCab form. As in 1974, the Explorer option was available in A, B, and C variations. Exterior colors listed for the Explorer pickups were Mexicali Red, Coronado Gold, and Hot Ginger metallic paint. (The latter color was not available for the SuperCabs.) Giving the Explorer added distinction was the new body side, color-keyed tape striping that ran from the rear of the pickup box and across the hood just ahead of the windshield base.

The Explorer interior of Kirsten Body Cloth with Corinthian grain vinyl bolsters was offered in Coral Red, Gold or Tan to correspond with the appropriate exterior color. Additional new Explorer features included a special hood ornament and, on models not requiring installation of the reduced noise package, bright exhaust extension pipes. Optional for SuperCab Explorer models were color-keyed flip seats, or the forward facing rear seat with Kiwi vinyl shoulder bolster.

For 1976 the F-100 and F-150 pickups carried new grille inserts with wider openings and rectangular black headlight nacelles.

Some XLT models were built without their red plastic XLT grille emblem and side body identification. Amber parking lenses were introduced mid-year. Front wheel disc brakes were now available for the 4x4 models.

Production began on November 3, 1975 of a 6.5 foot, 117in wheelbase Flareside model, a format last produced by Ford for the 1972 model year. Initially, the new version had 40 degree flareboards;

Engine line-up (1974)

Engine[1]	Horsepower/rpm	Torque/rpm (lb/ft)	Comp. Ratio	Carb.
240-6	106 at 3800	178 at 3400	8.1:1	1 bbl
300-6	113 at 3400	218 at 1800	7.9:1	1 bbl
302 V-8	145 at 4000	236 at 2000	8.0:1	2 bbl
360 V-8	157 at 4000rpm	265 at 2200	8.0:1	2 bbl
390 V-8	160 at 3600	295 at 2000	8.2:1	2 bbl
460 V-8	238 at 4200	380 at 2600	8.0:1	4 bbl

[1]Beginning in 1974 all power ratings were SAE Net.

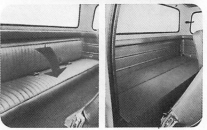

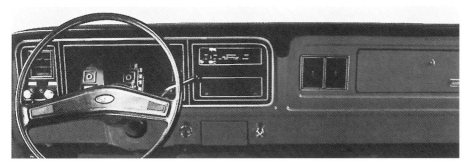

The Cruise-O-Matic transmission and four integral air conditioning outlets of this 1975 Explorer-equipped F-100 dash shows it has both Explorer B and C packages. (Courtesy Ford Motor Company)

These four views illustrate the various configurations of the SuperCab's cargo area. From top to bottom: The standard SuperCab, the optional jump seats, and the two positions of the optional forward-facing rear seat. (Courtesy Ford Motor Company)

A 1975 F-100 SuperCab with the Ranger XLT Package and Deluxe box cover. (Courtesy Ford Motor Company)

4-wheel drive systems: major specifications and availability (1974)

Engine	Std. 240 6[1]	360 V-8[2]	360 V-8
Transmission	4-speed NP435	4-speed NP435	Cruise-O-Matic
Transfer case	Dana 21 single speed	Dana 21 single speed	NP 230 Full-time
Ratios:	1:1	1:1	2.0:1, 1.0:1
Front axle	Dana 44	Dana 44	Dana 44
Capacity	3300lb	3300lb	3300lb
Std. ratio	3.73	3.54	3.50
Opt. ratio	4.09	4.09	none
Rear axle:	Ford[3]	Ford[4]	Ford[4]
Capacity:	3300	3300[5]	3000[5]
Std. ratio:	3.70	3.50	3.50
Opt. ratio:	4.11	4.11[6]	4.11[6]

[1]Not available in California. [2]Required in California. [3]Without limited slip. [4]With or without limited slip. [5]3600lb optional. [6]Not available in California.

later, both the short and long box models had 90 degree flareboards.

Job 1 was produced on April 5, 1976 at Ford's San Jose plant. All exterior, interior, functional, color, trim, standard, and optional features available for the regular Flareside models - except for the side-mounted spare tire carrier - were offered for the new short box F-100.

The Flareside pickup was also available with a new Pinstripe Accent

SuperCab v Regular Cab exterior dimensions (1975)

Model	Regular Cab		SuperCab	
Wheelbase (in)	116.8	133.0	138.8	155.0
Overall length (in)[1]	194.8	211.0	216.8	233.0
Cab extension (in)	0	0	22.0	22.0

[1]Without rear bumper.

F-100 and F-150 models & options prices (effective March 1, 1975)

F-100 Regular Cab
117 inch wheelbase models
Styleside $3495.70
GVW packages
    4850lb..$21.10
    5000lb..$55.60
    5350lb...$142.90
133 inch wheelbase models
Styleside or Flareside $3531.70
GVW packages
    4850lb..$21.10
    5100lb..$55.60
    5500lb...$140.75
F-100 SuperCab with 300 Six engine
138.8 inch wheelbase
Styleside $4010.70
GVW package
    5500lb..$85.25
155 inch wheelbase
Styleside $4046.70
GVW package
    5700lb..$85.25
F-100 SuperCab with 360 V-8 engine option
138.8 inch wheelbase
Styleside $4232.70
GVW package
5500lb $85.25
155 inch wheelbase
Styleside $4268.70
GVW package
    5700lb..$85.25
F-100 Regular Cab with 4x4 option
117 inch wheelbase
Styleside $4367.70
GVW package
    5600lb..$38.80
133 inch wheelbase
Styleside or Flareside $4403.70
GVW package
    5700lb..$27.45
F-150 Regular Cab
133 inch wheelbase
Styleside or Flareside $3818.85
F-150 SuperCab with 360 V-8 engine
138.8 inch wheelbase
Styleside $4540.55
155 inch wheelbase
Styleside $4576.55

continued next page

Package Option. All regular production paint colors were offered with this package, which consisted of these items:

Black-out painted grille inserts.

Low-gloss black rear channel bumper.

Tape pinstriping, available in black, white, and gold, on hood, body side cab and box, and tailgate.

Tailgate lettering - black FORD letters on trucks painted Wimbledon White, Silver Metallic, and Black. White letters used for other available colors.

All regular production options could be ordered with the Pinstripe Flaresides except for the following: Ranger XLT package, body side moldings, Tu-tone paint, argent rear channel bumper, bodyside accent panel, and dual body side tape stripes. If the Ranger option was ordered, the vinyl insert for the bedside molding was deleted. The price for this option was $197.40 for Custom level pickups, and $131.60 for those with the Ranger trim level. The Pinstripe option was offered in all standard Ford exterior colors as well as Coral, Chartreuse, Light Yellow, and Silver Metallic.

The F-150 was available in both 117in and 133in wheelbase variations, with either the NP 203 full-time or NP205 2-speed, part-time 4-wheel drive train. The latter system was paired with Cruise-O-Matic and the 360 V-8. The part-time system was available with either the standard 300 6-cylinder engine or the optional 360 V-8 and the 4-speed manual NP435 transmission.

In addition to the Explorer package, numerous other special edition models - including the Bicentennial Option Group and the XLT Luxury Group - were offered in 1976.

The special Explorer colors for 1976 were Jade Metallic, Blue Metallic, and Copper. The Explorer body side and

F-100 and F-150 models & options prices
(effective March 1, 1975) (continued)

Optional equipment	Price
F-150 SuperCab with 300 Six engine option	
138.8 inch wheelbase	
Styleside	$4318.55
155in wheelbase	
Styleside	$4354.55
Ranger trim level	
Regular Cab, Styleside	$273.60
Regular Cab, Flareside	$237.30
SuperCab, Styleside	$307.90
Ranger XLT trim level	
Regular Cab, Styleside	$448.70
Regular Cab, Flareside	$429.50
SuperCab, Styleside	$512.10
Engines	
302 V-8, required Calif. emissions, Regular Cab only,	
F-100, 4x2	$144.70
360 V-8, required Calif. emissions	$182.70
360 V-8 for SuperCab, F-150, required Calif. emissions	Std.
360 V-8 required Calif. emissions, for F-100 4x4	$182.70
360 V-8, required Calif. emissions, for F-150	$182.70
390 V-8, required Calif. emissions and Cruise-O-Matic,	
for F-100 4x2	$336.20
390 V-8., 4-bbl for SuperCab with 360 option,	
F-100 4x2, not avail. for Calif.	$153.60
390 V-8, 4-bbl, required Calif. emissions, Regular Cab,	
F-150	$336.20
460 V-8, required Calif. emissions and Cruise-O-Matic,	
Regular Cab, F-150	$411.60
460 V-8 for SuperCab, F-150, required Calif. emissions	
and Cruise-O-matic	$229.00
Transmissions	
4-speed manual transmission	
F-100, 4x2, 117in wheelbase	$123.10
F-100, F-150 4x2, 133in wheelbase	$123.10
All 138in,155in wheelbase	$123.10
2-speed NP205 transfer case for F-100, part time 4x4	
with 133in wb	$123.70
3-speed Cruise-O-Matic	
All 4x2, not avail. with 460 V-8	$301.90
F-150 for F-150 with 460 V-8 only	$312.20
F-100 full time 4x4	$301.90
Rear axles (std. ratios)	
3750lb Traction-Lok rear axle	$81.20
Optional axle ratios	$14.00
Air conditioner (required V-8, not avail. for 4x4)	$491.90
60amp alternator	$35.00
70amp-hr battery	$22.70
70amp-hr auxiliary battery	$61.10
Power brakes for F-100, 4 x2	$61.40
Body side accent panel for Styleside	
With Ranger or Ranger XLT	$90.80
Contour chrome rear bumper (Styleside only)	$46.10
Channel painted rear bumper (Flareside only)	$28.10
Stepside painted rear bumper (Styleside only)	$62.70
Carpeting delete with Ranger XLT	NC
Side-mounted spare tire carrier	
Left or right side, for 8ft. Styleside only	$16.10

continued over

hood striping now consisted of dual side portions running parallel to the side body cove and joining at the rear; a second set accented the raised hood section.

The Ranger XLT served as a base for the XLT Luxury Group Option, available for the Regular Cab F-100 and F-150 2-wheel drive Styleside models. Mandatory options required for its purchase included automatic transmission and power steering, and either AM or AM/FM stereo radio. Only three colors, all exclusive to the Luxury Group Option, were available: Tan Glow, Autumn Tan, and Polar White. A Dark Brown roof color was included with all three body colors. A White roof was available as a no-cost option with Autumn Tan and Tan Glow. A Tu-Tone roof delete option was available if a solid color format was desired. The interior was finished in a special Tan cloth and vinyl.

The package's content comprised these features:

Exterior:

Three coats of finish paint.

Special stainless steel wheel covers with a paint treatment color-keyed to the body.

Special hood ornament.

Special new filigree tape (dark brown only) on hood front and body side.

Body side molding with special brown vinyl insert.

Tailgate applique paint treatment with special brown paint on upper and lower tailgate appliques.

Interior:

Special low gloss Tan paint for roof, instrument panel, side and door panels.

Special simulated woodgrain applique on instrument panel cluster and glovebox door.

Tan steering wheel, steering column, transmission shift PRNDL housing, turn signal knob and shift knob.

F-100 and F-150 models & options prices
(effective March 1, 1975) (continued)

Option	Price
Left side mounted spare tire carrier for Flareside - (5in x 8in or larger mirrors recommended)	$18.20
Rear slide-out spare tire carrier	$27.00
Cigarette lighter (Custom Cab only)	$12.00
Convenience Group	$47.90
Cruise Control	$116.20
Custom Decor Group	$72.40
Oil bath air cleaner, not avail.for 460 V-8	$12.00
Engine block heater, single element	$14.30
Engine block heater, dual element, for all V-8 engines except 302	$28.50
Cooling Package	$30.00
Super Cooling Package with man. trans. and air cond. for 4x2 only with 360, 390 or 460 V-8	$48.70
With manual transmission and no air cond	$78.10
With Cruise-O-Matic and air cond	$70.70
With Cruise-O-Matic, and no air cond	$101.40
Required California exhaust emission for F-150	
For single fuel tank	$75.00
For dual fuel tanks	$110.60
Special engine emissions package for F-100	
For 6-cylinder engine	$45.00
For V-8 engines	$75.00
Reduced sound exhaust system	
For all series with V-8	$24.80
For F-150 with 390 or 460 V-8	NC
Ammeter, oil pressure gauges and fuel economy warning light	$19.70
Locking fuel filler cap, single tank	$6.60
Locking fuel filler cap, dual tanks	$13.20
Fuel tanks (in lieu of standard tank)	
17.5 gallon in-cab for F-100 and F-150, Regular Cab	$50.40
20.5 gallon fuel tank with 17.5 gallon tank mounted in cab	$145.00
Full-time 4-wheel drive for F-100 4x4	$85.00
Tinted glass, delete all windows	$20.00 credit
High output heater (not avail. for SuperCab)	$21.60
Dual electric horns	$9.80
Bright hub caps (Custom Cab only)	$13.10
Free-wheeling front hubs	$85.00
Roof clearance lights (5)	$30.00
Moldings, bright metal	
Narrow body side (Styleside only, not available with Ranger XLT)	$50.00
Body side with vinyl insert (Styleside only)	$75.40
Rocker panel delete	
Ranger and Ranger XLT Styleside	$20.90 credit
Option	Price
Ranger and Ranger XLT Flareside	$10.20 credit
Northland Special Package	
With air conditioning	$116.40
Without air conditioning	$148.50
Color Glow paint	$48.50
Two-tone paint	
Regular, includes beltline molding	$44.00

continued next page

New sew-style seat trim with soft Tan "Picton" cloth inserts, super soft Tan vinyl bolster, Saddle vinyl accent stripes, and rectangular buttons on upper bolster.

Tan super soft door trim with vinyl stripe and map pocket along lower panel.

Clear plastic window regulator handle knobs and bright door lock buttons.

Padded design headliner with bright metal surround moldings and three rectangular buttons.

Color-keyed vinyl-covered sun visors with extra padding. Passenger side visor had vanity mirror.

Back panel covered with 22 ounce spun nylon Tan cut-pile carpeting.

Bright metal moldings for parking brake, accelerator and brake pedals.

Color-keyed vinyl weather strips for the back window and door panel. Color-keyed windshield molding.

Color-keyed Tan safety belt, webbing, retractor trim covers and hooks.

Minor changes were made in the content of several F-100/F-150 options. Added to the Convenience Group were intermittent windshield wipers and map pockets. A new Visibility Group incorporated the old Light Package. The Protection Package now consisted of door edges, front bumper guards and front bumper strips. four-wheel drive models were available with the 19.3 gallon in-cab auxiliary fuel tank. The optional power steering for all models now incorporated the power system in the steering box. The F-100s GVW range was extended from 4600 to 5700lb; in 1975 the range had started at 4650lb. That of the F-150 was now 6050 to 6400lb, which included the 150 Special with F-250 running gear and a GVW of 6150lb.

Minor changes were made in the engine line-up for 1976. The 300 six was no longer listed as a delete option for the

F-100 and F-150 models & options prices
(effective March 1, 1975) (continued)

Option	Price
Deluxe (Styleside only)	
Custom Cab (includes bright body side and tailgate moldings and bright taillight bezels	$123.10
Ranger (includes bright body side moldings)	$73.10
Ranger XLT	$73.10
Combination Regular and Deluxe Custom Cab (includes bright body side and tailgate moldings and bright taillight bezels	$149.00
Ranger (includes bright body side moldings)	$99.00
Ranger XLT	$99.00
Body side tape stripe (for Styleside only, not available with Deluxe or Combination two-tone paint options)	$32.40
Pickup box cover, regular (8ft Styleside only)	$412.30
Pickup box cover, deluxe (8ft Styleside only)	$544.50
Standard cover with sliding front window	$471.00
Deluxe cover with sliding front window	$603.20
Protection Group (includes door edge and front bumper guards)	$32.80
AM push button radio	$74.30
AM/FM stereo push button radio	$262.30
Black or white painted texture roof	$59.00
Rear full width seat for SuperCab	$160.60
Dual center-facing seats for SuperCab	$139.50
Heavy duty black vinyl	$20.70
Knitted vinyl	
Custom Cab	$16.00
Ranger and Ranger XLT	NC
Supersoft vinyl for Ranger XLT	NC
Shock absorbers	
Heavy duty front and rear	$20.70
Dual shoulder harnesses (included black seat belts)	$36.40
Heavy duty front springs	$9.00
Rear springs	
1475lb progressive (for 4650 and 4700lb GVW only)	$21.10
1675lb progressive (for 4650 and 4700lb GVW only)	$22.80
1675lb progressive (for 4850, 5000, 5100, 5200lb. GVW only)	$2.20
1675lb single-stage (for F-100 4x4; 5250 and 5200 GVW)	NC
(for 4850, 5000, 5100, 5200lb GVW only)	$2.20
Rear springs	
400lb auxiliary (F-100)	$33.70
415lb auxiliary	$33.70
Power steering	
Integral	$161.00
Linkage (for F-100 4x4)	$177.40
Chrome tie-down hooks	$32.70
Right side tool storage box (for 8ft Styleside only)	$51.10
Bright 15in wheel covers	$35.30
Mag-style 15in wheel covers (F-100 only)	$66.50
Flipper-type rear quarter SuperCab windows	$60.00
Sliding, locking rear window, tinted glass only	$58.70
Interval windshield wipers	$30.80

F-150; the 360 V-8 with 2-bbl. carburetor was now standard for the F-100 4x4.

Exterior colors carried over from 1975 were Raven Black, Candyapple Red, Midnight Blue Metallic, Bahama Blue, Hatteras Green Metallic, Glen Green, Sequoia Brown Metallic, Chrome Yellow, Wimbledon White, and the optional Medium Green Glow and Ginger Glow colors. New for 1976 were Mecca Gold, Indio Tan, Castillo Red, Copper Metallic, and Bali Blue. Added during the model year were several other colors - Silver Metallic, Mecca Gold, Coral, Chartreuse, and Light Yellow. The interior colors, coded to the exterior finish, consisted of black, tan, red, blue or green. The Custom cab continued to be available with the heavy duty black vinyl trim.

For the 1977 model year Ford made changes in the F-100/F-150 design which, rather than focusing on appearance, were intended to strengthen their reputation for durability, performance, and value. The primary visual change was the use of new interior and exterior emblems. Unlike 1976, when the model designation was mounted low on the front fenders, and the trim level identification was found on the pickup box, for 1977 they were joined together and positioned on the cowl just ahead of the windshield base. Also apparent was the 1977 model's fuel filler door which replaced the body color cap used in 1976.

All F-100/F-150 interiors had new dash-mounted trim level identification. Jade replaced Green in both the Custom interior trim color selection and the optional trim level color selections. The Custom interior also had a new horizontal - instead of vertical - seat sew-style.

Six new exterior colors were offered. Debuting as standard colors were Dark Jade Metallic, Light Jade, Medium Copper, and Light Blue. Two new optional glamour colors were Cinnamon Glow and Jade Glow. Carried over from 1976 were Raven Black, Wimbledon White, Candyapple Red, Castillo Red, Silver Metallic, Midnight Blue Metallic, Bahama Blue, Chrome Yellow, Indigo Tan, and Copper Metallic.

Engine line-up (1975)

Engine availability

300 6-cylinder	Standard for F-100, F-150, delete option for F-150 SuperCab
302 V-8	Optional for F-100, except 4x4 and SuperCab
360 V-8	Standard for F-150 SuperCab, optional for F-100, F-150
390 V-8, 2-bbl	Optional for F-100 except 4x4
390 V-8,4-bbl	Optional for F-150 except 4x4
460 V-8, 4-bbl	Optional for F-150 except 4x4

Power ratings

302 V-8

Compression ratio 8.0:1
Net horsepower .... 130 at 3800rpm
Net torque (lb/ft) .... 222 at 2000rpm
Carburetion.................................... 2 barrel

360 V-8

Compression ratio 8.0:1
Net horsepower .... F-100: 145 at 3800rpm; F-150: 145 at 3600rpm
Net torque (lb/ft) .... F-100: 264 at 2200rpm; F-150: 263 at 2000rpm
Carburetion.................................... 2 barrel.
Compression ratio 8.2:1
Net horsepower .... 2-bbl 156 at 3400rpm; 4-bbl.:195 at 4000rpm (190 at 4000rpm for noise legislated areas)
Net torque (lb/ft) .... 2-bbl 292 at 2000rpm. 4-bbl 312 at 2400rpm (292 at 2600rpm for noise legislated areas)
Carburetion:................................... 2 or 4 barrel

460 V-8

Compression ratio 8.0:1
Net horsepower .... 245 at 4200rpm (230 at 4000rpm for noise legislated areas)
Net torque (lb/ft) .... 371 at 2600rpm (362 at 2600rpm for noise legislated areas)
Carburetion.................................... 1 barrel

Rear view of the 1975 Explorer package as installed on the F-100 SuperCab. (Courtesy Ford Motor Company)

Key features of the Explorer Package, shown here on a 1975 F-100, included a bright exhaust pipe extension and bright box rails (8 foot box only). (Courtesy Ford Motor Company)

Ford's F-150 was available in 4x4 form in 1976. (Courtesy Ford Motor Company)

The pickup box on the 1976 ½ F-100 Flareside had a 90 degree flange. (Courtesy Ford Motor Company)

The Pinstripe Accent Package had blacked-out painted inserts. (Courtesy Ford Motor Company)

Left: A profile of a 1976 ½ F-100 Flareside with the Pinstripe Accent Package. The tape pinstriping was available in black, white or gold. (Courtesy Ford Motor Company)

The 1977 Explorer's door trim panel consisted of a special insert with a bright molding. (Courtesy Ford Motor Company)

Left: Major exterior features of the 1977 Explorer Package are evident in this view of an F-100 Custom Styleside. (Courtesy Ford Motor Company)

The XLT Luxury Group Option for 1976 added many splendid features to F-100 Stylesides equipped with the Ranger XLT Package. (Courtesy Ford Motor Company)

This 1977 F-150 Ranger XLT has the 8 foot Styleside box. Optional equipment includes Deluxe Tu-Tone paint, rear bumper and mirrors. (Courtesy Ford Motor Company)

This 1977 F-100 Custom Styleside with Explorer package has optional box rails and whitewall tires. (Courtesy Ford Motor Company)

The Ranger XLT interior for 1977 is shown installed on an F-150 equipped with both 4-wheel drive and Cruise-O-Matic. (Courtesy Ford Motor Company)

The vinyl seat trim of the 1977 Custom Cab was offered in black, red, tan, blue or jade. (Courtesy Ford Motor Company)

The Custom Decor Group option was offered for 1977 Regular Cab models only. Among its features were knitted vinyl seat trim and color-keyed floor mats. (Courtesy Ford Motor Company)

The Ranger interior for 1977 was both distinctive and practical. (Courtesy Ford Motor Company)

F-100/F-150 engine power ratings (1977)

Engine	Application	
300 6-cylinder	F-100	F-150[1]
Compression ratio	8.9:1	8.0
Net horsepower	119 at 3200rpm	114 at 3200rpm
Net torque (lb/ft)	252 at 1600rpm	227 at 1800rpm

[1] F-150 rating for California was 118 horsepower at 3600rpm and 205lb/ft at 2200rpm

302 V-8	F-100	F-150[2]
Compression ratio	8.4:1	8.4:1
Net horsepower	136 at 3600rpm	136 at 3600rpm
Net torque (lb/ft)	245 at 2000rpm	245 at 2000rpm

[2] Available for 2-wheel drive F-150 only

351 V-8	F-100[3]	F-150[4]
Compression ratio	8.0:1	8.4:1
Net horsepower	162 at 3800rpm	163 at 3800rpm
Net torque (lb/ft)	282 at 2000rpm	267 at 2200rpm

[3] Horsepower rating for California was 165 horsepower at 3800rpm
[4] Ratings for California were 161 horsepower at 3800rpm and 265lb/ft at 2200rpm

400 V-8	F-100 (2-bbl)	F-150 (4-bbl)[5]
Compression ratio	8.0:1	8.0:1
Net horsepower	175 at 3600rpm	169 at 3600rpm
Net torque (lb/ft)	326 at 2000rpm	303 at 2200rpm

[5] California ratings were 167 horsepower at 3600rpm and 302lb/ft at 2200rpm

460 V-8	F-100/F-150	California
Compression ratio	8.0:1	8.0:1
Net horsepower	245 at 4200rpm	234 at 4000rpm
Net torque (lb/ft)	371 at 2600rpm	362 at 2600rpm

Power team changes were substantial. Replacing the 360 and 390 cu in engines were 351 and 400 cu in V-8s, both with 2-barrel carburetors. The 351 V-8 was standard for 4x4 models destined for California. A 400 cu in V-8 with 4-barrel carburetor was offered for 4x4 models. Both engines were based on passenger car versions with design and material modifications required for the more severe conditions associated with truck use. Among these were special intake and exhaust valves with chrome-plated stems, heavy duty copper-lead connecting rod bearings, and larger oil pan. All 400 cu in V-8 engines with manual transmissions had a standard 12 inch clutch with a 158.8sq in surface area.

Major changes (that were also incorporated into the 351 engine) were made in the 302 V-8 engine cylinder heads, intake manifolds and pistons. The cylinder heads featured a revised combustion chamber design that, along with the new pistons, increased compression ratio and improved burning of the fuel/air mixture to help reduce emissions. The cylinder heads also had larger cooling passages for improved sparkplug and exhaust valve cooling. The size of the intake manifold passages was reduced to increase the air/fuel mixture for more complete combustion. This change also improved engine response at lower rpm. In total, these developments increased engine octane tolerance, thus reducing pinging or knocking under heavy load.

All 302 V-8 engines ordered for use in California had a new Ford-produced variable venturi carburetor providing a more constant air velocity through the venturi.

A DuraSpark ignition system with high spark voltages was standard with all engines. Helping to reduce maintenance costs, the oil change interval for normal service was extended to 7500 miles. The mileage between oil filter changes was now 15,000 miles after an initial 7500 mile oil and filter change.

Greater use was made of pre-coated steel and galvanized steel: the radiator support panel was constructed of the latter material. New front and rear fender plastic splash shields were installed on all F-100/F-150 models. The front fender plastic shields were the first such applications on an American pickup. Added to the list of components manufactured of pre-coated metal (coated one side) were the front fenders, tailgate, lower radiator reinforcement, and cab rear corner. A zinc-rich primer was applied to the underside of the box floorpan. Seldom noticed, but appreciated when needed, was the new, heavy duty standard equipment scissors-type jack.

A new rear window defroster, identical to that used on Ford cars, was introduced for both Regular Cab and SuperCab models.

The optional Deluxe two-tone paint now included an upper vinyl insert molding on the top and bright moldings on the bottom and rear This allowed the fender well and rocker panel regions to be painted in the main body color.

Availability of both air conditioning and speed control was extended for 1977: air conditioning was offered with all engines, and speed control could be ordered with the 351 and 400 cubic inch V-8 engines with 2-barrel carburetors. A new High Altitude option was also available. Heavy duty front springs were incorporated into the heavy duty rear spring option. Other option changes included new LR78x15D steel-belted radial ply tires for the F-100 2-wheel drive

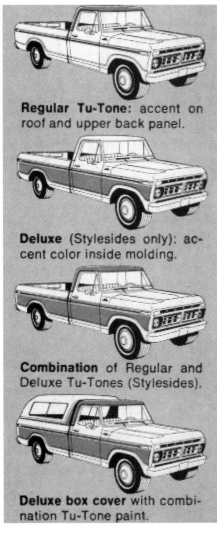

Regular Tu-Tone: accent on roof and upper back panel.

Deluxe (Stylesides only): accent color inside molding.

Combination of Regular and Deluxe Tu-Tones (Stylesides).

Deluxe box cover with combination Tu-Tone paint.

These four views illustrate the variety of tu-tone color combinations offered in 1977. (Courtesy Ford Motor Company)

Regular Cab models, an AM/FM monaural radio, 15in forged aluminum wheels, an AM/FM monaural five push button radio, box rails for 8 foot Styleside models, padlocks for underframe spare tire installation, and wing nut-type key locks for other installations. The underframe option included an enclosure to protect the padlock from mud and dirt.

A late availability option, Raised White Letter sport tires, was offered for F-100/F-150 2-wheel drive models. Added to the Ranger XLT package for Styleside models was a 'Race Track' body side molding system. The Ranger option featured a new 'Chain Mail' design vinyl upholstery.

F-100 and F-150 prices (effective February 7, 1977)

F-100 Regular Cab
117 inch wheelbase models
Styleside or Flareside $3988.45
GVW packages
    5250lb $98.15
133 inch wheelbase models
Styleside or Flareside $4038.45
GVW packages
    5100lb $33.90
    5400lb $131.95
F-100 SuperCab
139in wheelbase model
Styleside $4398.45
GVW packages
    5500lb $102.00
155in wheelbase model (not available in California)
Styleside $4440.45
GVW packages
    5650lb $102.00
F-150 Regular Cab
133in wheelbase models
Styleside or Flareside $4348.75
F-150 SuperCab
139in wheelbase model
Styleside $4700.05
155in wheelbase
Styleside $4752.05
F-150 Regular Cab with 4x4 option
117in wheelbase
Styleside or Flareside $5343.05
133in wheelbase
Styleside or Flareside $5394.05
GVW Package
    6350lb $54.00

Optional equipment   *Price*
Custom Decor Group $115.00
Free Wheelin' Option ....$139.50-$352.70
(depending on model and equipment)
Ranger trim level
Regular Cab, Styleside $326.90
Regular Cab, Flareside $289.70
SuperCab, Styleside $350.70
Ranger XLT trim level
Regular Cab, Styleside $570.30
Regular Cab, Flareside $549.80
SuperCab, Styleside $637.70
XLT Luxury Group $394.80
XLT Luxury Group, Tu-Tone roof delete $10.00
Engines
302 V-8, 2-bbl. (F-100)
    Regular cab only) $87.20
    302 V-8, 2-bbl., (F-150, 4x2, NA in Calif.) $120.00
    351 V-8, 2-bbl. (required in Calif with F-150 4x4) $212.70
    400 V-8, 2 bbl. $371.60
    460 V-8, F-150 4x2 ....$467.70

continued next page

F-100 and F-150 prices (effective February 7, 1977) (continued)

Optional equipment	Price
Transmissions	
4-speed manual transmission.	$142.00
Cruise-O-Matic	$319.00
Optional axle ratios	$20.00
3750lb Traction-Lok rear axle	$159.90
Full-time 4-wheel drive (F-150) required V-8 and Cruise-O-Matic	NC
Air conditioner	$519.50
60amp alternator	$42.70
Box rails	$69.00
Power brakes (F-100)	$68.20
Chrome rear bumper (Styleside only)	$64.00
Painted rear bumper (Flareside only)	$41.10
Stepside painted rear bumper (Styleside only)	$67.00
Cab lights	$33.10
Carpeting delete (Ranger and Ranger XLT only)	NC
Cigarette lighter (Custom Cab only)	$16.00
Cruise Control	$130.70
Rear window defroster without air conditioning	$86.90
with air conditioning	$44.30
Oil bath air cleaner, not avail.for 460 V-8	$14.00
Engine block heater, single element	$16.10
Engine block heater, dual element, for all V-8 engines except 302	$32.00
Super Cooling Package	$54.90-$114.10
(depending upon equipment ordered)	
Ammeter, oil pressure gauges	$25.00
Color-keyed, throw-in floor mats	$19.30
Tinted glass, all windows	$29.70
Tinted glass, windshield only	$21.00
High output heater	$24.40
Dual electric horns	$11.10
Bright hub caps (Custom Cab only)	$15.00
Moldings, bright metalbody side (Styleside only, not available with Pinstripe accent package)	$56.10
Body side with vinyl insert (Styleside only, not available with Pinstripe accent package)	
Without Deluxe or Combination Tu-Tone	$84.90
With Deluxe or Combination Tu-Tone	$38.20
Narrow Pin Tape Stripes (Custom and Ranger Styleside only)	$43.30
Convenience Group	$41.80
Light Group	$32.30
Northland Special	
With air conditioner	$186.20
Without air conditioner	$222.20
Protection Group	$48.90
Glow Color Paint	$54.70
Combination Tu-Tone Paint	
Custom Cab	$260.00
Ranger	$195.80
Ranger XLT	$109.80
Deluxe	
Custom Cab	$230.00
Ranger	$149.70

continued over

The content of the limited edition 1977 Explorer Package was revised to include special Bright Blue and Dark Brown metallic exterior paints, as well as eleven other colors. The Explorer's exterior striping for Styleside models was available in Red, Blue, White or Tan. It now consisted of a narrower lower body stripe, and a slightly thinner upper section that widened at the rear to surround an Explorer nameplate, mounted higher on the pickup box than in 1976. The hood striping was also revamped. The Explorer interior featured a Logan Plaid cloth seat with vinyl bolsters.

Three color combinations were offered: Red with White bolsters, Blue with Blue bolsters, and Brown with Tan bolsters. Color-keyed Red, Tan, White or Black mag-type wheel covers were used with 15 inch wheels on 2-wheel drive models. They were color-keyed to the tape stripes except for the Black wheels which were used for trucks with Blue stripes. 4-wheel drive models with 15 inch wheels were available only with Black mag-style wheel covers. Bright wheel covers were used on 2-wheel drive models with 16.5 inch wheels. Bright hub caps were installed on 4x4 models with 16.5 inch wheels. All models with 16 inch wheels had bright hub caps. The FORD tailgate letters on Styleside models were color-keyed to the body side tape stripes.

A new Free Wheelin' option had these features:
Exterior:
Full-length body side tape stripes with a 5-color rainbow effect.
Front pushbar in low-gloss black with brackets for mounting fog lights.
Blacked-out (charcoal painted) grille with argent accents.
Special tailgate applique with black FORD letters and orange accent.

F-100 and F-150 prices (effective February 7, 1977) (continued)

Optional equipment	Price
Ranger XLT	$90.00
Regular	$53.10

Pickup Box Covers

Deluxe	$612.00
Deluxe with sliding front window	$677.90
Standard	$463.30
Standard with sliding front window	$529.30
AM push button radio	$79.00
AM/FM monaural radio	$131.60
AM/FM MPX radio	$176.40
Rainbow tape stripe	$133.60
Black or white painted texture roof	$66.40
Optional equipment	Price
Deluxe seat belts	$13.30

Seat trims

Heavy duty black vinyl	$23.50

Knitted vinyl

Custom Cab	$37.80
Ranger and Ranger XLT	NC
Super soft vinyl for Ranger XLT	NC

Shock absorbers

Heavy duty front and rear	$22.70
Anti-theft spare tire lock	$13.20
Heavy duty front springs	$8.10
Power steering	$172.90
Rear full width seat for SuperCab	$180.60
Dual center-facing seats for SuperCab	$156.90
Chrome tie-down hooks	$36.80
Right side tool storage box (for 8ft.Styleside only)	$64.50
Full 15in wheel covers	$42.00
Mag-style 15 wheel covers	$74.90

Forged aluminum wheels

Custom and Ranger	$250.00
XLT	$208.10
Flipper-type rear quarter SuperCab windows	$67.70
Sliding, locking rear window, tinted glass only	$74.40

The interior of the new 1978 Ranger Lariat featured cloth seat upholstery with Super soft vinyl trim. (Courtesy Ford Motor Company)

This view of the vinyl headliner used for the 1978 Ranger Lariat illustrates its button-quilted design. (Courtesy Ford Motor Company)

Interior:

Black door panels with pleated silver vinyl trim inserts and red tape molding.

Black floor mats with Custom; black carpeting with Ranger.

Bright instrument panel molding with red accents.

Super soft seat trim with black grained vinyl bolsters; silver vinyl inserts with red accents. Raised White Letter tires were a required option for this package. When ordered for the 'Shorty' 6.5 foot Flareside pickup, the Free Wheelin' Package provided a black channel rear bumper and tape pinstriping. A low gloss rear bumper was also available for the Styleside version.

The pace of change in the pickup field continued to increase as the seventies drew to a close. At Ford Motor Company, nearly four out of every ten new vehicles sold were trucks, two-thirds of which were pickups. The youth market impact upon truck sales was evident as nearly 30 per cent of all pickups were purchased by individuals under the age of 30. Within the pickup truck market, the popularity of 4x4 models continued to grow, with their

New rectangular headlights were standard on all 1978 F-Series pickups, except for the base Custom models. (Courtesy Ford Motor Company)

80

continued on page 97

Series F-100 Pickup
Body Length: 6½ ft. (also 8-ft. Express)
Max. Gross Vehicle Weight: 5,000 lbs.
Wheelbases: 110 and 118 inches

A standard 1956 F-100 6.5ft bed pickup powered by the Power King V-8. (Courtesy Ford Motor Company)

Apparent in this view of a 1956 F-100 with Custom Cab option are the 'Lifeguard' steering wheel and 'high-dial' instrument panel introduced in 1956. (Courtesy Ford Motor Company)

Colour gallery

A 1957 F-100 Skyline with 6.5ft box and Custom Cab option. (Courtesy Ford Motor Company)

82

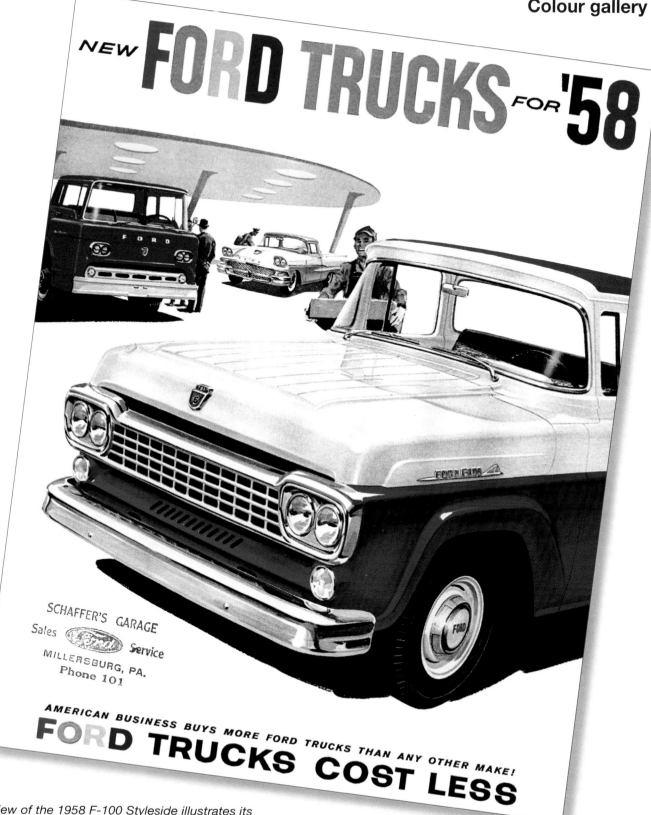

This view of the 1958 F-100 Styleside illustrates its redesigned grille. (Courtesy Ford Motor Company)

Ford touted the new 1959 F-100 4x4 as a truck capable of climbing sixty degree grades. (Courtesy Ford Motor Company)

Right, top: The two-tone color combination of this 1960 F-100 Custom Cab Styleside pickup consists of Monte Carlo Red and Corinthian White. (Courtesy Ford Motor Company)

Right, bottom: The horizontal bar grille design of the 1959 F-100 was replaced in 1960 by a unit combining larger headlight bezels and a mesh insert. The 1959 version had air intakes located at the bottom of the grille. For 1960, they were more prominently positioned in the lower edge of the hood. (Courtesy Ford Motor Company)

Both the revised model identification and the Custom Cab upholstery trim pattern used for the 1958 F-100 are apparent in this perspective. (Courtesy Ford Motor Company)

F-100 Styleside 6½' Box—gives you a full 56-cu. ft. load capacity on 110-inch wheelbase. Maximum GVW: 5,000 lb.

2

©1959. Ford Motor Co., Dearborn, Michigan

The best of the new
...*CERTIFIED ECONOMY, too!*

A 1962 F-100 Styleside with the Custom Cab option pulls away from a Flareside pickup. (Courtesy Ford Motor Company)

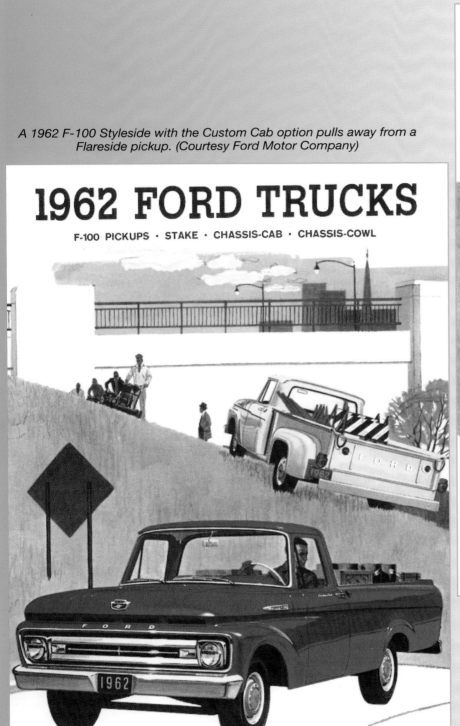

1962 FORD TRUCKS

F-100 PICKUPS · STAKE · CHASSIS-CAB · CHASSIS-COWL

Full-time economy that only <u>starts</u> with Ford's low price!

A 1962 Styleside F-100 with the Custom Cab and Two-Tone paint options. (Courtesy Ford Motor Company)

A ground-view perspective of a 1963 F-100 4x4 Flareside pickup. (Courtesy Ford Motor Company)

FORD
FOUR-WHEEL DRIVE
SALES GUIDE
MARKET DATA AND SALES INFORMATION

The Styleside version of the 1964 F-100 4x4 was based on a 120 inch wheelbase chassis. (Courtesy Ford Motor Company)

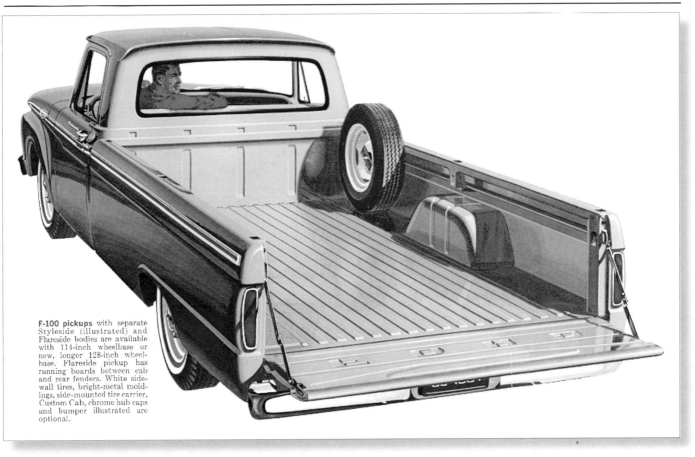

F-100 pickups with separate Styleside (illustrated) and Flareside bodies are available with 114-inch wheelbase or new, longer 128-inch wheelbase. Flareside pickup has running boards between cab and rear fenders. White sidewall tires, bright-metal moldings, side-mounted tire carrier, Custom Cab, chrome hub caps and bumper illustrated are optional.

The 1964 F-100 Styleside's new separate box had double-walled side panels and tailgate. (Courtesy Ford Motor Company)

A 1971 F-100 Styleside Custom equipped with the Explorer B Package. (Courtesy Ford Motor Company)

1971 EXPLORER

F-100/F-250 PICKUPS

PRICE REDUCED UP TO $308*

Available in Sport Custom and Custom

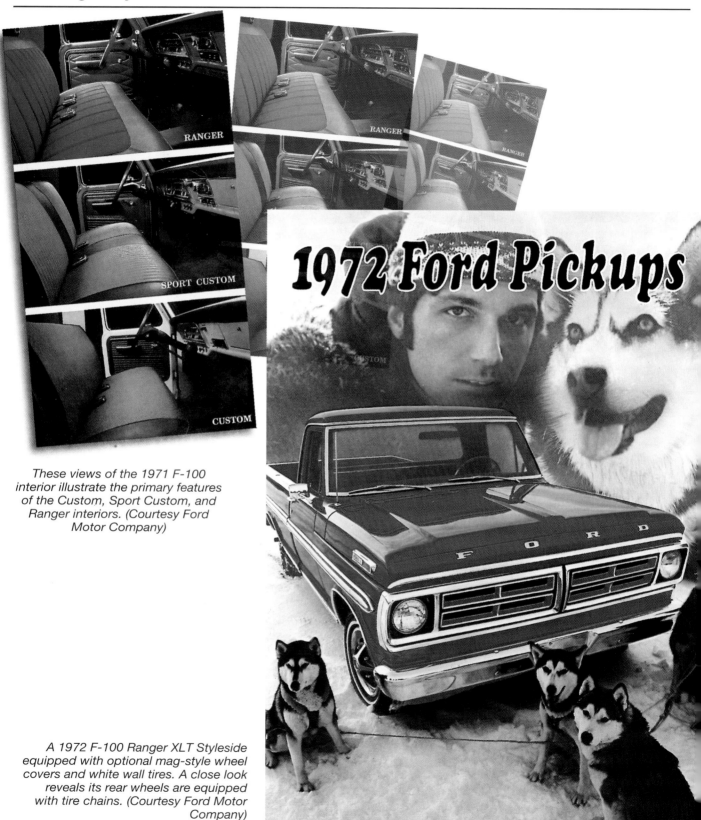

These views of the 1971 F-100 interior illustrate the primary features of the Custom, Sport Custom, and Ranger interiors. (Courtesy Ford Motor Company)

A 1972 F-100 Ranger XLT Styleside equipped with optional mag-style wheel covers and white wall tires. A close look reveals its rear wheels are equipped with tire chains. (Courtesy Ford Motor Company)

Explorer SuperCab in Mexicali Red

Front view of the 1975 Explorer package as installed on the F-100 SuperCab. (Courtesy Ford Motor Company)

A 1981 F-150 Custom SuperCab. (Courtesy Ford Motor Company)

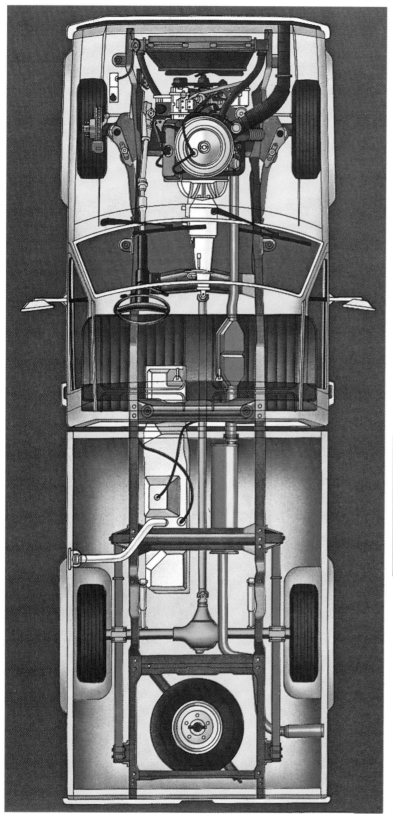

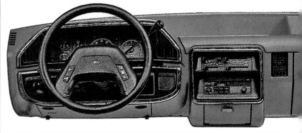

A perspective of the 1987 XLT Lariat dash panel. It featured full instrumentation, and an indicator light for the standard rear anti-lock brake system. (Courtesy Ford Motor Company)

Left: An overhead X-ray view of a 1982 F-100 Styleside equipped with the 232 cubic inch V-6 engine. (Courtesy Ford Motor Company)

The F-150 XLT Lariat Styleside was Ford's luxury pickup for 1985. (Courtesy Ford Motor Company)

The available engines for 1989. (Courtesy Ford Motor Company)

4.9 LITER IN-LINE 6   5.0 LITER V-8   5.8 LITER V-8

Ford said the 1992 F-150 with the Sport Appearance Package was for "... the owner who wanted to stand-out in the crowd". (Courtesy Ford Motor Company)

Left: Except for the addition of a '4x4' decal on the box sides of F-150 4wd models, there were no external changes to the F-150 for 1991. During the model year a Touch Drive (push button) electronic transfer case became available for F-150 4x4 models. Ford reported that 68.3 per cent of its 1991 model pickups were ordered with V8 engines. (Courtesy Ford Motor Company)

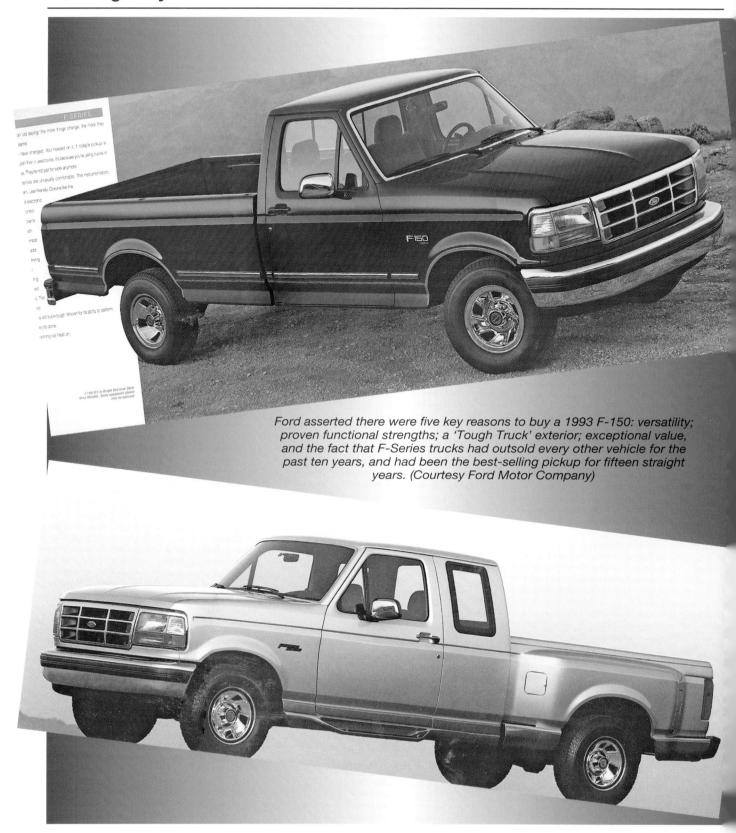

Ford asserted there were five key reasons to buy a 1993 F-150: versatility; proven functional strengths; a 'Tough Truck' exterior; exceptional value, and the fact that F-Series trucks had outsold every other vehicle for the past ten years, and had been the best-selling pickup for fifteen straight years. (Courtesy Ford Motor Company)

A new 'egg-crate' grille made the 1978 F-Series pickups easy to identify. This F-150 Ranger has optional 10-hole forged aluminum wheels. (Courtesy Ford Motor Company)

share of the market increasing to nearly 25 per cent. Here, too, the youth market was influential as over 30 per cent of all 4x4 pickups were bought by customers under 30. Ford noted that "... the shifts in market trends have placed increased emphasis upon appearance, comfort and convenience.

"More and more buyers now want their pickups to offer the same kind of styling, handling, performance and wide range of convenience features that have come to be associated with the modern automobile.

"However, because trucks are still called upon for rugged usage, whether for work or play, durability is still the number one buying motive. 'Built Ford Tough' is more than just a slogan; it remains the number one priority in the design and manufacture of F-Series pickups."

While not offering any dramatic changes (an all-new F-Series pickup was still two years away), Ford did endow its

1978 models with a measured blend of technical and styling changes sufficient to give a sales lead of 132,132 units over Chevrolet in the full-size pickup category.

The most apparent exterior change combined a new argent one-piece egg crate grille insert with a bright surround, a recontoured chrome front bumper, and low-mounted front parking/turn signal lights. Initially, four new exterior colors - Tan, Green, Dark Brown Metallic, and Tangerine - were introduced. In February 1978, another color, Maroon, was added. Carried over from 1977 were Raven Black, Dark Jade Metallic, Chrome Yellow, Bahama Blue, Silver Metallic, Bright Red, Wimbledon White, Cinnamon Glow, Light Jade, Midnight Blue Metallic, Candyapple Red, Silver Metallic, Jade Glow, Medium Copper, Bright Yellow, Light Blue, and Prime.

Saddle and Bright Blue replaced Tan and Medium Blue in the interior color selection. A new, low-gloss, color-keyed

paint was used on the instrument panel with matching interior components. A modified steering column permitted use of car-type steering wheels (with an argent peripheral horn pad stripe) and tilt columns. A lane-change feature was incorporated into the turn-signal operating lever.

Additional sound-proofing resulted from improved door and cowl sealing and retuned body insulator mounts.

A realignment of trim series for 1978 brought the F-Series into closer competition with Chevrolet which had, for several years, offered four trim levels to Ford's three. Ford noted that this change "makes it easier for a prospect to step up from one trim level to the next by providing more attractive price increments." Ford's new trim levels, and their Chevrolet counterparts, were as follows:

Ford	Chevrolet
Custom	Custom Deluxe
Ranger	Scottsdale

A 1978 F-150 Styleside with the rainbow tape striping, blackout grille, and black front bumper of the Free Wheelin' option. The 5-slot forged aluminum wheels, and raised white letter tires were optional. (Courtesy Ford Motor Company)

This 1979 F-150 Ranger Lariat Styleside has optional turbine wheel covers. (Courtesy Ford Motor Company)

FORD TRUCKS

Ranger XLT   Cheyenne
Ranger Lariat   Silverado

With the exception of the woodgrain applique panel for the glovebox door, and the new black steering column, the content of the Custom trim level was unchanged for 1978.

Added to the Ranger packages were rectangular headlights. The Ranger

XLT, in addition to these headlights, had a new "Westminister" patterned cloth and vinyl seat trim with vertical pleats without bolsters. New sun visors finished in Corinthian grain were, like the seat trim, color-keyed to the exterior. The center retaining clip and brackets were of color-keyed plastic.

The Ranger Lariat Package included

the following items in addition to, or in place of, Ranger XLT features:

Exterior
'Race Track' molding.
Cowl-mounted "Ranger Lariat" emblem.
A stamped aluminum applique covering for the upper tailgate depression. The applique had a black center section and the access area for the tailgate handle was bright aluminum.
Deluxe two-tone paint. A delete paint option was available.

Interior
Bright door lock buttons.
Trim panels with a soft trim insert and bright black-paint filled moldings and map pockets.
Padded design headlining with peripheral bonding and four rectangular buttons (six on the SuperCab). The headliner was color-keyed vinyl and had sound absorbing material.
Deluxe seat belts. These were the same as those used on the Custom level, except the webbing and boot stiffeners were color-keyed and a bright mini-buckle was used.
Picton cloth seat trim with Super soft vinyl and accent striped rectangular bolsters. The SuperCab rear seat had Corinthian vinyl.

As this list shows, many new options were available for the F-100 and F-150 pickups:
Chrome rear step bumper.
Carpeted cowl sides (Ranger XLT only).
Dura-weave Polyknit seat trim.
Inside locking hood release.
Security Lock Group (included locking gas cap(s), locking glovebox door,

Overdrive manual transmission ratios (1978)

	4.9/5.0 liter	5.8 liter
First	3.25	3.01
Second	1.92	1.78
Third	1.00	1.00
Fourth	0.78	0.78
Reverse	3.25	3.01

inside hood release and spare tire lock with regular underframe tire carrier. It was not available with the slide-out tire carrier).

Chrome-plated grill insert (included bright headlight doors, except for the Custom).

Deluxe Comfort Vent heater (included larger heater core than standard model, a stronger blower and four outlets. It was not available with air conditioning).

Handling Package (included front stabilizer bar, heavy duty 1.375in diameter front and rear shock absorbers with freon bag, and heavy duty front springs. Radial tires were recommended with this option.

Simulated leather-wrapped steering wheel (required power steering).

Maintenance-free 68amp battery.

Auxiliary maintenance-free 68amp battery.

Bright rocker panel moldings.

Wheellip moldings for Custom level.

Low-mount, 9in x 6in bright or black Western mirrors.

Swing-out bright Recreation mirrors. Pushbar.

AM radio with digital clock, included digital display of radio frequency.

Radio Flexibility Option.

CB radio, available with any radio. Included special antenna and microphone-mounted controls.

GT bar.

Vanity visor mirror. This mirror was illuminated and color-keyed (white with Custom).

Forged aluminum wheels either 5-hole or 10-hole, 15 x 6.0.

White painted styled steel wheels (set of five).

15 inch, 3-spoke sport-type steering wheel with soft skin foam padding,

F-100 and F-150 prices (1978 and 1979)

	1978	1979
F-100 Regular Cab		
117in wheelbase models		
Styleside or Flareside	$4221.45	$4548.45
GVW package	$144.15	$128.30
133 in wheelbase models		
Styleside or Flareside	$4297.45	$4629.45
GVW packages		
5200lb	$40.00	$42.90
5600lb	$14.15	$128.30
F-100 SuperCab		
139in wheelbase model		
Styleside	$4648.45	$5397.45
GVW package	$108.20	$124.10
155in wheelbase model (not available in California)		
Styleside	$4724.45	$5478.45
GVW package	$102.00	$124.10
F-150 Regular Cab		
133in wheelbase models		
Styleside or Flareside	$4600.65	$5004.60
F-150 SuperCab		
139in wheelbase model		
Styleside	$4952.60	$5546.60
155in wheelbase model		
Styleside	$5028.05	$5628.05
F-150 Regular Cab with 4x4 option		
117in wheelbase model		
Styleside or Flareside	$5674.05	$6453.05
133in wheelbase model		
Styleside or Flareside	$5750.05	$6587.05
GVW Package	$25.75	NC
F-150 SuperCab with 4x4 option		
155in wheelbase model		
Styleside	$6757.05	$7653.05

Option	Price	
302 V-8	$177.70	$240.80
351 V-8	$309.30	$373.70
400 V-8		
For F-150 4x2 models and Regular Cab 4x4	$480.30	$556.80
For F-150 SuperCab 4x4	$171.00	$183.10
4-speed manual transmission (1979 F-150 only)	$152.00	$162.70
	$222.70	
(credit of 4x4 SuperCab)		
460 V-8 (for F-150 only)	$538.20	$618.70
4-speed manual, overdrive transmission	$181.40	$194.10
Cruise-O-Matic	$349.00	$385.30
Heavy duty oil cooler	$73.50	$78.70
Traction-Lok rear axle	$175.00	187.40
Free Wheelin' A Package		
Custom Regular Cab	$309.80	$311.50
Ranger Regular Cab	$174.40	$218.70

continued next page

F-100 and F-150 prices (1978 and 1979) (continued)

Option		Price
Flareside Custom Regular Cab	$221.90	$281.60
Flareside Ranger Regular Cab	$147.90	$248.30
Free Wheelin' B Package		
Custom Styleside Regular Cab	$548.20	$641.50
Ranger Styleside Regular Cab	$397.50	$512.40
Ranger Package		
Styleside Regular Cab	$275.00	$294.40
Flareside Regular Cab	$226.40	242.30
SuperCab	$321.00	$343.60
Ranger XLT		
Styleside Regular Cab	$410.60	$439.40
Flareside Regular Cab	$361.90	$337.90
SuperCab	$456.60	$514.00
Ranger Lariat		
Styleside Regular Cab	$668.50	$715.30
Flareside Regular Cab	NA	$581.60
Ranger Lariat Tu-Tone delete	-$95.40	-$95.20
Air conditioner	$554.00	$603.60
60amp alternator	$45.00	$48.20
Power brakes (F-100)	$74.00	$81.40
Chrome rear bumper (Styleside only)	$73.10	$78.20
Chrome rear step bumper	$138.10	$147.80
Black painted channel rear bumper (Flareside only)	$47.00	$50.30
Stepside argent painted rear bumper (Styleside only)	$72.00	$77.20
Front push bar bumper	$64.30	$68.90
Fog lamps	$90.70	$97.20
Cab lights	$35.00	$37.50
Carpeting delete (Ranger XLT, Ranger Lariat only)	NC	NC
Cigarette lighter (Custom Cab only)	$17.00	$18.30
Cruise Control	$138.60	$148.30
Rear window defroster without air conditioning	$92.20	
With air conditioning	$47.00	
Oil bath air cleaner	$15.00	$16.10
Engine block heater, single element	$17.20	$18.50
Engine block heater, dual element, for all V-8 engines except 302	$34.00	$36.50
Super Cooling Package with air conditioning	$58.30	$62.50
Without air conditioning	$93.20	$99.80
Convenience Group		
Custom, Ranger, Ranger XLT	$49.70	$53.20
Ranger Lariat	$38.50	$41.20
Simulated leather steering wheel	$64.30	$68.90
Sport steering wheel	$52.00	$55.70
Ammeter, oil pressure gauges	$29.70	$31.80
Tinted glass, all windows	$32.99	$34.40
High output heater	$26.00	$27.80
Dual electric horns	$11.90	$12.80
Forged, 5-slot aluminum wheels		
Custom trim	$265.20	$283.90
Ranger, Ranger XLT, Ranger Lariat	$249.30	$266.80

continued over

stainless steel spokes and a blue Ford oval in center (required power steering).

Tilt steering wheel. Required power steering and Cruise-O-Matic.

Ford strengthened its position in the 4-wheel drive pickup field by offering the long wheelbase F-150 SuperCab in 4x4 form for 1978. The 4x4 SuperCab used new two-leaf front springs that were both thicker than comparable multi-leaf springs and tapered to provide a constant stress distribution.

Also offered was a new 4-speed overdrive manual transmission for all 2-wheel drive models, which was available with the 4.9 liter, 300 cubic inch, 6-cylinder as well as either the 5.0 liter, 302 cubic inch, or 5.8 liter, 351 cubic inch, V-8 engine.

Ford also offered the 300 cubic inch engine in a heavy-duty form for the F-150 Regular and SuperCab models. This optional engine was fitted with heavy-duty pistons, heavy-duty intake and exhaust valves and extra-cooling radiator. It was not available in California.

In addition, a new "Free Wheelin'" Styleside Package B was offered that included all the features of the original "Free Wheelin'" option (which was now identified as Package A), plus a tubular black painted GT bar, a spare tire lock with underframe carrier and five styled steel 15in x 6in wheels painted Chrome Yellow. White painted wheels were available as a customer option.

In 1978 annual truck sales, for the first time, exceeded the four million mark. Ford was the sales leader with 1,365,718 units sold. With full-size pickups representing over 60 percent of the truck market, the sale of 864,046 F-Series pickups made them the number one selling car or truck nameplate in the world. Moreover, with nearly 50 percent of all 1978 F-150 models sold with the optional Ranger, Ranger XLT or Ranger Lariat trim groups, the F-Series was well positioned to appeal to buyers who wanted their light trucks to be attractive and comfortable as well as rugged.

Ford vice president and Ford Division general manager Walter S. Walla, introduced Ford's 1979 truck line by noting that "Ford's success in the growing truck market can be attributed to outstanding product content, fuel economy and performance, more of which we expect to deliver in 1979."

With the first major redesign of the F-Series in eight years scheduled for 1980, changes for 1979 - aside from the use of catalytic converters for the F-150 models - were cosmetic only. Nine new exterior colors were offered: Maroon Metallic, Medium Vaquero Glow, Light Medium Blue, Coral, Light Sand, Dark Brown Metallic, Medium Blue Glow, Gold Metallic and Walnut Glow. Continued from 1978 was Raven Black, Wimbledon White, Candyapple Red, Silver Metallic, Dark Blue Metallic, Bright Yellow, Dark Jade Metallic and Light Jade. Joining these were two new interior colors: Red and Sand. In addition, Black, Blue and Jade were also available. Rectangular headlights with argent doors and bright surrounds were now standard on the Custom model. On all models except the Custom, bright headlight doors were included with the chrome grille option.

Ford promised its dealers that a new Accent Tu-Tone exterior paint combination provided a "great way for your customers to individualize their Styleside pickups." This option, limited to use on 133 inch wheelbase models, included a two-tone roof, wide and narrow tape stripes around the body side sculptured depression

F-100 and F-150 prices (1978 and 1979) (continued)

Option	Price	
Forged, polished, 10-hole aluminum wheels		
Custom trim	$326.50	$349.40
Ranger, Ranger XLT, Ranger Lariat	$310.70	$332.50
Styled steel wheels		
Custom trim	$124.00	$187.80
Ranger, Ranger XLT, Ranger Lariat	$108.10	$170.60
Mag-style wheels		
Custom trim	$79.50	$85.20
Ranger, Ranger XLT, Ranger Lariat	$62.80	$67.30
Moldings, bright metal		
Body side (Custom Styleside only)	$59.00	$63.20
Body side with vinyl insert		
Custom Styleside	$89.00	$95.30
Ranger Styleside	$30.00	$32.20
Bright rocker panel	$37.90	$40.70
Wheellip molding	$21.10	$22.70
Convenience Group		
Custom, Ranger, Ranger XLT	$49.70	$53.20
Ranger Lariat	$38.50	$41.20
Light Group	$34.30	$36.80
Northland Special		
With air conditioner	$229.10	
Without air conditioner	$267.50	
Protection Group	$52.70	$56.40
Glow Color paint	$57.90	$62.00
Tu-tone Paint		
Regular	$55.00	$59.00
Deluxe (Styleside only)		
Custom Cab	$244.00	$289.30
Ranger	$158.70	$198.10
Ranger XLT	$95.60	$130.40
Combination (Styleside only)		
Custom	$276.10	$323.50
Ranger	$207.70	$250.40
Ranger XLT	$116.50	$152.80
Ranger Lariat	$55.00	$59.00
Box rails	$69.00	$73.90
Chrome grille		
Custom	$26.10	$27.90
Ranger, Ranger XLT, Ranger Lariat	$37.90	$40.70
Pickup Box Covers		
Deluxe	$648.90	$694.40
Deluxe with sliding front window	$718.70	$769.10
Standard	$491.20	$525.70
Standard with sliding front window	$561.10	$600.40
AM push button radio	$86.00	$92.20
AM push button radio with digital clock	$134.90	$144.40
AM/FM monaural radio	$143.30	$153.50
AM/FM stereo radio	$186.90	$207.00
CB radio	$315.30	$337.40
Rainbow tape stripe	$141.60	-
Chromatic tape stripe		
With Freewheelin' Package	-	$201.50
Without Freewheelin' Package	-	$443.60

continued over

A 1978 F-100 Styleside Custom pickup with the standard chrome front bumper and argent hubcaps. (Courtesy Ford Motor Company)

This 1978 4x4 F-150 Flareside has an aftermarket GT bar. The 15in x 8in painted-style wheels were available after November 1, 1978. (Courtesy Ford Motor Company)

Option	Price	
Deluxe seat belts	$14.50	$15.60
Seat trims		
Heavy duty black vinyl	$24.90	$26.80
Knitted vinyl		
Custom Cab	$40.20	$43.10
Ranger and Ranger XLT	NC	NC
Dura-weave vinyl	$40.20	$43.10
Vinyl Chain Mail for Ranger XLT and Lariat		NC
Shock absorbers		
Heavy duty quad front and rear for F-150 only)	$74.00	$79.30
Heavy duty rear springs		
1475lb for F-100	$40.00	$42.90
1675lb for F-100	$44.00	$47.20
Heavy duty front springs		
Regular and SuperCab, 4x2	$10.00	$10.80
Regular and SuperCab, F-150 4x4	$67.00	$71.80
Tilt wheel	$72.00	$77.20
Power steering		
4x2 models	$191.00	$207.00
4x4 F-150 Regular Cab	$211.0	std equip
Rear full width seat for SuperCab	$191.50	$204.90
Dual center-facing seats for SuperCab	$166.40	$178.10
GT bar	$99.00	$106.00
Chrome tie-down hooks	$39.00	$41.80
Right side tool storage box (for 8ft Styleside only)	$68.50	$73.30
Full wheel 15in covers		
Custom	$41.10	$44.00
Ranger (and Ranger XLT and Ranger Lariat for 1979)	$25.00	$26.90
Mag-style 15in wheel covers		
Custom	$79.50	$85.20
Ranger, Ranger XLT (and Ranger Lariat for 1979)	$62.80	$67.30
Sport Custom wheels		
Custom	-	$93.60
Ranger, Ranger XLT, Ranger Lariat	-	$76.40
Forged aluminum wheels		
Custom	$265.20	$283.90
Ranger and Ranger XLT (and Ranger Lariat for 1979)	$249.30	$266.80
Polished Forged Aluminum wheels Custom	$326.50	$349.40
Ranger and Ranger XLT (and Ranger Lariat for 1979)	$310.70	$332.50
Styled steel wheels		
Custom	$124.00	$187.80
Ranger (and Ranger Lariat for 1979)	$108.10	$170.60
Flipper-type rear quarter SuperCab windows	$71.10	$76.90
Sliding, locking rear window tinted glass only	$82.90	$88.90

and black tailgate applique letters on an orange background. The wide body side tape stripe was available in four colors: Blue, Red, White and Sand, accented by the narrow stripe in Tangerine.

The side body pinstriping for the Flareside Free Wheelin' Package was revised to include a portion of the front fender above the body side depression and the roof's B-pillar. This chromatic tape stripe was also listed as a separate option for all Styleside models. Flareside models were also offered with revised pinstriping. A new sand color was available for either the Standard or Deluxe pickup box cover. Also debuting in 1979 was an optional mag-type 15in. wheel cover with silver-grey metallic finish spokes on a black background. Beginning on November 10 1978, a new sport wheel cover replaced the mag-type wheel cover option for 4x4 models.

The availability range of several carry-over options was extended for 1979. The 4x4 F-150 could now be ordered with power steering. The tilt steering wheel option, previously available only with Cruise-O-Matic, was now offered on trucks with 4-speed manual transmission. The Super Cooling Package previously offered only on trucks with V-8 engines could now be ordered with all engines. All optional stereo radios had upgraded speakers with enhanced bass reproduction and minimal distortion.

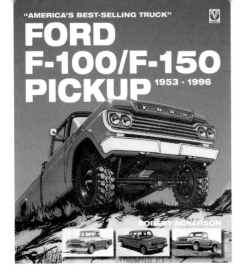

"AMERICA'S BEST-SELLING TRUCK"

FORD F-100/F-150 PICKUP
1953 - 1996

ROBERT ACKERSON

6
1980-1986

For 1980, Ford introduced a new generation of F-100 and F-150 models that, said Philip E. Benton, Jr., Ford Motor Company vice president and Ford Division general manager, "... retain the best of the past, but [with] fresh styling, chassis innovations and powertrain advancements which have been designed and engineered ... to give American pickup buyers a more fuel-efficient yet fully functional truck line."

The new F-Series, developed at a cost of 700 million dollars, retained the same wheelbase and bed dimensions as the 1979 models, but were three inches shorter in overall length, two inches narrower, and two inches lower. This downsizing was accomplished by reducing front overhang and space between body panels. These changes, plus a weight reduction achieved by the increased use

of plastic, aluminum, fiberglass, and lighter gauge steel for several steel components, joined a shortened frame and new wind tunnel-tested, more aerodynamic styling in contributing to improved fuel economy. Ford reported that these changes reduced aerodynamic horsepower requirements by 12.8 per cent for the F-100/F-150 4x2, and by 15.3 per cent for the F-150 4x4.

Subtle appearance changes gave the new trucks a more contemporary look whilst retaining what Ford described as the traditional F-Series 'Macho' look. One of the more apparent exterior changes was a larger windshield, slightly recurved and Butyl-mounted for improved protection against water leaks and noise. Its use increased cab glass area by nine per cent (seven per cent on the SuperCab). Other revisions included a bright windshield surround (standard for all models), bolder

A 1980 F-100 Styleside Ranger with optional sport wheel covers. (Courtesy Ford Motor Company)

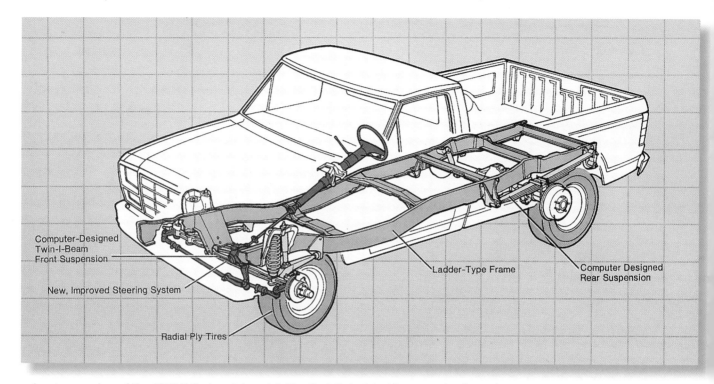

Computer-Designed
Twin-I-Beam
Front Suspension

New, Improved Steering System

Radial Ply Tires

Ladder-Type Frame

Computer Designed
Rear Suspension

A cut-away view of the 1980 F-Series pickup detailing its fully isolated frame, revised steering, new standard radial ply tires, and computer-designed front and rear suspension. (Courtesy Ford Motor Company)

egg crate grille, wraparound taillights that eliminated the need for separate side-marker lamps on Styleside models and a larger, more swept-back front bumper.

In addition, the new trucks had a smoother overall appearance with fewer exposed welds and screws. SuperCab models had a new 'Twin Window' for the back cab section. Also introduced for the SuperCab were optional 'Captain's Chairs' with a reclining feature and center console. Added to all trim levels above Custom was a brushed aluminum lower body side molding. The Lariat had a new tape stripe that ran on the top of the front fender and up the B pillar. It was not available with the Regular or Deluxe Tu-Tone options.

Improved corrosion protection was provided by the use of large one-piece, tub-type front fender aprons molded from non-rusting polypropylene. The F-Series underbody was redesigned to reduce the number of 'mud pockets' where corrosion could begin and spread. In addition, the lower body side sheet metal was recontoured to reduce stone chipping and abrasion from gravel and dirt thrown up by the wheels.

The series and trim identification

was relocated from the front cowl to a position just above and behind the front wheel wells. The truck's larger windshield allowed larger wiper blades and a resultant increase of 26.6 per cent in wiping area. A corresponding innovation was a new dual-port washer nozzle that more efficiently distributed the washer fluid. This system also provided for easier service of the fluid nozzle, wiper motor, linkage, arm, and blade.

Flareside models had new bolt-on fiberglass rear fenders with a chamfered design intended to improve airflow. A concealed fuel filler cap was positioned on the left side. The Styleside pickup's tailgate design permitted easy removal by disconnecting the support cables and lifting the tailgate off its hinges.

Ten new exterior colors were offered for 1980 Medium Grey Metallic, Dark Silver Blue Metallic, Midnight Blue Metallic, Medium Blue, Dark Pine Metallic, Light Medium Pine, Dark Chamois Metallic, Light Chamois, Sand Glow, and Chamois Glow. Retained from 1979 were Raven Black, Wimbledon White, Candyapple Red, Silver Metallic, Light Sand, Walnut Glow, and Maroon. A new Victoria two-tone paint treatment positioned the

accent color on the hood, upper fender, around the door window and the lower body side.

In spite of the new model's reduced exterior dimensions, interior space remained essentially unchanged. Headroom and shoulder room were about the same as in 1979, whilst leg room was increased by approximately 1 inch to 41 inches. The seat position control was relocated to the front of the seat for easier operation. Fore-and-aft seat travel was increased by half-an-inch or eleven per cent.

A new color-keyed instrument panel, molded from a new Lexan material, had a center accessory pod and a row of warning lights across its top. On trucks with automatic transmission, the gear selector was instrument panel mounted. The glovebox liner had two cup holder depressions and an integral coin/token slot. International symbols were provided on controls, gauges, and warning lights. Tri-color temperature controls were included with air conditioners and heaters. New slide-type door locks were positioned below the armrests for easier operation and increased anti-theft protection. In the same vein, a locking steering column and

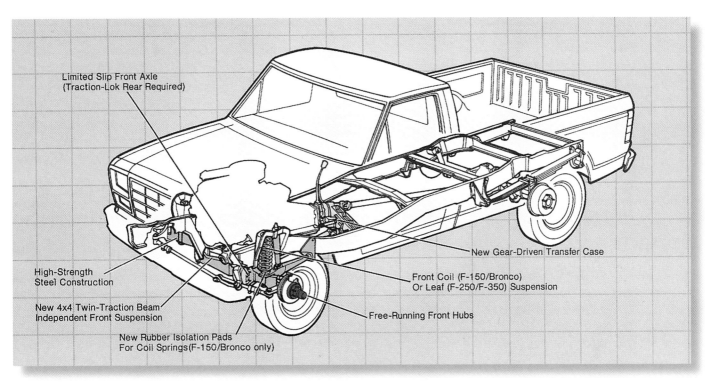

Limited Slip Front Axle
(Traction-Lok Rear Required)

High-Strength
Steel Construction

New 4x4 Twin-Traction Beam
Independent Front Suspension

New Rubber Isolation Pads
For Coil Springs(F-150/Bronco only)

New Gear-Driven Transfer Case

Front Coil (F-150/Bronco)
Or Leaf (F-250/F-350) Suspension

Free-Running Front Hubs

A cut-away view of the 1980 4x4 F-150 pickup illustrating its new design and features. (Courtesy Ford Motor Company)

inside hood release (with an optional key lock) were standard.

The ignition switch was steering column-mounted and had a hardened lock cylinder to help guard against disassembly. A new mini-fuse panel, easily accessible under the dash panel, used new-shaped fuses for easy identification and replacement. The vent window lock was relocated to face inboard, making it more resistant to outside tampering. An in-dash storage compartment for coins, gum, etc., was also standard. The cigarette lighter was located in the ashtray compartment. Three defroster outlets were provided for improved windshield defrosting action. Other interior features included color-keyed sun visors, garnish moldings at the sides and top of the windshield, and all-vinyl seat trim. The use of new sound insulation, including a double-panel roof with a steel inner panel, reduced overall interior noise level by around ten per cent.

Interior colors for 1980 were color-keyed to the exterior and consisted of Caramel, Medium Blue, Red, Black, Sand or Pine (except for the SuperCab models).

The optional air conditioning had a 36 per cent larger condenser, and a new

plate fin for improved discharge of excess heat to the surrounding air. Two registers (one in 1979) supplied a more equitable distribution of cooled air to the interior.

Incorporated into the steering linkage was a second toe adjustment permitting steering geometry toe-in to be set while maintaining proper centering of the steering gear. Faster steering ratios provided improved road performance. All models had new rubber spacers positioned between the front coil spring and the spring seat. Their purpose was to help reduce the transfer of road shock and noise through the frame. Radial tires were now standard for all F-100 and F-150 2-wheel drive models.

The F-150 4x4 pickup had a new, completely independent coil spring front suspension. Each side of the new system was mounted on high-strength steel arms that were pivoted at their inboard ends (a first for a domestic manufacturer). The front differential, with an integral, Ford patented skid plate, was part of the left suspension arm. This set-up eliminated the need for CV joints. Other design changes, such as single stamping suspension arms, reduced the total number of components, thus lowering unsprung weight by approximately 50 pounds.

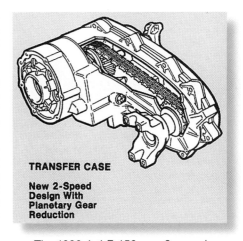

TRANSFER CASE

**New 2-Speed
Design With
Planetary Gear
Reduction**

The 1980 4x4 F-150 new 2-speed transfer case. (Courtesy Ford Motor Company)

A new part-time New Process Model 208 transfer case provided a redesigned gear selector so that the most used positions - 2-wheel drive, high gear (2H), and 4-wheel drive high (4H) - were forward towards the dash, more out of the way of a center seat occupant. The new transfer case gear ratios were 2.61 (L) and 1.1 (H). A standard '4x4' light indicated when 4-wheel drive was selected. Manually-

F-100/F-150 powertrain availability (1980)

Engine	Transmission	F-100	F-150	F-150 4x4
300 Six	3SM	Std.	Std.	NA
	4SM	NA	NA	Std.
	4SMOD	Opt.	Opt.	NA
	Auto.	Opt.	Opt.	NA
302 V-8	3SM	Opt.	Opt.	NA
	4SM	NA	NA	Opt.
	4SMOD	Opt.	Opt.	NA
	Auto.	Opt.	Opt.	Opt.
351 V-8	3SM	NA.	Opt.	NA
	4SM	NA	Opt.	Opt.
	4SMOD	NA	Opt.	NA
	Auto.	NA	Opt.	Opt.

Transmissions
3SM: 3-speed manual transmission.
4SM: 4-speed manual transmission.
4SMOD: 4-speed manual overdrive transmission.
Auto: SelectShift 3-speed automatic transmission.

A 1980 F-150 Custom with the Explorer Package and optional bright low-mount Western mirrors, chrome rear bumper, and whitewall tires. (Courtesy Ford Motor Company)

operated, free-wheeling front hubs were also standard. Optionally available were TractionMatic locking hubs which provided the same driver convenience as full-time 4-wheel drive without the increased on-road wear of front-end components. Fuel economy of the 4x4 improved slightly over its 1979 counterpart.

With neither the 400 nor 460 cubic inch V-8 engine offered, the powertrain availability for the F-100 and F-150 for 1980 was as shown in the table above.

In addition to those previously mentioned, a number of new options - along with several revised carry-over options - were offered for 1980. The new items included AM/FM radios with either cassette or 8-track tape players and two speakers; an electronic digital clock with time, date and elapsed time features; a Sport Instrumentation Package with oil pressure gauge, ammeter, tachometer and trip odometer; an underhood tool box; skid plates; and an extra capacity air cleaner.

The Light Group was revised to include an underhood light on a retractable cord, a headlights 'on' warning light, and an interior reading light. The cruise control option now included a 'Resume' switch that, when depressed, allowed the driver to automatically accelerate to the previously set speed after the system had been deactivated by the brakes. The CB radio offered direct access to Channel 9, and an automatic scanner.

Ford also revised the Free Wheelin'

Packages for 1980 -
Package A: Pinstriping (in place of the 1979 multi-color accent stripes) or optional deluxe Tu-Tone paint (Flareside only), blackout grille and headlight doors and sport wheel covers.

Package B: (available for 4x2 models beginning in February 1980). All of Package A plus fog lamps, bumper guards, Handling Package, bright rear contour bumper (Styleside only), bright rear channel bumper (Flareside only), 10-hole aluminum wheels (in place of wheel covers), simulated leather-wrapped steering wheel, and Sports Instrumentation Package. Styleside 4x4 models also had a GT bar and white styled wheels in place of the 10-hole aluminum wheels.

Featured colors for the 1980 Explorer Package were Dark Chamois Metallic, Midnight Blue Metallic, and Candyapple Red. The Explorer was offered in eight other colors Raven Black, Wimbledon White, Medium Gray Metallic, Maroon, Dark Silver Blue Metallic, Medium Blue, Light Caramel, and Chamois Glow. Body side stripes were offered in either White or Orange. Four variations of the Explorer Package were available
Package A -
   Custom trim package.
   Explorer diecast nameplate.
   Explorer hood ornament.
   Deluxe wheel covers (bright hubcaps for F-150 4x4).
   Box rails.

A 1980 F-150 Flareside 4x4 with the Free Wheelin' package, deluxe Tu-Tone paint, and styled steel wheels. (Courtesy Ford Motor Company)

Wheellip moldings.

Chrome grille.

Plaid cloth and vinyl seats (available in either Medium Blue, Red or Caramel) in Ranger sew style.

Ranger door trim panel with bright surround molding and Plaid cloth insert above armrest.

Knitted vinyl seat trim (in lieu of Plaid cloth trim) with Ranger door trim without cloth insert.

SuperCab rear seat trim in Corinthian vinyl.

Package B -
Ranger Package A.
Ranger trim (less body side molding).
Power steering.

The 1980 Ranger Lariat instrument panel was fitted with a polished woodtone applique, and a bright 'Ranger Lariat' script. (Courtesy Ford Motor Company)

Explorer Packages prices (1980)

Package A
F-100, F-150 4x2 .... $270.40
F-150 4x4 .... $245.40

Package B
F-100, F-150 Regular Cab 4x2 .... $939.60
F-150 Regular Cab 4x4 .... $494.60
F-150 SuperCab 4x2 .... $943.80
F-150 SuperCab 4x4 .... $528.80

Package C
F-100, F-150, Regular Cab 4x2 .... $1729.70
F-150 Regular Cab 4x4 .... $1314.70
F-150 SuperCab 4x2 .... $1733.90
F-150 SuperCab 4x4 .... $1318.90

Package D
F-100, F-150 Regular Cab 4x2 .... $2352.60
F-150 Regular Cab 4x4 .... $1937.60
F-150 SuperCab 4x2 .... $2330.10

F-100 and F-150 prices (1978,1979 and 1980)

	1978	1979	1980
F-100 Regular Cab			
117in wheelbase models			
Styleside or Flareside	$4221.45	$4548.45	$5391.70
GVW package	$144.15	$128.30	$123.10
133in wheelbase models			
Styleside or Flareside	$4297.45	$4629.45	$5478.70
GVW packages			
5200lb	$40.00	$42.90	$123.10
5600lb	$14.15	$128.30	NA
		(5500lb)	
F-100 SuperCab			
139in wheelbase model			
Styleside	$4648.45	$5397.45	NA
GVW package	$108.20	$124.10	NA
155in wheelbase model (not available in California)			
Styleside	$4724.45	$5478.45	NA
GVW package	$102.00	$124.10	NA
F-150 Regular Cab			
117in wheelbase model	NA	NA	$5584.60
133in wheelbase models			
Styleside or Flareside	$4600.65	$5004.60	$5671.60
F-150 SuperCab			
139in wheelbase model			
Styleside	$4952.60	$5546.60	$6287.50
155in wheelbase model			
Styleside	$5028.05	$5628.05	$6374.50

continued next page

F-100 and F-150 prices (1978,1979 and 1980) (continued)

	1978	1979	1980
F-150 Regular Cab with 4x4 option			
117in wheelbase models			
Styleside or Flareside	$5674.05	$6453.05	$7347.10
133in wheelbase models			
GVW package	NA	NA	$45.00
Styleside or Flareside	$5750.05	$6587.05	$7431.10
GVW package	$25.75	NC	$45.00
F-150 SuperCab with 4x4 option			
155in wheelbase model			
Styleside	$6757.05	$7653.05	$8145.40

Option	Price		
302 V-8	$177.70	$240.80	$315.00
351 V-8	$309.30	$373.70	$476.60
400 V-8			
For F-150 4x2 models and Regular Cab 4x4	$480.30	$556.80	NA
For F-150 SuperCab 4x4	$171.00	$183.10	NA
460 V-8 (for F-150 only)	$538.20	$618.70	NA
4-speed manual transmission (1979 F-150 only)	$152.00	$162.70*	$175.00
*(credit of $222.70 for 4x4 SuperCab)			
4-speed manual, overdrive transmission	$181.40	$194.10	$240.70
Cruise-O-Matic (SelectShift)	$349.00	$385.30	$408.20
F-150 (1980)	NA	NA	$233.20
Heavy duty oil cooler	$73.50	$78.70	$48.10
Traction-Lok rear axle	$175.00	187.40	$197.00
Dana Limited slip front axle (1980)	NA	-	$197.00

Free Wheelin' Packages 1978/1979

Free Wheelin' Package A

Custom Regular Cab	$309.80	$311.50
Ranger Regular Cab	$174.40	$218.70
Flareside Custom Regular Cab.	$221.90	$281.60
Flareside Ranger Regular Cab..	$147.90	$248.30

Free Wheelin' Package B

Custom Styleside Regular Cab	$548.20	$641.50
Ranger Styleside Regular Cab..	$397.50	$512.40

Ranger Package

Styleside Regular Cab	$275.00	$294.40
Flareside Regular Cab	$226.40	242.30
Super Cab	$321.00	$343.60

Ranger XLT

Styleside Regular Cab	$410.60	$439.40
Flareside Regular Cab	$361.90	$337.90
SuperCab	$456.60	$514.00

Ranger Lariat

Styleside Regular Cab	$668.50	$715.30
Flareside Regular Cab	NA	$581.60

Free Wheelin' Packages 1980

Free Wheelin' Package A

Custom	$406.80
Ranger and Ranger XLT (Styleside)	$281.10
Ranger XLT (Flareside)	$185.40
Ranger Lariat	$171.20

continued over

Optional wheels and covers for 1980 were from top white painted styled steel; 10-hole forged aluminum with a clear plastic coating; Sport covers, and 5-slot brushed forged aluminum wheels with a clear plastic cover. (Courtesy Ford Motor Company)

Rear view of a 1980 F-150 Ranger XLT 4x4 Styleside showing its XLT plaque and brushed aluminum tailgate applique. (Courtesy Ford Motor Company)

Automatic transmission.
Package C -
  Ranger Package B.
  Air conditioning.
  Tinted glass.
  Tilt steering wheel.
  Speed control.

Package D -
  Ranger Package C.
  Sports Instrumentation.
  Convenience Group.
  Ranger XLT trim minus body
  side molding.
  Light Group.

Poor economic conditions, high inflation and rising gasoline prices ravished the American pickup truck market in 1980. Ford sales declined from 718,158 in 1979 to 475,998 in 1980. The F-Series, by a margin of 35,080 units over Chevrolet, were the nation's best selling full-sized pickups, but clearly Ford's new generation of downsized pickups needed further improvements in fuel economy if sales erosion was to stop.

This 1980 F-150 Ranger Styleside is equipped with the Exterior Protection Group, which included bright door edge guards, front bumper guards, and front bumper rub strip. Wheels are the optional 10-hole polished forged aluminum type. (Courtesy Ford Motor Company)

F-100 and F-150 prices (1978,1979 and 1980) (continued)

	1978	1979	1980
Free Wheelin' Package B			
Custom			$1266.40
Ranger and Ranger XLT (Styleside)			$1140.70
Ranger XLT (Flareside)			$1045.00
Ranger Lariat			$1030.80
F-150 4x4 models			
Custom			$1235.20
Ranger and Ranger XLT (Styleside)			$1109.50
Ranger Lariat			$999.70
Ranger Lariat Tu-Tone delete	$95.40	$95.20	NA
Optional axle ratios	$21.00	NA	NA
3750lb Traction-Lok rear axle	$175.00	NA	NA
Full-time four-wheel drive (F-150)			
Required V-8 and Cruise-O-Matic	NC	NA	NA
Air conditioner	$554.00	$603.60	$611.00
60amp alternator	$45.00	$48.20	$52.00
Power brakes (F-100)	$74.00	$81.40	$78.10
Chrome rear bumper (Styleside only)	$73.10	$78.20	$84.00
Chrome rear step bumper	$138.10	$147.80	$156.10
Black painted channel rear bumper (Flareside only)	$47.00	$50.30	NA
Stepside argent painted rear bumper (Styleside only)	$72.00	$77.20	$93.10
Front push bar bumper	$64.30	$68.90	NA
Fog lamps	$90.70	$97.20	$215.20
Cab lights	$35.00	$37.50	$40.00
Carpeting delete (Ranger XLT Ranger Lariat only)	NC	NC	NA
Cig. lighter (Custom Cab only)	$17.00	$18.30	$19.00
Cruise Control	$138.60	$148.30	$150.40
Rear window defroster without air conditioning	$92.20	NA	NA
With air conditioning	$47.00		
Oil bath air cleaner	$15.00	$16.10	NA
Engine block heater, single element	$17.20	NA	$26.60
Engine block heater, dual element, pre-1980 for all V-8 engines except 302	$34.00	$36.50	$53.10
Extra cooling package	NA	NA	$49.70
Super Cooling Package with air conditioning	$58.30	$62.50	$63.90
Without air conditioning	$93.20	$99.80	$106.90
Convenience Group			
Custom, Ranger, Ranger XLT	$49.70	$53.20	$77.80
Ranger Lariat	$38.50	$41.20	$49.70
Simulated leather steering wheel	$64.30	$68.90	$73.70
Sport steering wheel	$52.00	$55.70	NA
Ammeter, oil pressure gauges	$29.70	$31.80	
Tilt steering wheel	NA	NA	$83.10
Tinted glass, all windows	$32.99	$34.40	$36.10
High output heater	$26.00	$27.80	$86.20
Comfort Vent heater	NA	NA	$183.70
Halogen headlights 1980-beginning Nov 1979	NA	NA	$39.50
Dual electric horns	$11.90	$12.80	$14.80

continued next page

F-100 and F-150 prices (1978,1979 and 1980) (continued)

	1978	1979	1980
Bright hub caps	NA	NA	$18.60
Forged, 5-slot aluminum wheels			
Custom trim	$265.20	$283.90	$310.60
Ranger, Ranger XLT, Ranger Lariat	$249.30	$266.80	$292.00
Forged, polished, 10-hole aluminum wheels			
Custom trim	$326.50	$349.40	$380.70
Ranger, Ranger XLT, Ranger Lariat	$310.70	$332.50	$362.20
Styled steel wheels			
Custom trim	$124.00	$187.80	$160.80
Ranger, Ranger XLT, Ranger Lariat	$108.10	$170.60	$142.00
Mag-style wheels			
Custom trim	$79.50	$85.20	NA
Ranger, Ranger XLT, Ranger Lariat	$62.80	$67.30	NA
Moldings, bright metal			
Body side (Custom Styleside only)	$59.00	$63.20	NA
Body side with vinyl insert			
Custom Styleside	$89.00	$95.30	NA
Ranger Styleside	$30.00	$32.20	NA
1980 Lower body side protection with vinyl insert			
Custom	NA	NA	$148.60
Custom with Deluxe, Combination or Victoria Tu-Tone	NA	NA	$41.50
Ranger, Ranger XLT	NA	NA	$41.50
Bright rocker panel	$37.90	$40.70	NA
Wheellip molding	$21.10	$22.70	$25.00
Convenience Group			
Custom, Ranger, Ranger XLT	$49.70	$53.20	$77.80
Ranger Lariat	$38.50	$41.20	$49.70
Light Group	$34.30	$36.80	$108.30
Northland Special with air conditioner	$229.10	NA	NA
Without air conditioner	$267.50	NA	NA
Protection Group	$52.70	$56.40	$67.00
Glow Color Paint	$57.90	$62.00	66.40
Tu-Tone Paint			
Regular	$55.00	$59.00	$62.00
Deluxe (Styleside only)			
Custom Cab	$244.00	$289.30	$302.40
Ranger	$158.70	$198.10	$195.30
Ranger XLT	$95.60	$130.40	195.30
Ranger Lariat	NA	NA	$123.50
Combination (Styleside only)			
Custom	$276.10	$323.50	$336.40
Ranger	$207.70	$250.40	229.30
Ranger XLT	$116.50	$152.80	$229.30
Ranger Lariat	$55.00	$59.00	$157.40
1980 Flareside			
Custom	NA	NA	$362.70

continued over

A 1980 F-150 Ranger Styleside 4x4 with Free Wheelin' pinstripe. (Courtesy Ford Motor Company)

A 1980 F-150 Custom Flareside 4x4 model with the Free Wheelin' option. (Courtesy Ford Motor Company)

Rear view of a 1980 F-150 Custom Flareside 4x4 model with the Free Wheelin' option and Deluxe Tu-Tone paint option in place of pinstripes. (Courtesy Ford Motor Company)

Ford's response was encapsulated in a terse announcement "The 1981 Ford pickup trucks feature two industry exclusives - the only six-cylinder pickup with a city rating of 21 miles per gallon, and the only eight-cylinder pickup available with an Automatic Overdrive transmission." Ford Division general manager, Philip E. Benton, explained that "... these outstanding fuel economy advances, coupled with all of the other features in what is still the only completely new generation of pickup truck for the 1980s, signify the company's continuing leadership in truck technology.

"This kind of fuel economy excites Ford dealers and provides obvious

F-100 and F-150 prices (1978,1979 and 1980) (continued)

	1978	1979	1980
Ranger XLT	NA	NA	$159.90
Box rails	$69.00	$73.90	$79.00
Chrome grille			
Custom	$26.10	$27.90	NA
Ranger, Ranger XLT, Ranger Lariat	$37.90	$40.70	NA
1980 All models	NA	NA	$31.10
Pickup Box Covers			
Deluxe	$648.90	$694.40	NA
Deluxe with sliding front window	$718.70	$769.10	NA
Standard	$491.20	$525.70	NA
Standard with sliding front window	$561.10	$600.40	NA
AM push button radio	$86.00	$92.20	$97.00
AM push button radio with digital clock	$134.90	$144.40	NA
AM/FM monaural radio	$143.30	$153.50	$153.10
AM/FM stereo radio	$186.90	$207.00	$242.00
CB radio	$315.30	$337.40	$361.10
1980			
AM/FM stereo radio with 8-track tape player			$345.00
AM/FM stereo radio with cassette tape player			$351.10
Rainbow tape stripe	$141.60	NA	NA
Chromatic tape stripe			
With Free Wheelin' Package	NA	$201.50	NA
Without Free Wheelin' Package	NA	$443.60	NA
1980			
Free Wheelin' pin stripes	NA	NA	NC
Deluxe seat belts	$14.50	$15.60	$16.80
Seat trims			
Heavy duty black vinyl	$24.90	$26.80	$28.70
Knitted vinyl			
Custom Cab	$40.20	$43.10	$46.10
Ranger and Ranger XLT	NC	NC	NC
Dura-weave vinyl	$40.20	$43.10	-
Vinyl Chain Mail for Ranger XLT and Lariat	NA	NC	NA
Shock absorbers			
Heavy duty front and rear	NA	NA	$28.10
Heavy duty quad front and rear for F-150 only)	$74.00	$79.30	$84.90
Heavy duty rear springs			
1475lb for F-100	$40.00	$42.90	NA
1675lb for F-100	$44.00	$47.20	NA
1980 with base payload	NA	NA	$45.00
Heavy duty front springs			
Regular and SuperCab, 4x2	$10.00	$10.80	-
Regular and SuperCab, F-150 4x4	$67.00	$71.80	NA
1980 all models	NA	NA	$12.20
Tilt wheel	$72.00	$77.20	$63.10
Power steering			
4x2 models	$191.00	$207.00	NA
4x4 F-150 Regular Cab	$211.00	Std. equip.	NA
1980 All models	NA	NA	$215.00
Rear full width seat for SuperCab	$191.50	$204.90	$219.30

continued next page

benefits to our customers. Fuel economy leadership, combined with product leadership and sales leadership, should give us a larger share of a pickup truck market which is beginning to turn around." In reality, the decline did not stop as F-series sales for the 1981 calendar fell to 432,134 units.

Ford's efforts to improve the efficiency of its pickups were commendable. Based on 1981 EPA fuel economy labels, Ford had the lowest overall and base powertrain fuel consumption for full-sized domestic, 2-wheel drive pickups, at 21 and 20 miles per gallon respectively. Ford also had the best overall label for full-size domestic 4x4 pickups, which were rated at 18mpg.

To attain these results Ford made the 4.9 liter, 300 cubic inch 6-cylinder the standard engine for all F-100 and F-150 models. In addition, a 4-speed overdrive transmission was offered for the F-150 4x4.

New for 1980 was a 4.2 liter V-8 for the F-100. Based on the 5.0 liter V-8 and offered for the F-100 only in 1981 and 1982, it was the smallest V-8 available in an American pickup. Also utilized were lower axle ratios. For example, the standard axle ratio for the F-100 with 3-speed manual transmission in 1980 was 2.741; for 1981 it was 2.471.

The new automatic overdrive transmission was available on F-100 and F-150 2-wheel drive models with the 5.0 liter V-8. In third gear (direct drive) the flow of torque was split so that 40 per cent was transmitted through the torque converter. The remaining 60 per cent was transmitted mechanically through solid connections to the driveshaft. The overdrive ratio was 0.671. Thus, when the transmission shifted into overdrive at 40mph, engine speed was reduced by approximately one-third. In overdrive, fourth gear, flow

F-100 and F-150 prices (1978, 1979 and 1980) (continued)

	1978	1979	1980
Dual center-facing seats for SuperCab	$166.40	$178.10	$190.60
GT bar	$99.00	$106.00	$132.40
Chrome tie-down hooks	$39.00	$41.80	$44.80
Right side tool storage box (for 8ft Styleside only)	$68.50	$73.30	NA
1980 Underhood tool box	NA	NA	$77.50
Full wheel 15in covers			
Custom	$41.10	$44.00	$43.60
Ranger (and Ranger XlT and Ranger Lariat for 1979, 1980)	$25.00	$26.90	$25.00
Mag-style 15in wheel covers			
Custom	$79.50	$85.20	NA
Ranger, Ranger XLT (and Ranger Lariat for 1979)	$62.80	$67.30	NA
Sport Custom wheels			
Custom	NA	$93.60	$96.50
Ranger, Ranger XLT, Ranger Lariat	NA	$76.40	$77.90
Forged aluminum wheels			
Custom	$265.20	$283.90	$310.60
Ranger and Ranger XLT (and Ranger Lariat for 1979, 1980)	$249.30	$266.80	$292.00
Polished forged aluminum wheels			
Custom	$326.50	$349.40	NA
Ranger and Ranger XLT (and Ranger Lariat for 1979)	$310.70	$332.50	NA
Styled steel wheels			
Custom	$124.00	$187.80	NA
Ranger (and Ranger Lariat for 1979)	$108.10	$170.60	NA
Flipper-type rear quarter SuperCab windows	$71.10	$76.90	NA
Sliding, lockable rear window, tinted glass only	$82.90	$88.90	$102.20
Electric digital clock	NA	NA	NA
Sports Instrumentation Package	NA	NA	NA
Captain's chairs for SuperCab	NA	NA	NA
Automatic locking front hubs (4x4)	NA	-	NA
Skid plates (4x4)	NA	NA	NA
Extra capacity air cleaner	NA	NA	NA
Underhood tool box	NA	NA	NA

Engine specifications (1981)

4.9 liter 6-cylinder
Bore x stroke.......... 4.00in x 3.98in
Displacement .... 300cu in
Compression ratio.. 8.91
Carburetion 1-barrel
Net horsepower...... 122 at 3000rpm
Net torque .... 255lb/ft at 1400rpm

4.2 liter V-8
Bore x stroke.......... 3.68in x 3.00in
Displacement .... 255cu in
Compression ratio.. 8.21
Carburetion 1-barrel
Net horsepower...... 115 at 4000rpm
Net torque .... 206lb/ft at 1800rpm

5.0 liter V-8
Bore x stroke.......... 4.00in. x 3.00in
Displacement .... 305cu in
Compression ratio.. 8.41
Carburetion 2-barrel
Net horsepower...... 133 at 3400rpm
Net torque .... 233lb/ft at 2000rpm

5.8 liter V-8 (Available for F-150 only)
Bore x stroke.......... 4.00in. x 3.50in
Displacement .... 350cu in
Compression ratio.. 8.01
Carburetion 2-barrel
Net horsepower...... 136 at 3000rpm
Net torque .... 22lb/ft at 1600rpm

of engine power completely bypassed the torque converter and followed a direct mechanical path to the driveshaft.

Additional refinements for 1981 included the extension of radial tires to the F-150 4x4 model standard equipment, and the use of standard halogen headlights on all models, minor trim and color revisions of the Explorer Packages, and new options such as power windows and power door locks. For the first time, speed control was optional on both 2- and 4-wheel drive trucks with manual transmissions. 4-wheel drive F-150s were available with automatic locking front hubs and new 10R-15C steel-belted radial ply tires. The F-150 4x4 was also offered with a snowplow preparation package. A new tri-color tape could be applied with or without the Free Wheelin' package. The stripe flowed along the body, both above and below the chamfered character depression, to a location just behind

A 1981 F-150 4x4 Ranger Flareside with the Free Wheelin' B package and Deluxe Tu-Tone paint. (Courtesy Ford Motor Company)

3.8 liter V-6 engine specifications (1982)

Bore x stroke............3.81in x 3.38in
Displacement ....3.8 lts (232 cu in)
Compression ratio....8.65
Carburetion 1-barrel
Net horsepower ....110 at 4100rpm
Net torque................183lb/ft at
                         2450rpm

A 1981 F-150 Ranger Lariat Styleside. The brushed aluminum lower body side molding, black vinyl insert, and dual narrow tape stripe were exclusive to the Ranger Lariat. The 10-hole aluminum wheels were optional.
(Courtesy Ford Motor Company)

This 1981 F-150 Styleside Ranger has the optional dual fuel tank system, which allowed models with the 4.9 liter engine and 4-speed manual transmission a cruising range of 1102 miles. (Courtesy Ford Motor Company)

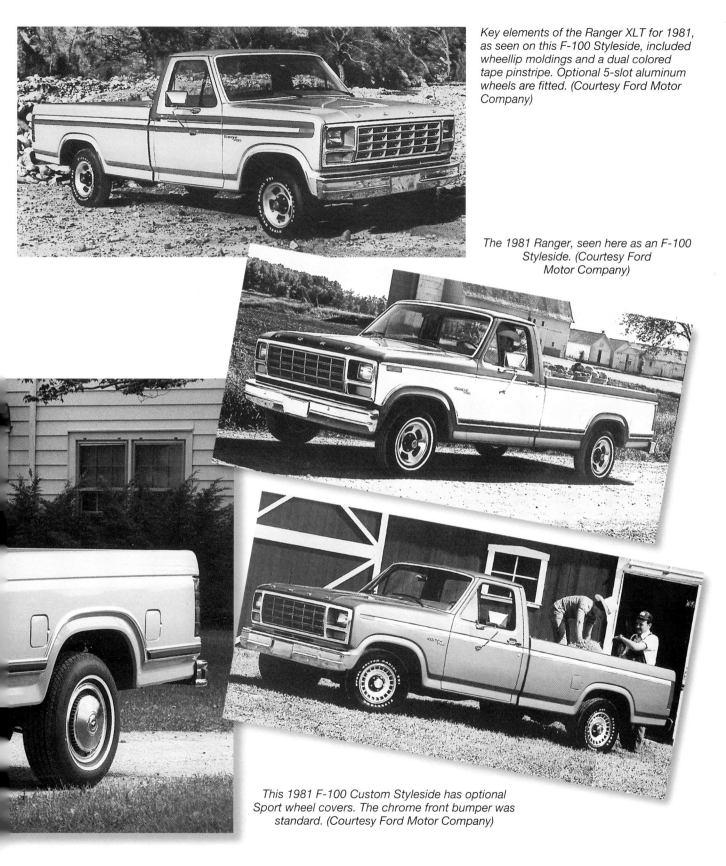

Key elements of the Ranger XLT for 1981, as seen on this F-100 Styleside, included wheellip moldings and a dual colored tape pinstripe. Optional 5-slot aluminum wheels are fitted. (Courtesy Ford Motor Company)

The 1981 Ranger, seen here as an F-100 Styleside. (Courtesy Ford Motor Company)

This 1981 F-100 Custom Styleside has optional Sport wheel covers. The chrome front bumper was standard. (Courtesy Ford Motor Company)

The optional wheel and wheel covers for 1982. From left to right cast aluminum wheels; white styled steel wheels; sport wheel covers; deluxe argent styled steel wheels, and the deluxe wheel covers. (Courtesy Ford Motor Company)

A standard trim 1982 F-150 Styleside with various options, including low-mount mirrors, accent tape stripe, auxiliary fuel tank, Sport wheel covers, argent rear step bumper, and whitewall tires. (Courtesy Ford Motor Company)

This 1982 F-150 XLT Lariat Styleside had numerous options, including cast aluminum wheels, Western mirrors, and a sliding rear window. (Courtesy Ford Motor Company)

the door. At that point the upper stripe swept up to the roof while the lower stripe continued back along the full length of the Styleside pickup box. The Ranger, Ranger XLT and Lariat Packages had new cloth-covered cut-and-score headliners.

Four new standard and three new extra-cost 'Glamour' exterior colors were available. The new standard colors were Tan, Dark Spruce Metallic, Fawn, and Medium Caramel Metallic. Continued from 1980 were Raven Black, Wimbledon White, Silver Metallic, Medium Gray Metallic, Candyapple Red, Maroon, Midnight Blue Metallic, Medium Blue, Dark Chamois Metallic, and Light Caramel.

The new extra cost paints were Medium Blue Glow, Medium Spruce Glow, and Fawn Glow. Three new interior color choices - Nutmeg, Fawn and Spruce Green - also debuted in 1981.

Following on the heels of the introduction of the 4.2 liter V-8 in 1981 was an all-new, 3.8 liter, 90 degree V-6 engine for the 1982 F-100. Although not available in California, this engine was offered with either the 4-speed overdrive or 3-speed automatic transmission as alternatives to its standard 3-speed gearbox. Many of its components, such as cylinder heads, pistons, accessory brackets, intake manifold, water pump, oil pump and integrated front housing for the oil pump, fuel pump, and distributor, were constructed of aluminum. A two-piece diecast intake manifold was used, as were one-piece forged connecting rods and a one-piece design camshaft which incorporated the fuel pump and distributor gear. The block was of a thin-wall, cast iron design. Plastic valve covers and a serpentine drivebelt were also used. Ford projected its fuel economy with the overdrive transmission at 28mpg highway and 18mpg EPA. Specifications of this engine were as shown in the table on page 116.

Other engine ratings and availability were unchanged from 1981.

A new C5 automatic transmission, providing mechanical direct drive in third gear, was introduced for both the V-6 and the 4.2 liter V-8 engines. Additional technical revisions were minimal, the front suspension ball joints were lubricated for life, and the front king pins redesigned to allow for up to three degrees of camber adjustment.

Minor exterior changes occurred for 1982. The grille was revised to include a blue Ford badge, and the windshield molding was recessed into the cab line. Several new options - styled steel and

Two views of the new-for-1982 XLS option as installed on an F-150 Styleside (top), and an F-150 Flareside (bottom). Key elements included blackout grille and headlight surrounds, black bumpers, and argent styled steel wheels with black hubs. (Courtesy Ford Motor Company)

cast aluminum wheels, electric remote-control mirrors and puncture-resistant tires - were offered.

As Ford's new compact pickup was given the name of 'Ranger,' the nomenclature of Ford's optional trim lines for the F-100 and F-150 were revised to 'Standard,' 'XL,' and 'XLT Lariat.' In addition, a new sport-oriented 'XLS' package was introduced (not available for the SuperCab).

Exterior colors carried over from 1981 were Tan, Dark Spruce Metallic, Fawn, Raven Black, Wimbledon White, Silver Metallic, Medium Gray Metallic, Candyapple Red, Maroon, and Midnight Blue Metallic. New colors introduced were Medium Blue Metallic, Bright Blue, Light Spruce, Dark Fawn Metallic, and Dark Brown Metallic. Only one optional

The front bumper guards and bumper rub strip of this 1982 XL Styleside were part of the Exterior Protection Group option. (Courtesy Ford Motor Company)

glamour color, Light Spruce Glow, was available. Joining Nutmeg and Fawn as interior color choices were Dark Blue, Red, and Black.

The short life of the 4.2 V-8 came to an end at the conclusion of the 1982 model run. While its place in the F-series line-up was left vacant, the 4.9 liter 6-cylinder was now offered with automatic overdrive transmission. The only other technical development of note for 1983 was the use of a new cast center rear axle.

Added to the F-100/F-150 standard equipment was a day/night interior mirror. Although the XLT Lariat trim designation was changed to XLT, its content remained virtually intact. The only significant revision was the replacement of the mid-body side and wheellip molding and black tape stripe with a lower body side protection molding. Added to the XLS package were 9in x 6.0in black low-mount Western swingaway mirrors. Ten new colors debuted in 1983 Light Teal Metallic, Light Harbor Blue, Light Charcoal Metallic, Dark Charcoal, Dark Red Metallic, Dark Teal Metallic, Desert Tan, Light Desert Tan, Copper, and Medium Walnut Metallic. The only colors retained from 1982 were Raven Black, Wimbledon White, Candyapple Red, Midnight Blue Metallic, and Bright Blue.

Trim packages (1983)

Standard trim (exterior)
- Chrome front bumper
- Bright grille surround
- Bright windshield molding
- Bright door-mounted mirrors
- Argent hub caps

Standard trim (interior)
- All-vinyl seat trim
- Folding seat back
- Glovebox
- Left door courtesy light
- Temperature gauge
- Color-keyed windshield pillar, header and cowl side trim panels
- Color-keyed door trim panels with foam-padded armrests
- Floor insulation
- Carpet texture rubber floor mat
- Inside hood release

XL (exterior) in addition to or in place of base standard features
- Bright hub caps
- Bright rear window molding
- Styleside upper body side molding (identical to paint break used with Deluxe Tu-Tone)
- Flareside body side surround tape and tailgate tape letters
- 'XL' nomenclature

XL (interior)
- Cloth and vinyl seat trim (knit vinyl optional)
- Passenger door courtesy light
- Bright door trim panel
- Color-keyed floor mat with full insulation
- Cigarette lighter
- Woodtone instrument cluster and center pod with woodtone insert
- Deluxe color-keyed seat belts
- Fully covered seat back

- Vinyl headliner
- Day/night mirror

XLT (exterior) in addition to or in place of XL features
- Brushed aluminum tailgate applique (Styleside only)
- Chrome tailgate release handle (Styleside only)
- Upper body side protection molding with vinyl insert
- Wheellip moldings
- 'XLT' nomenclature

XLT (interior)
- Color-keyed cut-pile carpeting with insulation to back of cab
- Full-length storage bin on lower door trim panel (without carpet insert)
- Storage shelf behind seat
- Deluxe steering wheel (woodtone insert)

XLS (exterior) in addition to or in place of base standard features
- Black gloss paint treatment on grille, grille surround moldings, headlight doors, front bumper, door handles and locks, front windshield, mirrors, tailgate handle
- Argent-styled steel wheels with black hub covers
- Black rear bumper
- 'XLS' tape stripe

XLS (interior)
- Brushed aluminum instrument panel applique
- Brushed aluminum steering wheel trim
- Cloth seat trim.
- Color-keyed carpeting.
- Color-keyed vinyl headliner.
- Deluxe seat belts (color-keyed)

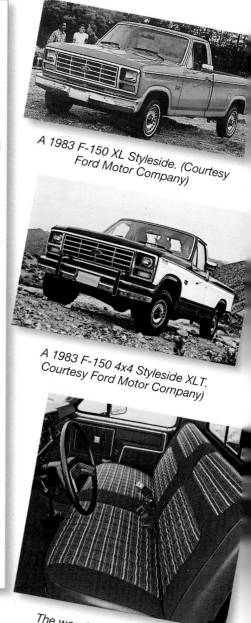

A 1983 F-150 XL Styleside. (Courtesy Ford Motor Company)

A 1983 F-150 4x4 Styleside XLT. Courtesy Ford Motor Company)

The woodtone appliques for the door panels and steering wheel of the 1983 XLT interior are apparent in this view. (Courtesy Ford Motor Company)

Interior developments included a new cloth insert material for cloth-and-vinyl seat trims, revised radio faceplate finish, and graphics for the radio as well as for the heater and air conditioner. The coat hook was moved from the left to the right side of the cab. Three new color choices were Dark Blue, Tan, and Teal (not available for SuperCab). Black and Red continued from 1982.

Added to the option list was a Deluxe Insulation Package. The optional digital clock now had stopwatch functions, and an easier reset operation.

The 1983 Explorer packages were refined to be more visibly distinct to other F-series trim levels, and to provide customers with greater ordering flexibility. Packages A and B were appearance packages whilst Package C was an equipment option. As a result of this realignment, Ford allowed customers to purchase either Package A or B in combination with Package C (also available as a separate option). The content of these packages was as shown in the table on page 121 (A and B could also be ordered with a special Explorer Tu-Tone paint treatment).

An era in Ford truck history ended in 1984 with a brief announcement from Ford: "The F-150 is the F-Series base model for 1984. The base 1984 model offers the same values as previous models with F-100 nomenclature; which is discontinued." Aside from its historical

A 1983 F-150 SuperCab in XLT form with optional cast aluminum wheels. (Courtesy Ford Motor Company)

A 1984 F-150 XLT 4x4 Styleside with optional deluxe Tu-Tone finish, bright low-mount Western mirrors, Protection Group, auxiliary fuel tank, sliding rear window, rear step bumper, raised white letter tires, chrome grille, and Sport wheel covers. (Courtesy Ford Motor Company)

significance, this development had limited impact upon Ford's pickup line since payloads were essentially unchanged from 1983 levels.

The position of the F-Series pickup as the best-selling vehicle in America - car or truck - since 1977 was strengthened by numerous new technical and design features. The most significant was a new High-Output (HO) 5.8 liter V-8 engine. This engine, available after November 1, 1983 for all F-150 models, was rated at 210 horsepower at 4000rpm and 304lb/ft of torque at 2800rpm. Based on the 5.8 liter 2-barrel V-8, the HO version's power-boosting modifications included a four-

barrel Holley 4180 carburetor, new camshaft, larger 17 inch air cleaner, lower back-pressure exhaust system with a heat crossover valve, and dual exhaust pipes. The HO's timing chain, camshaft sprocket and exhaust valves were more robust than those of the two-barrel version. The HO V-8 was delivered with a 63amp battery, a brushed aluminum air cleaner cover, painted black rocker arm covers, and stainless steel exhaust pipes.

The standard transmission for the 5.8 HO V-8 was the SelectShift 3-speed automatic. It was not available in California or with the 116.8 inch wheelbase F-150.

The 3.8 liter V-6 was dropped as an F-150 engine. The carry-over 4.9 liter 6-cylinder, 5.0 liter, and 5.8 liter V-8 engines were equipped with the EEC-IV computer electronic engine control, the features of which included a self-test to aid in system diagnosis, spark control for more precise ignition

Explorer packages (1983)

Explorer Package A (exterior)
    Explorer body side tape stripe treatment with matching tailgate letters
    Sport wheel covers
    Bright moldings on wheellips and rear window
Explorer Package A (interior)
    Unique horizontal pleat cloth and vinyl or knit vinyl seat trim
    Color-keyed seat pivot covers and black seat back trim
    XL-level door trim.headliner and moldings, floor mats and scuff plates
Explorer Package B (exterior). All of Package A plus the following
    Chrome grille and tailgate handle
    Chrome rear contour bumper (or step bumper at extra cost)
Explorer Package B (interior). All of Package A plus the following
    XLT-level door trim and carpet
    XL-level seat belts and woodtone instrument panels
Explorer Package C
    Air conditioning and tinted glass (both could be deleted)
    Tilt steering wheel with power steering and Fingertip Speed Control
    AM/FM monaural radio (others at extra cost).
    Auxiliary fuel tank
    Light and Convenience Groups

Even with no exterior appearance options, the 1984 standard trim F-150 Styleside was an attractive pickup. (Courtesy Ford Motor Company)

As illustrated by this view of a 1984 F-150 Styleside, it was possible to order the Explorer Package A with the tape stripe deleted. (Courtesy Ford Motor Company)

The chrome grille identifies this 1984 F-150 Styleside as being equipped with the Explorer Package. (Courtesy Ford Motor Company)

timing throughout the range of engine operations, and a 'Keep Alive' memory element that adjusted engine functions based on component wear.

The corrosion protection of the F-150 was improved by the use of pre-coated metal for the outer door panels. Styleside models had new two-sided galvanized steel inner side panels and rear crossmember. Forged steel axles were now used for the F-150's Twin-I-Beam front suspension. Drivetrain improvements included quicker and more crisp shifting of the four-speed manual overdrive transmission and a self-adjusting hydraulic clutch linkage. A new clutch/ignition feature required that the clutch pedal be fully depressed before the engine could be started. As a running change, 4-wheel drive models received a new front driveshaft slip yoke that extended the scheduled maintenance service interval from 7500 to 30,000 miles. Replacing the highway tread tires previously used for 2-wheel drive models were all-season tread tires. Similarly, the 4-wheel drive, multi-surface tread was replaced by an all-terrain design.

All F-150 trim levels now had a key-in-ignition warning buzzer as well as heavier 16oz carpeting for all floor carpet applications. The standard interior trim included argent instrument panel appliques, a one-piece coat hook, and textured metal surfaces inside the roof. Also added to the standard trim level were bright hub caps. Replacing the XL package's upper body side moldings were two-color dual body side stripes and wheellip moldings. The XLS trim package was canceled.

Ford offered 14 exterior colors, seven of them new, for the latest F-150: Raven Black, Polar White, Light Charcoal Metallic, Bright Canyon Red, Dark Canyon Red, Light Blue, Medium Blue Metallic,

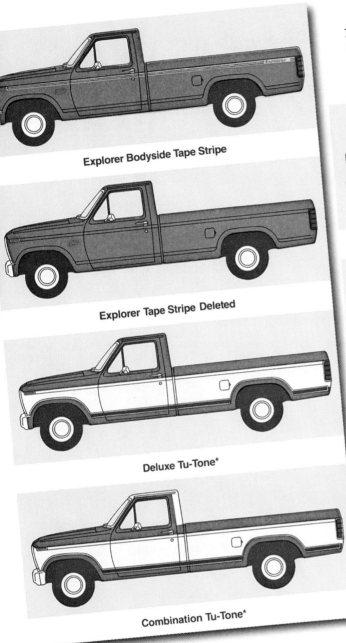

Explorer Bodyside Tape Stripe

Explorer Tape Stripe Deleted

Deluxe Tu-Tone*

Combination Tu-Tone*

These eight profiles illustrate the variety of appearances available for the 1984 F-150 Styleside equipped with the Explorer option. (Courtesy Ford Motor Company)

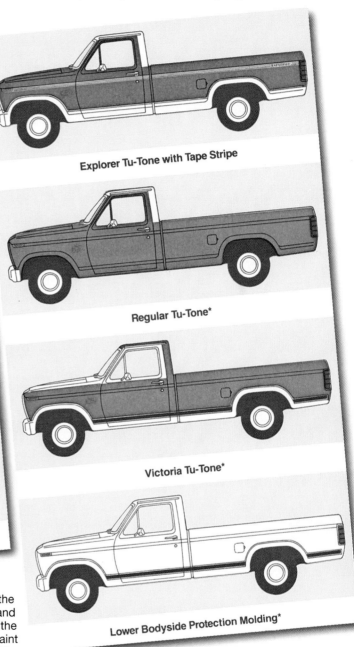

Explorer Tu-Tone with Tape Stripe

Regular Tu-Tone*

Victoria Tu-Tone*

Lower Bodyside Protection Molding*

Midnight Blue Metallic, Desert Tan, Walnut Metallic, Light Desert Tan, Medium Copper Metallic, Dark Teal Metallic, and the extra cost Bright Copper Glow glamour color. Interior color selection consisted of Charcoal, Dark Blue, Canyon Red, and Tan.

Only minor changes - such as replacing the XL-level seat belts used in 1983 with deluxe versions for the Explorer Package B - were made in the content of the Explorer trim packages. Added to the existing Explorer Packages was Package

D, which combined the contents of the A and B packages with the Explorer Tu-Tone paint and air conditioning. The Explorer D Package was also available with a tape stripe delete.

1985 was another year of technical and design refinement for the F-150. The optional side body molding was positioned below, instead of above, the side-marker lights. The Captain's Chair option for the SuperCab pickups

now included a zippered pouch with an external pocket mounted on the seat back. Use of electronic fuel injection in the 5.0 liter V-8 raised horsepower to 190 at 3800rpm. Maximum torque was now 285lb/ft at 2400rpm.

Ford's top trim level for the F-150 was identified as the XLT Lariat, and primary features included a brushed aluminum tailgate applique with a red reflective lower portion, and a bright tailgate release handle. The XLT Lariat interior featured a cloth seat trim and matching cloth inserts on door trim panels, map pockets, and carpeted lower door panels, and a soft-wrapped steering wheel with woodtone insert. Additions to the content of the intermediate level XL included new cloth and vinyl seat trim, and woodtone instrument panel appliques. Changes found in the standard trim level included black instead of bright door-mounted exterior mirrors, a new all-vinyl seat trim, and argent instrument panel appliques.

Only six of the 12 exterior colors for 1985 were carryovers: Raven Black, Bright Canyon Red, Midnight Blue Metallic, Dark Canyon Red, Dark Teal Metallic, and Light Desert Tan. The six other colors for 1985 were Silver Metallic, Light Regatta Blue, Dark Charcoal Metallic, Desert Tan Metallic, Wimbledon White, and Bright Regatta Blue Metallic. Interior colors, keyed to the exterior color, were Charcoal, Regatta Blue, Canyon Red, and Tan.

Prices of the 1985 models (effective January 2 1985) and selected options are shown in the nearby table.

1986 was a year of minimal exterior change, minor interior revision, moderate functional change, and elimination of many items from the F-150 option list.

Replacing the standard 15in x 5.5in wheels of the 4x2 F-150 were 15in x 6.0in wheels which were argent, rather than white, in color. A bright tailgate release handle was standard. Located on the front fenders below the F-150 series nomenclature on standard trim models was either a '4x2' or '4x4' plaque (as appropriate). Five new exterior colors were offered: Dark Grey Metallic, Medium Silver Metallic, Dark Spruce Metallic, Dark

F-150 prices (1985)

F-150 Regular Cab 1985
117in wheelbase

Styleside	$7799.00
Flareside	$7962.00

133in wheelbase

Styleside	$7965.00

F-150 SuperCab
139in wheelbase

Styleside	$9134.00

155in wheelbase

Styleside	$9300.00

F-150 4x4 regular Cab
117in wheelbase

Styleside	$9794.00
Flareside	$9967.00

133in wheelbase

Styleside	$9960.00

F-150 4x4 SuperCab
155in wheelbase

Styleside	$10,934.00

Engines

5.0 liter V-8	$426.00
5.8 liter V-8	$757.30

Transmissions

4-speed manual	$210.00[1]
4-speed manual overdrive	
Regular cab 4x2	$290.00[2]
All 4x4 models	$80.00
SelectShift automatic	$558.80
Automatic overdrive	$694.40

Options

Auxiliary oil cooler	$59.00
Traction-Lok axle	$238.00
Optional axle ratio	$42.10
Dana limited slip front axle	$238.00
Heavy duty air cleaner	$20.90
Air conditioning	$743.70
60amp alternator	$62.00
Heavy duty auxiliary battery	$179.00
Heavy duty maintenance-free battery	$53.00
Manual brakes	$95.00 credit
Argent rear step bumper	$120.00
Chrome rear step bumper	$189.00
Chrome rear bumper	$103.00
Clearance lights	$50.00
Electronic digital clock	$84.50
Console	$119.60

Convenience Group

Std trim	$126.50
XL trim	$111.50
XLT Lariat trim	$85.70
Engine oil cooler	$120.00
Extra engine cooling	$53.00
Super engine cooling	$142.00

continued next page

F-150 prices (1985) (continued)

Exterior Sound Package $12.70
     Auxiliary fuel tank $229.50
     Outside of frame fuel tank $177.60
     Ammeter and oil pressure gauges $40.00

Tinted glass
     Regular Cab $46.00
     SuperCab $58.20

Chrome grille $56.80

Handling Package
     All except 4x4 Regular Cab $124.10
     F-150 4x4 Regular Cab $218.20

Headliner and Insulation Package
     Regular Cab, standard trim $73.20
     Regular Cab, optional trim $19.50

Engine block heater
     4.9 and 5.0 liter $31.00
     5.8 liter $62.00
     High output heater $31.20
     Dual electric horns $17.90
     Automatic locking hubs $40.20
     Sport instrumentation $132.60
Light Group without Convenience Group $135.00
With Convenience Group $116.50
Cigarette lighter $30.00

Security Lock Group
     With single fuel tanks $52.70
     With dual fuel tanks $64.60

Mirrors
     Bright low-mount Western $88.60
     Bright swing-out recreational $96.00
Body side protection moldings $144.00
Wheellip moldings $41.20

Regular Tu-Tone paint
     Regular Cab/SuperCab Styleside with
     standard trim $342.80
     With XL trim $273.90
     With XLT Lariat trim $185.40

Regular Cab Flareside
     With standard trim $367.20
     With XL trim $172.20

Combination Tu-Tone
     Styleside
     With standard trim $385.90
     With XL trim $317.00
     With XLT Lariat trim $228.40

Victoria Tu-Tone
     With standard trim $438.40
     With XL trim $369.50
     With XLT Lariat trim $281.00
Power door locks/windows $292.60
Exterior Protection Group $64.10

Radios
     AM/FM stereo $100.00
     AM/FM stereo with cassette tape player $235.40
     Electronic AM/FM stereo search with
     cassette tape player $400.00
     Radio delete option .... $39.00 credit

continued over

Shadow Blue Metallic, and Colonial White. Also available were Raven Black, Bright Canyon Red, Light Regatta Blue, Dark Canyon Red, Light Desert Tan, and Desert Tan Metallic. Joining Regatta Blue and Canyon Red as interior colors were Medium Grey and Chestnut.

Technical revisions included incorporation of a pin tail front disc brake design and, for improved corrosion protection, an internal hem-flange sealer on the doors and hood. A cathodic electrocoat primer was also used.

The following items, previously optional for the F-150, were now included in its base equipment -

Dual electric horns.

60amp alternator.

Exterior Sound Package.

Ammeter and oil pressure gauges.

Cigarette lighter.

Glovebox lock.

Rear bench seat for SuperCab (rear Jump seat had been standard; it was now optional).

Auxiliary fuel tank for SuperCab.

Tinted glass for SuperCab.

Bright low-mount swing-away mirrors for SuperCab.

12 inch day/night mirror.

Chrome rear channel bumper for Flaresides (delete option status available).

The following design changes were made for 1986 -

A warning chime replaced the buzzer on XL and XLT Lariat Packages.

A chrome grille was added to XL trim for Flaresides and all XLT
Lariat applications.

The body side/tailgate surround tape stripes were deleted from Flareside models with XL trim.

The dual body side accent paint

F-150 prices (1985) (continued)

SuperCab rear bench seat	$150.50
Heavy duty front and rear shock absorbers	$34.00
Skid plates	
Without auxiliary fuel tank	$90.20
With auxiliary fuel tank	$165.10
Speed control	$195.00
Front and rear stabilizer bars	$78.40
Manual steering	$260.00 credit
Tilt steering wheel	$115.00
Deluxe wheel covers	$40.00
Sport wheel covers	$93.30
Deluxe Argent styled steel wheels	$230.00
White styled steel wheels	$174.00
Sliding rear window	$77.70
Captain's Chairs	$491.70
XL trim level	
Regular Cab, Styleside	$369.60
Regular Cab, Flareside	$494.10
SuperCab, Styleside	$319.90
XLT Lariat	
Regular Cab, Styleside	$655.10
SuperCab, Styleside	$607.00

[1](4x2 models, standard for 4x4)
[2](standard for SuperCab 4x2)

The ultimate Explorer for 1984 - an F-150 Styleside with the D Package. (Courtesy Ford Motor Company)

The mid-range XL level for 1985 was fitted with bright wheellip moldings and two-color side panel stripes. This F-150 4x4 XL Styleside has the optional Deluxe Tu-Tone paint, low-mount Western mirrors, a chrome rear step bumper, sliding rear window, auxiliary fuel tank, Sport wheel covers, and raised white letter tires. (Courtesy Ford Motor Company)

stripes in the XL trim for Styleside models was changed from two-color to single-color.

Secondary door seals were added to XL trim on Flareside models.

The coat hook was color-keyed rather than black.

P195/75R15SL steel-belted black sidewall all-season tires were standard for 4x2 F-150.

These options had their content revised for 1986

Speed control and tilt steering wheel combined into a new speed control/tilt steering wheel option - deleted as separate options.

Captain's Chairs - the console was added and deleted as a separate option.

The heavy duty battery was upgraded from 63amp-hr to 71amp-hr rating.

The mid-body side protection molding and wheellip moldings were combined into a single package.

A stationary underhood light replaced the movable work light in the Light Group.

Sports Instrumentation nomenclature

126

*The argent rear step bumper installed on this standard 1985 F-150 Styleside was an extra cost item.
(Courtesy Ford Motor Company)*

Optional wheels and wheel covers for 1985. From left to right: Deluxe argent styled steel wheels; Sport wheel covers; Deluxe wheel covers, white styled wheels. (Courtesy Ford Motor Company)

was changed to Tachometer and included a trip odometer.

The bright low-mount Western swing-away mirrors nomenclature was revised to bright low-mount swing-away mirrors.

Stabilizer bars were included only in handling packages.

The following options were not offered for 1986 -
Auxiliary battery.
Mid-body side protection molding.
Extra engine cooling.
Front limited slip axle.
Heavy duty air cleaner.

In-box spare tire carrier.
Manual brakes (delete option).
Mirrors not included (delete option).
Outside-of-frame fuel tank.
Regular Tu-tone paint.
White styled steel wheels.

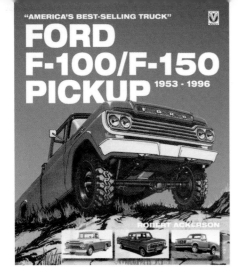

FORD F-100/F-150 PICKUP 1953 - 1996

ROBERT ACKERSON

7

1987-1996

The F-150's new aerodynamic look and numerous performance, comfort, and convenience features for 1987 virtually guaranteed it would continue as part of the F-series pickup team, which had been the industry's best selling vehicles for the past nine years.

In the words of Robert L. Rewey, Ford Division general manager, "The 1987 F-Series pickup meets the challenges of today's marketplace and will help to ensure that Ford dealers remain the industry's tough-truck leaders. F-Series changes are evolutionary and are designed to upgrade truck quality, performance and convenience features.

"The F-Series pickup is one of the automotive industry's most successful vehicles - an industry pacesetter, as well as a technological leader. The F-Series look for 1987 is more aerodynamic, enhancing fuel economy and reducing wind noise."

Technical features added for 1987 included multiple-port electronic fuel injection on the standard 4.9 liter 6-cylinder engine, which improved cold weather starting whilst also increasing horsepower by 20 per cent and torque by 6 per cent. A new air induction system featured a tuned cast aluminum plenum and branched intake manifold with individual runners for greater efficiency and torque at low engine speeds. Also used for the 4.9 liter engine was a new fast-burn cylinder head design. As a running model year change, new hydroelastic engine mounts were adopted for the 4.9 liter engine. These mounts, plus the use of aluminum driveshafts, helped reduce noise levels in the 1987 F-150. Both the 4.9 and 5.0 liter engines had a serpentine accessory belt drive for 1987.

Refinements to the 5.0 liter V-8 included the use of low-tension piston rings for reduced internal friction, and a 'Second Generation' EEC-IV electronic engine control that improved management of fuel and spark. Enhancing serviceability of the 5.0 V-8 was its new universal air cleaner and engine oil dipstick. Front end accessory drive and cooling component revisions reduced noise level and vibration in the 5.0 liter engine.

No longer offered for the F-150 was the 3-speed manual transmission. In its place was a Warner T-18 4-speed manual (for which a New Process 435 unit could be substituted). The standard rear axle (49 State) for the F-150 was 2.73. Optional were ratios of 3.08 and 3.55 (standard for California). The F-150 4x4 had a standard (49 State) axle ratio of 3.08 with 3.55 (standard for California) and 4.10 optional.

All F-150 models had an all-new, anti-lock brake system utilizing an electronic sensor, an on-board computer, and special control valves. Collectively, these items helped the driver bring the vehicle to straight stops in hard braking situations by preventing the truck's rear wheels from locking up in most situations, regardless of truck load or road conditions. This industry first had its own diagnostic system and did not require adjustment.

Now standard were twin-tube, gas-pressurized shock absorbers for improved ride. The Twin-I-Beam front suspension was redesigned to incorporate adjustable caster and camber for longer tire wear and easier alignment. A new heavier duty tailgate with improved latching system was used for Styleside pickups. All radios were now electronic and incorporated a digital clock.

Styling changes were apparent from virtually every angle of the F-150. At the front was a new fender, and hood sheet metal with a new grille; a larger front

A 1987 F-150 XLT Lariat Styleside. Its standard Sport wheel covers have been replaced by optional Deluxe argent styled steel wheels. (Courtesy Ford Motor Company)

A 1987 F-150 XL Styleside 4x4. Among the standard features were bright, low-mount swingaway mirrors, bright wheellip moldings, and dual accent bodyside paint stripes. In place of the standard XL bright hub caps are optional Deluxe argent styled steel wheels. (Courtesy Ford Motor Company)

F-150 engine power ratings (1987)

Engine.. 4.9 liter 6-cylinder
Horsepower .... 145 at 3400rpm
Torque .... 265lb/ft at 2000rpm
Compression ratio 8.8:1
Induction system .... Six port-mounted fuel injectors

Engine.. 5.0 liter V-8
Horsepower .... 185 at 3800rpm
Torque .... 270lb/ft at 2400rpm
Compression ratio 9.0:1
Induction system .... Eight port-mounted fuel injectors

Engine.. 5.8 liter HO V-8
Horsepower .... 190 at 3800rpm
Torque .... 295lb/ft at 2600rpm
Compression ratio: 8.3:1
Induction system: .... Four Venturi downdraft carburetor

bumper with integral spoiler, and new, aero-style impact-resistant headlights with replaceable halogen bulb (which did not require any special tools to change). Previous units had been of sealed beam design. At the rear was new box outer panel sheet metal with larger rounded wheel openings, and new taillight lenses. All series had new trim identification plaques.

A new lower body side and wheellip molding was included in the XLT Lariat trim for Styleside models. A black rub stripe was incorporated into the front bumper used for XL and XLT Lariat trim packages. It was also included with the optional chrome rear step bumper. Styleside pickups with the XLT Lariat option had a new tailgate applique. Added to the XLT Lariat Package were bright headlight bezels, cloth sun visors with a band on the left visor, sport wheel covers and, on Regular Cab models, tinted glass. Replacing the XL trim for Flareside models was the XLT Lariat trim. The vinyl front bench seat used in 1986 for the SuperCab was replaced by a standard knitted vinyl seat.

The F-150 interior had a new instrument panel with four air registers and side window demisters. The panel had black appliques (woodgrain with optional trim) with a center-mounted speedometer, back-lit gauges, and redundant indicator light for coolant temperature and oil pressure. A right door light switch was now standard. A safety belt comfort regulator feature was included with the combination lap/shoulder belts. New door trim panels and seat trim/sew styles were also used, as was a new steering wheel. An electronic AM radio was standard.

Common to all trim levels were black accents for door handles, window regulators, door lock buttons, dome light

bezel, door scuff plates, and seat pivot covers. A cloth 'flight bench' seat was used with the Regular Cab XLT Lariat trim, which included a center fold-down armrest with two cup holders, and raised seat back at outboard seating positions. Improved vent window sealing reduced cab noise level at highway speeds. Access to the fuses - through a removable panel below the steering wheel - was easier and quicker than in previous trucks. Five extra fuses were provided. A 72amp-hr battery was standard with an 84amp-hr battery as optional.

Additional new convenience features included a see-through brake master cylinder reservoir, and a tethered fuel filler cap. Windshield washer reservoir capacity was increased from 62 to 80 ounces; the capacity of the radiator overflow reservoir was also increased. Corrosion protection was improved by increased use of one- and two-sided galvanized body panels.

Exterior colors offered for 1987 were Raven Black, Dark Grey Metallic, Medium Silver Metallic, Bright Canyon Red, Light Regatta Blue, Alpine Green Metallic, Dark Canyon Red, Dark Shadow Blue Metallic,

Colonial White, Desert Tan Metallic, and Light Chestnut. The interior trim colors were Medium Grey, Regatta Blue, Canyon Red, and Chestnut.

The F-150 4x4 had a new front drive axle end with a unicast hub and rotor assembly. The 4x4 transfer case was also of a new design which reduced shifting effort. The addition of a constant displacement hydraulic pump - which provided lubrication whenever the driveshaft was turning - allowed vehicles with manual locking hubs to be towed unlimited distances at speeds of up to

Apparent on this 1987 F-150 XLT Lariat SuperCab are its standard bright low-mount swingaway mirrors, chrome front bumper, lower body molding, and bright wheellip moldings. The standard Sport wheel covers have been replaced by optional Deluxe argent styled steel wheels. (Courtesy Ford Motor Company)

5-speed, all-synchromesh transmission ratios (1988)	
First	3.90:1
Second	2.25:1
Third	1.49:1
Fourth	1.00:1
Fifth:	0.80
Reverse:	3.41:1

A 1988 F-150 Custom with optional auxiliary fuel tank. The black exterior mirrors were standard. (Courtesy Ford Motor Company)

These two views of the 1989 XLT Lariat SuperCab interior show the rear bench seat in upright and folded positions. (Courtesy Ford Motor Company)

A 1989 F-150 XL Regular Cab. (Courtesy Ford Motor Company)

55mph, without having to disengage the driveshaft.

Added to the option list was a new Roof/Rocker Tu-Tone paint treatment in which the accent color was applied to the roof and lower body side. On trucks with the XLT Lariat trim, the lower body side and wheellip moldings were replaced by a two color tape installed at the lower paint break. The same tape replaced the dual accent paint stripes and wheellip moldings on XL trim-equipped models.

Options revised for 1987 included the following:

Lower paint break molding/tape revamped on Deluxe and Combination Tu-Tones.

Paint color of vanes on sport wheel covers was changed from light argent to dark argent.

Deluxe argent styled-steel wheels included larger 8 inch rim width when

ordered with P235 tires.

The under instrument panel courtesy light was removed from the Light Group. Options no longer offered for the F-150 included the Victoria Tu-Tone paint, deluxe wheel covers, high-output heater, manual steering, electronic AM/FM stereo seek/scan radio with cassette tape player, and Exterior Protection Group.

For the eleventh year in succession, the F-Series models were the leaders in the full-sized pickup market segment, with sales of 550,125 units and the best-selling vehicles of any type - car or truck - in the US for the sixth year in a row. They were also the only models to exceed the half-million mark in US sales.

Just in case anyone had missed the point, Robert L. Rewey reminded the media at the introduction of the 1988 F-Series trucks that "... trucks are not what

Key features of the 1988 F-150 XLT Lariat includes sport wheel covers, lower body side molding, and bright wheellip moldings. (Courtesy Ford Motor Company)

E40D ratios (1990)	
First	2.71:1
Second	1.54:1
Third	1.00:1
Fourth	0.71:1
Reverse	2.18
Converter	2.30

they used to be; they have become more civilized - the vehicle of choice for millions of buyers in the U.S." Supporting Rewey's view was a 1985 market survey indicating that 65 per cent of the light trucks in the US were purchased predominantly for personal use, an increase of 8 per cent since 1977.

Three major developments characterized the 1988 F-150 pickups: multi-port electronic fuel injection on the 5.8 liter V-8; replacement of the standard 4-speed manual transmission with a new 5-speed overdrive unit supplied by Madza, and introduction of a new F-150 4x4, 139 inch wheelbase SuperCab model.

The fuel injected 5.8 liter V-8 now developed 210 horsepower at 3800rpm and 315lb/ft of torque at 2800rpm. Availability was extended to include California.

New exterior colors for 1988 were Scarlet Red, Cabernet Red, Bright Regatta Blue Metallic, Deep Shadow Blue Metallic, and Dark Chestnut Metallic. Continued from 1987 was Raven Black, Dark Grey Metallic, Medium Silver Metallic, Alpine Green Metallic, Colonial White, Desert Tan Metallic, and Light Chestnut. For the F-150 interior, Scarlet Red replaced Canyon Red.

As in 1988, the F-150 received only moderate updates for the 1989 model year. The exterior was identified by a new Light Argent/Black grille in place of the Black grille formerly used for the Custom model. This format was also used for XL models ordered under Ford's Preferred Equipment Package option plan. All other

The 1988 XLT Lariat interior provided an all-cloth bench seat with a folding center armrest and cup holder depressions. (Courtesy Ford Motor Company)

trim levels had a chrome/Dark Argent grille. Tinted glass became standard for the Regular Cab models (it was already standard for the SuperCabs). No changes were made in exterior color selection for 1989. Deleted from the interior color selection were Medium Grey and Regatta Blue, replaced by Dark Charcoal (also identified as Granite in Ford's initial September 7, 1988 press release), and Crystal Blue.

Changes in option content and availability were also modest in nature. A 'Floormat-In-Lieu-Of-Carpet' option was offered for the XLT Lariat. Added to the XLT Lariat package was an AM/

FM stereo radio with digital clock. New Captain's Chairs for the SuperCab included a tip/slide mechanism on both driver and passenger side to improve rear seat ingress/egress. They also had a new sew style and folding inboard armrests. Although no longer offered as a separate option, heavy duty front and rear shock absorbers were still available as part of the Handling and Heavy-Duty Suspension Packages. No longer available was the Roof/Rocker Tu-Tone paint option. Still offered as an alternative to the standard 5-speed overdrive transmission for F-150 pickups with either the 4.9 or 5.0 liter engines was the Warner T-18 4-speed

The 1991 Nite was available in only in black. It could be ordered in either 2x4 or 4x4 drive with either the 5.0 liter or 5.8 liter engine. (Courtesy Ford Motor Company)

that had been reintroduced during the 1988 model year.

Thomas Wagner, who, after managing the Lincoln-Mercury Division, succeeded Robert L. Rewey in 1988 as Ford Division general manager, built on the words of his predecessor in introducing the 1990 F-Series trucks. "Light trucks," he noted, "are very much a part of today's lifestyles. Trucks are being used not just as farm-to-market or plant-to-user haulers, but for a variety of personal and recreational needs. Trucks go racing and belong just as much at home or in front of the country club as they do down on the farm or at a remote construction site."

Added to the powertrain choices for the 1990 F-150 (Job #1 for the F-Series pickup was completed on July 24, 1989), and replacing the older C-6 automatic was Ford's electronically-controlled 4-speed automatic transmission (E4OD), originally introduced in 1989 for F-250 and F-350 models with a gross vehicle weight rating of over 8500 pounds. Its electronic shift and converter clutch controls were integrated into the on-board computer of Ford's fourth generation electronic control system (EEC-IV) for improved fuel economy, smoother shifting, and more accurate service diagnostics.

A late availability of this transmission was scheduled for models with 4.9 and 5.0 liter engines.

Introduced as standard equipment late in the 1989 model year and continued for 1990 were automatic locking hubs for the 4x4 models; manual locking hubs remained available as an option. The fuel pump was now of a high-pressure, in-tank design. Standard for all 133 inch wheelbase Regular Cab models was a new 18.2 gallon aft-of-axle fuel tank.

Exterior changes were limited to inclusion of the cargo box light as standard equipment, and a chrome grille (which was no longer offered as an F-150 option) with the XL trim.

Changes in option content involved consolidation into a single heavy duty service package of the heavy duty battery, super cooling radiator, and skid plate options. Similarly, the Light/Convenience Group option consolidated the previously separate Light and Convenience Group options. Regular Cab models were now available with a single fuel tank option rather than the old auxiliary fuel tank.

The 1990 F-150 Regular Cab model was offered (on a late availability status) with two new 'dress-up' options: Sport Packages A and B. Package A included

unique body side and tailgate tape treatment and body color deluxe styled steel wheels. Package B comprised Package A, plus a black tubular bumper and a light bar with off-road lamps.

Also debuting as an F-150 option in 1990 was a set of deep dish forged aluminum wheels. No changes were made in the interior color selection, but replacing Light Chestnut as an exterior color choice was Tan. Phased in during the 1990 model year was the use of two-sided galvanized dash panel and tailgate components for improved corrosion protection.

1991 was another year of modest change for the F-150. Aside from the addition as a late availability change of a '4x4' decal on the box sides of F-150 4-wheel drive pickups, and inclusion of deep dish forged aluminum wheels in two Preferred Equipment Packages, there were no exterior changes for 1991. A new color - Emerald Green Metallic - replaced Alpine Green Metallic as an exterior color selection. The 'Touch Drive' electric shift transfer case option that was originally scheduled for "delayed availability" in 1990 was rescheduled for "late availability" for the F-150 4x4 models with the 5.0 liter engine and automatic overdrive transmission.

Interior revisions were also of a minor nature: an AM/FM stereo radio was included in the XL trim package, and models with XLT Lariat trim now had a standard tachometer.

In terms of option content and availability the net result of changes made for 1991 was very limited. A new body side Tu-Tone paint option for both Regular Cab and SuperCab models positioned the accent color on the body side and tailgate below the two-color tape stripe paint breaks. It also included body side/wheellip moldings. Exclusive to F-150 Styleside pickups with the XLT Lariat trim was a new Lower Accent Tu-Tone paint option. Reinstated as separate options were the heavy duty battery, Super Cooling system, and Skid Plate. Along with the Combination Two-Tone and in-box spare tire carrier, the Heavy-Duty Service package was discontinued. Replacing the body color deluxe wheels in the Sport Appearance Packages were deep dished forged aluminum wheels.

During the model year Ford also offered a Monotone Sport Model option for the F-150 Regular Cab with XLT Lariat trim. No longer offered as a free-standing option were the lower body side and wheellip moldings.

Determined to maintain the F-Series number one sales position in a market where over 20 per cent of all pickups were purchased by women, Ford expanded the F-150's appeal in 1991 with the introduction of the Nite model. Depicted as a "street machine with a sleek look, ample power and adept road-handling capabilities," the Nite was initially available as a Regular Cab model in either 4x2 or 4x4 form, and a 117 inch or 133 inch wheelbase. Subsequently, it became available in SuperCab form. The exterior, in XLT Lariat trim, was all-black with special blue or red tape and graphics. Included as standard equipment was a handling package, forged-aluminum deep-dish wheels, and a rear step bumper. Nite badges were located on the quarter

Right: A 1991 F-150 XL with the Sport Appearance option. (Courtesy Ford Motor Company)

A rear view of the 75th Anniversary Edition of the 1992 F-150. (Courtesy Ford Motor Company)

A 1991 F-150 XLT Lariat SuperCab with optional deep-dish forged aluminum wheels and auxiliary fuel tank. (Courtesy Ford Motor Company)

Two attractive F-150 options for 1993; the hood cover and bed liner. (Courtesy Ford Motor Company)

panels, tailgate, and instrument panel.

Interior colors were Dark Charcoal and Blue with the Blue exterior stripe, and Dark Charcoal and Red with the Red exterior stripe. Monogrammed Nite floor mats were also provided, as was a sliding rear window, air conditioning, AM/FM stereo with cassette and clock, and the Light/Convenience Group.

Engine choices were the 185 horsepower 5.0 liter V-8, or the 210 horsepower 5.8 liter V-8. An upgraded handling package - along with a 4.10 rear

axle ratio and a modified exhaust system for the 5.8 liter V-8 - were offered later in the model year.

The F-150 was depicted by Ford as having a new "aero-tough" look for 1992. Key characteristics of this fashion included a new grille, more rounded front end styling, new tailgate lettering, and new body side moldings. Inside the latest F-150 was a new instrument panel with black appliques, new clusters, a larger locking glovebox, and rotary air conditioning and heater controls. New door trim panels included a reflector with Custom and XL trim levels, and a light/reflector for the XLT Lariat trim. The seat trim patterns were also revised. Offered for all models were new bright electric aerodynamic mirrors.

Returning to the F-150 line-up (late availability) for the first time since 1987 was a short wheelbase Flareside model in either Regular Cab or SuperCab form. During the model year four new colors were offered for the Flareside: Cabernet Red, Bright Red, Twilight Blue Clearcoat Metallic, and Medium Platinum Clearcoat.

The 4x4 F-150 models were now available with extra cost 15in x 7.5in OWL all-terrain tires. Added to the

F-150's optional wheels were 15in x 7.0in argent-styled steel wheels, and 15in x 7.5in chrome-styled steel wheels. The body side accent paint stripe previously standard for XL models became an option for 1992 (with delayed availability).

Now included with the Light/Convenience Group on Regular Cab models was a removable mini-console that attached to the bench seat. The optional Captain's Chairs and cloth flight bench seats included a power lumbar support. Added to the front bench seats were adjustable head restraints for the outboard seating positions.

Ford offered a limited edition 75th Anniversary F-150 pickup package to commemorate production of the first Ford truck, a one-ton model, in 1917. This option was available only for F-150, 133 inch wheelbase 4x2 models equipped with the XLT trim, Preferred Equipment Package 498A and an argent rear step bumper. Exterior colors offered for the Anniversary model were Cabernet Red, Bright Red, Dark Grey Metallic, Bright Regatta Blue Metallic, Deep Shadow Blue Metallic, Emerald Green Metallic, Raven Black, Oxford White, and Colonial White. The package featured graduated silver (turquoise on white trucks) body side and tailgate tape stripes that were the same as those offered for the Sport Appearance Package. Color-keyed 75th Anniversary logos and installment instructions were included in the glovebox for dealer application.

In the process of realigning the F-150's trim levels for 1993, Ford

The available optional wheels for 1993 were, from left to right, argent styled steel, deep-dish aluminum, and chrome styled steel. (Courtesy Ford Motor Company)

A 1993 F-150 XLT Regular Cab. (Courtesy Ford Motor Company)

A 1993 F-150 XLT SuperCab. (Courtesy Ford Motor Company)

streamlined its Preferred Equipment Packages, deleting the dual-body side paint stripe and 15in sport wheel cover options, as well as the Sport Appearance and Custom Upgrade Packages. More significant was the replacement of Custom by XL for the base F-150 model. The 1992 XL level was therefore deleted for 1993. The XLT Lariat trim package was identified as the XLT.

An improved electronic speed control system provided both faster response and enhanced speed-holding capability. Its speed tap up/down feature had 1mph increments. During the model run a redesigned rear bench seat was installed in SuperCab models.

Regular Cab models were offered in these colors for 1993: Light Mocha, Medium Mocha Metallic, Dark Mocha Metallic,

Cabernet Red, Bright Red, Medium Silver Metallic, Dark Grey Metallic, Bright Regatta Blue Metallic, Deep Shadow Blue Metallic, Emerald Green Metallic, Raven Black, and Colonial White. SuperCab and Flareside models color selection consisted of Light Mocha (Styleside only), Medium Mocha Clearcoat Metallic (Styleside only), Mocha Frost Clearcoat Metallic (Styleside only), Cabernet Red, Bright Red, Wild

Among the options on this 1994 F-150 XLT Flareside is an exterior side step. (Courtesy Ford Motor Company)

Strawberry Clearcoat Metallic (Styleside only), Bimini Blue Clearcoat Metallic, Twilight Blue Clearcoat Metallic, Medium Platinum Clearcoat, Silver Clearcoat Metallic, Raven Black, Colonial White (Styleside only), Oxford White, Electric Red Clearcoat Metallic (Flareside only), and Iris Clearcoat Metallic (Flareside only). The interior colors offered were Crystal Blue, Scarlet Red, Dark Charcoal, and Medium Mocha.

All developments of the 1993 model year played supporting roles to the F-150 Lightning model. This high-performance pickup was the creation of Ford's Special Vehicle Team (SVT), comprised of engineering and marketing personnel responsible for designing, developing,

and marketing limited edition, high-performance vehicles for the enthusiast market. Its philosophy focused on design refinement, improving attributes of current models and, hopefully, making them image leaders for Ford. Specific attention was paid to the vehicle's powertrain and chassis to provide the balance of power and handling representative of vehicles purchased by motoring enthusiasts.

In that context, the SVT provided the Lightning with a high-output engine based on the 5.8 liter V-8. In true classic racing-improving-the-breed form, it was equipped with GT-40-type cylinder heads, a tuned intake manifold, tubular stainless steel headers, larger intake and exhaust valves, high-flow ports, high-rate capacity fuel

pump and injectors, revised combustion chamber design, redesigned air filter for improved air flow, and a dual exhaust system. Other upgrades for the basic 5.8 liter V-8 included high-silicon aluminum pistons, a special camshaft for optimized valve tuning, and a cartridge-type, oil-to-water exchanger to control lubricant temperatures. The engine's control computer was programed to deliver crisp throttle response, a clean exhaust, and acceptable fuel economy. Lightning engine output was 240 horsepower at 4200rpm, and 340lb/ft of torque at 3200rpm.

The only transmission offered for the Lightning was the E4OD electronically-controlled 4-speed automatic. For this application it was recalibrated to handle

the Lightning's power, and fitted with an auxiliary transmission oil cooler. A 4.0 inch diameter aluminum driveshaft combined sufficient torque capacity with minimal weight. A 4.10:1 rear axle was used, along with a limited-slip differential.

The Lightning's suspension was modified to utilize larger diameter stabilizer bars and recontoured front coil and rear semi-elliptical springs. Heavy duty gas pressurized Monroe Formula GP shock absorbers, and 17 inch cast aluminum wheels with P275/60HR17 black sidewall tires were also used. The steering system was revised with a larger pitman arm and improved-response power steering control valve.

Interior and exterior features of the Lightning were based upon the XLT trim level, and a Preferred Equipment Package that included air conditioning, power door locks/windows, electronic AM/FM stereo radio with cassette, digital clock and four speakers, speed control, tilt steering wheel, six-way adjustable performance bucket seats with power lumbar, and floor console.

The bucket seats were cloth covered and the steering wheel was wrapped in perforated leather. Instrumentation included a 6000rpm tachometer,120mph speedometer, and a full array of secondary gauges. Major exterior features included a color-keyed rear step bumper (a color-keyed tubular bumper was optional), color-keyed grille and headlamp bezels, and a color-keyed front bumper with integral air dam and fog lamps. The Lightning was available in either Raven Black or Bright Red. The only interior color offered was Charcoal.

In Ford's words: "For all intents, the F-150 Lightning is a Mustang GT with a cargo bed."

For 1994 exterior changes included

a center high-mounted stoplamp, and a black - rather than bright- aero mirror. Additional clearcoat colors were offered in a paint selection that contained fifteen new colors. The clearcoat metallic colors were Desert Copper, Electric Red, Sunrise Red, Iris, Brilliant Blue, Royal Blue, Deep Forest Green, Tobago Green, Light Opal, and Tucson Bronze. Black and Crimson were also available as clearcoats. Rounding out the color selection were Oxford White, Raven Black, and Colonial White. Three new colors - Ruby Red, Royal Blue, and Opal Grey - joined Medium Mocha as interior colors for 1994.

Environmentalists applauded Ford's action in making the F-150 available with a CFC-free air conditioning system.

All F-150 models had a standard driver side air bag as well as driver and passenger side door intrusion beams. A stainless steel exhaust was also standard, as was - with automatic transmission - a brake/shift interlock system. Other functional changes made in 1994 were discontinuation of the 4-speed manual transmission, and replacement of the automatic overdrive transmission (ADO) for the 5.0 liter V-8 with the 4R70W 4-speed automatic. A new Off-Road Package included skid plates for the transfer case and fuel tank, Handling Package, and unique '4x4' off-road decal.

New options for 1994 included, for the XLT, an electrochromic rearview mirror which automatically dimmed at night to reduce headlamp glare. This option also contained vanity mirrors and auxiliary visors. Also debuting in 1994 was a Security Group option consisting of remote keyless entry and anti-theft alarm system, and a premium AM/FM stereo radio with cassette tape player or compact disc player.

During the model run several new or

revised items were phased into production. Among these was a premium cloth 40/20/20 convertible console bench seat with power lumbar support as an option for the XLT. In a similar fashion, a six-way power driver's seat with a 40/20/20 convertible console bench seat was made available for the SuperCab models.

At the start of the model year Ford introduced new 139 inch wheelbase and 155 inch wheelbase SuperCab S, and Special models with lower levels of equipment content than the XL versions.

For 1995 Ford expanded the upper reaches of the F-150's market realm with the top-of-the line new F-150 Eddie Bauer Series. Indirectly admitting that such a F-150 was long overdue, Ford noted that it had "... teamed up with Eddie Bauer ten years ago to create what has become a popular line of personal-use utility vehicles and vans combining the best attributes of style, ruggedness and comfort.

"Now there's a Ford F-Series superbly outfitted to live up to the name Eddie Bauer."

Major features of the Eddie Bauer F-150, offered for all Regular Cab and SuperCab Styleside 4x2 or 4x4 models, included a slotted front bumper, Eddie Bauer floor mats, SuperCab privacy windows (also available as a new separate option, this feature included a sliding rear window), convertible console seat, electric outside mirrors, color-keyed cab steps (also offered as an option for XLT Styleside), lower accent Tu-tone paint treatment, forged aluminum deep dish wheels, and all elements of the XLT trim level. All SuperCab, Flareside and Eddie Bauer models had clearcoat paint (most Regular Cab models also had this finish). The SuperCab was no longer available with rear jump seats. A rear bench seat was optional with the Special version and could be deleted from the XL SuperCab. A premium cassette system was no longer offered for the F-150. The Security Group option of 1994 was identified as the Remote Keyless Entry/Anti-Theft Group.

With an all-new F-150 scheduled for unveiling as a 1997 model during the 1996 calendar year, the 1996 F-150 was little changed from its predecessor (although all Flareside models were discontinued). The XLT body side molding aft of the rear wheels was discontinued and the XLT front bumper now was of a 'diesel' slotted type on all models. The XLT instrument panel and door insert was black instead of color-keyed, as was the base floor covering. Also noted was the use of a bright instead of black ignition key insert.

During the model run, seats with integrated head restraints and revised sew patterns were phased in. Except for Bright Red, Raven Black, Oxford White, and Colonial White, exterior colors for the 1996 were all new and included the following clearcoat metallic colors: Light Saddle, Toreador Red, Dark Toreador Red, Moonlight Blue, Reef Blue, Pacific Green, Silver Frost, and Portofino Blue. No longer offered as an F-150 option were the Electrochromic rearview and illuminated visor vanity mirrors. The anti-theft system was deleted from the remote Keyless Entry System.

Changes to the American pickup during the 44 years of F-100/F-150 production had been seismic in character. The vehicle's primary reason for existence was functionality, but it became a common sight in all settings - urban, rural, suburban, off-road, and in racing.

New model changes occurred far less frequently in the pickup field than in the passenger car market. But these long time frames meant that, when change did take place, it was dramatic in fashion, broad in scope, and often revolutionary in nature. In 1997, such a time came for the Ford F-150.

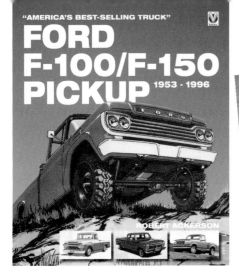

FORD F-100/F-150 PICKUP

1953 - 1996

ROBERT ACKERSON

8

Discovering, restoring, & showing a 1948 F-1 pickup

Two views of Dave Marquart working on his 1948 F-1 in the early stages of its restoration. Several points of interest are apparent including the hole in the cab for the fuel tank filler line, and the small rear window. Beginning in 1951, the area of the window was increased by 50 per cent. (Courtesy Dave Marquart)

Little is known of the background of the 1948 F-1 that was featured in Ford's '50 Years of F-Series: History of America's Favorite Truck' celebration in 1998 before it was rescued from a junkyard and restored by David Marquart of Akron, New York.

"It came right out of a junkyard," he recalls. "It wasn't one of those massive junkyards. There were maybe 50 or 100 vehicles and this truck was laying out in the back. The owner was starting to clean everything up and I asked him what he wanted for 'that old truck' and I ended up buying it for $200.

"It was scrap ... there wasn't a whole lot left of it but I thought, 'what the heck, we'll give it a try.' A friend of mine and I brought it home on a flatbed. It rolled off the truck right into my shop. I started taking it apart and in an hour the back end of the truck was off."

Dave offers a straightforward explanation for taking seven years to complete the truck's restoration: "You only have so many hours in the day and you only have so much money. And the money would dry up and I would put it aside until I had more money."

Even when funds were available, the project didn't always progress smoothly. "I started that truck in 1982," he notes, "and there wasn't the after market parts that there are now. Now you can buy pretty much anything. Back then it wasn't quite as easy, so it took quite a while to find certain parts.

"The very last parts that I found, the stainless steel grille bars, took me years to locate. Beginning in late '48 Ford discontinued those grille bars and went to a solid grille instead of what I have, which is a Beige background with the grille bars."

Dave began the Ford's restoration by removing the body, cleaning the frame, and rebuilding the entire rolling chassis. "Making it roll is important," he emphasizes. "That is what I did first; getting everything all-new ... going through everything, making sure everything was good or all-new. You then have something that can move. There was no front end, there was no

Two views of the F-1's rear fenders mounted on a special support platform built by Dave Marquart to facilitate their repair. (Courtesy Dave Marquart)

"I like to work on my truck outside so I used to roll it out into the driveway. Just made it a lot easier," said Dave. (Courtesy Dave Marquart)

back end, and no motor. Everything is bare bones and you can roll it from one spot to another. I like to work on it outside so I would roll it out into the driveway; just makes it a lot easier.

"I then found a parts truck in Tennessee along with many parts. I would try to do one section at a time, the body, the cab, front clip, etc., from start to finish. On a pickup truck everything is a bolt-on part, so you can do each piece, put it back on the truck and then move on to the next item. It worked out pretty well. I bought a brand new box for it because the bed took the most abuse in pickup trucks."

Restoring the F-1 interior is relatively simple and straightforward. "The only upholstery on the truck, explains Dave, "is the front seat. The doors have nothing. They're just all metal. The only thing I sent out was the seat and I had that done at an upholstery shop. A kit is available for the side panels, back, and ceiling that screws into place."

Dave's F-1 is powered by the 95hp, 6-cylinder 'Rouge 226' and has the optional 4-speed, non-synchro gearbox with a floor-mounted shift lever. As he explains, this makes for an interesting combination on the road. "It has plenty of pep. But it's no race car, and with that old non-synchro transmission I'm not going to

win any drag races with it. You have to double-clutch everything. The transmission whines like crazy. But for its purpose, it's fine.

"Back then pickups were made to work and that's why when a truck was done, it was junk. It was used up. They were using them on farms and they weren't worried about what the thing looked like, they were worried

This view of the F-1 illustrates Dave Marquart's assertion that one of the most attractive aspects of restoring a vintage pickup is its relative ease of assembly; nearly everything is a bolt-on part. (Courtesy Dave Marquart)

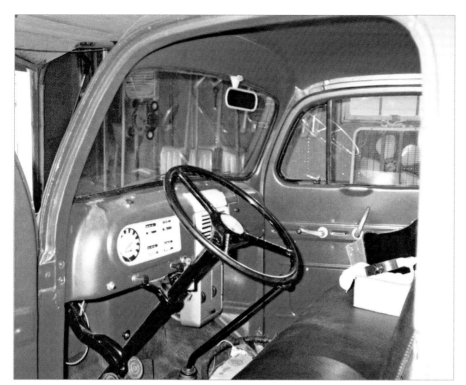

The F-1 interior was a no-frills work environment. Instrumentation included (from left to right): speedometer, gauges for fuel level, engine coolant temperature, oil pressure, and ammeter. (Courtesy Dave Marquart)

The Marquart F-1 was equipped with the optional passenger-side windshield wiper. (Courtesy Dave Marquart)

A view of the F-1 nearing the end of body restoration. (Courtesy Dave Marquart)

As on other early 1948 F-1 models, Dave Marquart's truck has a Tucson Tan grille backer panel with five bars mounted on it. Attached to each bar was a chrome grille piece. In August 1948, the chrome parts were removed and the grille bars were painted silver with red pinstriping on each bar. For the 1949 models the pinstriping was not applied. (Courtesy David Marquart)

Depending on the source, the 1948 F-1 had either black or body-color wheels. Dave Marquart, aware of this discrepancy, opted for the latter and painted his truck's wheels Vermilion Red. (Courtesy David Marquart)

about it doing a job. Its purpose was to work.

"It doesn't ride bad. Actually, it rides pretty good. Basically because of drivability, last year I took the 'hockey puck' tires off and put a set of radials on it. They were 6-ply nylon tires and unless it was above 85 degrees, they shook the brains out of your head for the first five minutes." So I didn't like that and I wanted to drive the truck more so I put a set of radials on it just so it was more drivable."

The 1948 F-1's standard equipment provided only the driver with a windshield wiper and sun visor. This F-1 has the optional passenger-side wiper and visor. "They work just like normal vacuum wiper blades," says Dave, "you jump on it - they stop. I try not to drive it in the rain anyway."

Dave has nothing but praise both for Ford's treatment and care of his truck when it was included in the celebrations for the F-Series' 50th anniversary, and the hospitality that was extended to him and his wife.

"Everything went smooth as silk," he recalls. "There never was a problem. They came out after we talked on the phone and they wanted to take it to the International Auto Show in Detroit, and they sent a truck out to pick it up. My truck never got damaged. When it was displayed at the International Automobile Show in Detroit, they had people there, cleaning it, wiping it down, and so there were no problems. During the auto show they brought my wife and me to Detroit and we stayed at the Ritz-Carleton. They were very nice people. We went to the show, and had a tour of Ford's World Headquarters."

During 1998 the truck was also part of several other exhibits, including the commemoration of NASCAR's 50th Anniversary in New York City.

The 1948 F-1 pickup's box was a carry-over design, dating back to the 1938 pickups. (Courtesy David Marquart)

The beautifully proportioned lines of the 1948 F-1 justify its status as a classic pickup. (Courtesy David Marquart)

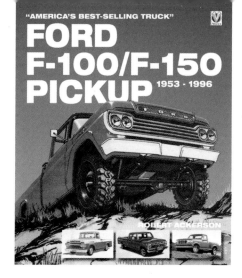

Dave Dorf's 1953 F-100 as purchased in 1985. (Courtesy Dave Dorf)

9

Restoring & driving early 1950s F-100s

David Dorf and Gerald Frisbe, owners of 1953 and 1956 F-100 pickups respectively, are typical examples of contemporary truck enthusiasts. Both express admiration for the simple, undiluted form of the early F-100s. "I've always liked the early fifties Ford pickups very much. They just have a very nice line to them," says David.

Both men have found the experience of a frame-off restoration of an F-100 a challenging - but most certainly not overwhelming - proposition. Both agree that restoring a truck is much easier than a car of the same vintage. There is essentially no interior trim, and very little chrome embellishment; in essence, the truck consists of three major elements: cab, box, and the front cowl.

"It's important to set realistic, intermediate goals," says David. "For most people, restoring a truck is not something that is done over a one or two year span of time. It's a lot of work.

"It's crucial, at the onset of restoring an F-100, to do some preliminary research on features and accessories that were offered for the F-100. This knowledge is valuable when you find a restorable F-100 in assuring that you are acquiring an original vehicle, not one that has been modified. It is also important to acquire a sense of current values of F-100 pickups.

"Too often," David continues, "people pay too high a price for a truck, and by the time they go through the restoration process they have so much invested that

they seldom can recover their costs. Know at the beginning the market value of a fully-restored vehicle and then determine what your restoration costs may be - consider your skills, ability; how much work you can do yourself - how much work you will have to farm out. This information helps determine how much you should spend for a reasonably sound vehicle."

Concurring with these thoughts, Gerald adds, "To get a truck restored, you are going to have to spend a great deal of money, and you can't begin by spending thousands of dollars on the truck before it's restored."

"People very often underestimate how much work is involved in a restoration." adds David. "They get overwhelmed when they realize the size of the task they are facing. It takes a lot of time; you need a lot of space - not just for the vehicle - but also for all the parts, once you disassemble the vehicle." When a part has been dismantled, David recommends that its components are placed in a clear plastic bag, along with a notation concerning the bag's contents and key aspects of reassembly. These, in turn, can be stored in boxes for easy access and cleaning.

Both David and Gerald emphasize the need, literally from the first moment a part is removed from the F-100, of keeping a log and taking plenty of photographs. "Absolutely keep a log" says David, "and note the position of certain parts;

The F-100 was the subject of a frame-off restoration. The chassis has been rewelded where needed, sandblasted and painted, and the rear end rebuilt. (Courtesy Dave Dorf)

The refinished cab remounted on the F-100 frame (Courtesy Dave Dorf)

A view of the partially completed interior through the rear window. (Courtesy Dave Dorf)

The primed pickup box temporarily installed to check alignment with the cab. (Courtesy Dave Dorf)

Numerous components have been installed at this point in the F-100's restoration. (Courtesy Dave Dorf)

At this point in the restoration, the F-100's inner front fenders have been installed. (Courtesy Dave Dorf)

the way nuts and bolts face, small, but crucial details such as that. Three or four years down the road it is going to be very difficult to remember those types of things that are vital for a proper restoration."

"I'm always writing myself notes," says Gerald, "about how different things go together and how they relate to each other." He is emphatic about the importance of photos in a restoration project that stays on track. "My advice," he says, "to anyone restoring a truck is to get a camera and about fifty rolls of film. Take pictures - different views of everything before you take it apart because something that you swear you will be able to put together, you'll find you can't."

David notes that "I also keep a very complete log of all the parts I've purchased and their cost - whether new, reproduction or junkyard parts. Then, at the end of restoration, I know, short of my labor cost, what my investment in the truck is." Concerning parts, David is a strong advocate of the use of original as opposed to replacement parts wherever possible. A careful search of local junkyards and part-scouting trips in the country often yield surprising results, he reports. "Most people" adds David, "are pretty good when you stop to talk with them. And often they will let you take whatever parts you need. There are a lot more F-100s sitting around than you might think."

David also suggests getting to know the oldest parts man at nearby Ford dealerships, since they are often the individuals who remember the old parts and know where they may be stored.

A prime prerequisite for a successful F-100 restoration, in David's view, is a truck with a reasonably good body. "Mechanically, you can fix up an F-100 without a great deal of difficulty, but once you start patching the body, invariably you have to go back and redo your work. Like all vehicles, the F-100 has certain weak spots. The rear windows used to leak and water would run down the cab and into the back of the cab corners. Eventually, dust and dirt would collect in the pocket, get wet and rot the body out."

Gerald notes that "... the bed is prone to rust in many areas, particularly where the rear fender meets the running board. Another prime area for rust is above the headlights in the front fender."

On trucks that have seen heavy duty, David also cautions that stress cracks can develop between the rivets connecting the crossmembers to the side rails. But, overall, David feels that the F-100's frame and springs are very heavy and that they typically held up very well.

"I generally look for a vehicle with as good a body as possible and one that has the correct knobs and small trim pieces, because," says David, "some of those items are very difficult to find." Gerald adds that "I had to get my front fenders from another truck in Arizona. The only metal part for the F-100 that I know is available is the valence behind the front bumper and under the grille. The rest you have to search for and find something that's in better shape than what you have."

Both agree that driving their vintage F-100s is an experience quite unlike that provided by a modern counterpart. "It drives differently because we are accustomed to driving modern trucks." says Gerald. "One of the big things you notice is when you go to stop. In a modern truck with power brakes, you just tap your foot and you stop. With the F-100 you really have to pick your leg up and stand on the pedal. There's nothing wrong with the truck, that's just the way they were.

"It rides fine - it's not as comfortable as my 1994 F-150, but it's darn close and I've taken it for trips lasting several hours.

"It's not fast - 40 to 45mph is a good cruising speed. It's also a little louder than a newer truck. It doesn't have sound insulation around the firewall, so you hear the air cleaner and other mechanical sounds.

"It corners OK. It has that big steering wheel and you have to grab hold of it and slow down and turn it around the corner. It doesn't compare to a modern truck. It acts like a truck did back in the mid-fifties."

David Dorf's first generation F-100 has proven both reliable and fun to drive since its restoration. "All-in-all," he notes, "it rides pretty good. I can go down the highway at 60mph with ease. It has the highest rear axle ratio Ford offered back then and its engine has been very carefully balanced. That helps a great deal since Ford didn't do that great a job of balancing the old flathead back in 1953.

"Acceleration is also quite good. The Ford V-8 has a lot of low end torque and it can move right along. However, it doesn't

Much work remains, but much has already been accomplished. (Courtesy Dave Dorf)

FORD

The F-100 with the majority of front end reassembly completed. A great deal of time was expended in aligning the front fenders and hood. (Courtesy Dave Dorf)

With the restoration project entering its final stages, the F-100's refurbished grille has been installed. Note the finished rear fenders hanging on the shop wall. (Courtesy Dave Dorf)

The completed engine compartment. (Courtesy Dave Dorf)

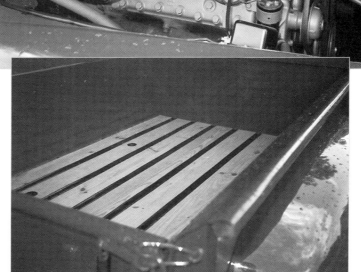

shift very fast and I find it quite practical to often double-clutch.

"Ride, by modern standards, is fairly harsh and stiff. After all, it does have an I-beam front suspension that isn't very forgiving!" Both the steering and braking characteristics of the 1953 F-100 are dramatically different to those of its modern counterpart. "The steering is loose by contemporary standards" David explains, "and, as far as the brakes are concerned, you have to really put your foot into them.

"You also get a lot of outside noise in the cab. There isn't much soundproofing except for a thin insulation blanket over the headliner. There's nothing in the door panels and all the interior surfaces are basically hard, so there is little or no sound absorption."

But with great visibility and a ventilation system that puts modern efforts to shame, the F-100 offers a great deal of pure, honest motoring pleasure. Designed primarily for work, the F-100's minor drawbacks fade in perspective to its numerous virtues. As David Dorf says about its idiosyncrasies, "those are the kind of things that make it interesting."

Yellow Pine was selected for the F-100 bed boards. (Courtesy Dave Dorf)

Dave Dorf's F-100 after restoration. It has been driven 9000 miles. (Courtesy Dave Dorf)

A quality restoration seldom goes unnoticed at local car and truck shows. (Courtesy Dave Dorf)

The completed F-100 interior. Note the factory radio and heater. (Courtesy Dave Dorf)

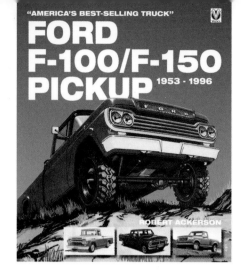

Index